Hitler's Fortresses
in the East

Hitler's Fortresses in the East

The Sieges of Ternopol', Kovel', Poznan and Breslau, 1944–1945

Alexey V. Isaev

Edited and Translated by Richard W. Harrison

Pen & Sword
MILITARY

First published in Great Britain in 2021 by
Pen & Sword Military
An imprint of
Pen & Sword Books Ltd
Yorkshire – Philadelphia

Copyright © Alexey V. Isaev 2021
Copyright © English Translation Pen & Sword Books 2021

ISBN 978 1 52678 395 0

Printed and bound by CPI Group (UK) Ltd, Croydon, CR0 4YY

Pen & Sword Books Limited incorporates the imprints of Atlas,
Archaeology, Aviation, Discovery, Family History, Fiction, History,
Maritime, Military, Military Classics, Politics, Select, Transport,
True Crime, Air World, Frontline Publishing, Leo Cooper, Remember
When, Seaforth Publishing, The Praetorian Press, Wharncliffe
Local History, Wharncliffe Transport, Wharncliffe True Crime
and White Owl.

For a complete list of Pen & Sword titles please contact

PEN & SWORD BOOKS LIMITED
47 Church Street, Barnsley, South Yorkshire, S70 2AS, England
E-mail: enquiries@pen-and-sword.co.uk
Website: www.pen-and-sword.co.uk

Or

PEN AND SWORD BOOKS
1950 Lawrence Rd, Havertown, PA 19083, USA
E-mail: Uspen-and-sword@casematepublishers.com
Website: www.penandswordbooks.com

Contents

List of Illustrations

1. The commander of a motorized battalion of automatic riflemen, Captain G.T. Dobrunov (in the centre) with comrades next to a BA-64 armoured car. 4th Guards Tank Corps, 60th Army.
2. I.D. Chernyakhovskii, commander of the 60th Army, photographed in the summer of 1944. In his command post as commander of the Third Belorussian Front, after being promoted to general and receiving his second star (Hero of the Soviet Union) (29 July 1944).
3. I.I. Lyudnikov, commander of the 15th Rifle Corps. The successful storming of Ternopol' would facilitate his appointment as an army commander in Belorussia.
4. An abandoned Panther from the 7th Panzer Division on the street in Ternopol'. (TsAMO)
5. A knocked-out *Sturmgeschütz* assault gun on the street in Ternopol'. (TsAMO)
6. A knocked-out SU-152 self-propelled gun in Ternopol'. (TsAMO)
7. A parachute-dropped supply container on the roof of one of the buildings in Ternopol' (from a newsreel clip).
8. A burnt-out transport glider on the street in Ternopol'. (TsAMO)
9. Soviet infantry in the street fighting for Ternopol'.
10. The railway station in Ternopol'. (TsAMO)
11. A Maxim machine gun team putting its weapon in order.
12. A panoramic view of the approaches to Kovel' from the roof of the railway station.
13. The Catholic church in Kovel'. An enormous structure built in the 1930s.
14. An He-111 bomber abandoned on the airfield at Poznań. In all, according to Soviet data, about 150 aircraft of various types were captured in the Poznań area.
15. A sketch of one of the typical Poznań forts.
16. General V.I. Chuikov, commander of the 8th Guards Army.
17. A ditch around one of Poznań's forts. Gun limbers have been positioned in the ditch, which was probably used as a storehouse for artillery equipment.
18. Fort Rauch in Poznań. A photograph from the beginning of the twentieth century.
19. Embrasures in one of the casemates of the fortress's citadel.
20. Soviet officers by a redoubt in the fortress's citadel.
21. A building destroyed by heavy artillery on the approaches to the central part of the old city. It had been turned into a centre of resistance by the Germans and suffered heavily during the assault.

Translator's Introduction

This study contains a number of terms that may not be readily understandable to the casual reader in military history. Therefore, I have adopted a number of conventions designed to ease this task. For example, major Soviet field formations (i.e., First Belorussian Front) are spelled out in full, as are similar German formations (i.e., Army Group South). Soviet armies are designated using the shortened form (i.e., 60th Army). German armies, on the other hand, are spelled out in full (i.e., Fourth Panzer Army). In the same vein, Soviet corps are designated by Arabic numerals (i.e., 4th Guards Tank Corps), while the same German units are denoted by Roman numerals (i.e., XLVIII Panzer Corps). Smaller units (divisions, brigades, etc.) on both sides are denoted by Arabic numerals only (i.e., 357th Infantry Division, 322nd Rifle Division).

Given the large number of units involved in the narrative, I have adopted certain other conventions in order to better distinguish them. For example, Soviet armoured units are called tank corps, brigades, etc., while the corresponding German units are denoted by the popular term 'panzer'. Likewise, Soviet infantry units are designated by the term rifle, while the corresponding German units are simply referred to as infantry.

Elsewhere, a *front* is a Soviet wartime military organization roughly corresponding to an American army group. Throughout the narrative the reader will encounter such names as the Belorussian and First Ukrainian Fronts, etc. To avoid confusion with the more commonly understood meaning of the term front (i.e., the front line), italics will be used to denote an unnamed *front*.

Many of the place names in this study are hyphenated, such as Kamen'-Kashirskii. In these cases, the names are separated by a single hyphen, which is to distinguish them from the recitation of a particular line of separate locales, often countered in such works, such as Yezerna–Kozlov–Plaucha Mala–Zborov. In the latter case, the individual villages and towns are separated by en-dashes.

The work subscribes to no particular transliteration scheme, because no entirely satisfactory one exists. I have adopted a mixed system that uses the Latin letters 'ya' and 'yu' to denote their Cyrillic counterparts, as opposed to the 'ia' and 'iu' employed by the Library of Congress, which tends to distort proper pronunciation. Conversely, I have retained the Library of Congress's 'ii' ending (i.e., Chernyakhovskii), as opposed to the commonly-used 'y' ending. I have also retained the apostrophe to denote the Cyrillic soft sign.

As always, place names in Eastern Europe present a special problem in spelling, as so much depends on which country controlled an area at a particular time. I have chosen to spell/transliterate locales according to how they were written at the time of the events in question. Thus Poznań retains the Polish spelling of Poznań and not the pre-First World War Posen, despite its conquest by the Germans in 1939. Breslau is Breslau throughout, as it was a part of Germany until 1945, when it was acquired by Poland and renamed Wroclaw. Kovel' is transliterated as such, as its spelling has not changed since 1939. However, since Russian was the dominant language of the Soviet Union, I have elected to spell Ternopol' as it would have been transliterated from the Russian, and not as Ternopil', in line with the new Ukrainian transliteration. I have also avoided the German Tarnopol.

The work contains endnotes by the author. They have been supplemented by a number of appropriately-identified editor's notes, which have been inserted as an explanatory guide for a number of terms that might not be readily understandable to the foreign reader.

Preface

The development of events along the Soviet-German front, which were unfavourable for the German army, forced the German leadership to look for new methods and forms of fighting. One of these was the concept of the so-called fortresses, which were towns and cities defended in complete isolation. The author of this method is considered to be Hitler himself, namely in his Directive No. 11 of 8 March 1944, which became the guiding document for the choice and construction of fortresses. Strictly speaking, in the early stages of the war with the USSR the Wehrmacht also adopted tactics quite close to that of fortresses. Units and formations that ended up isolated took up an all-round defence and sought to hold out, while awaiting a relief attack from outside. It is enough to recall Kholm, Demyansk and Sukhinichi (von Gilsa's group) in the 1941–2 winter campaign, and Millerovo and Chertkovo in the winter of 1942–3 as examples. However, during 1944–5 the concept was taken to its logical conclusion.

It was planned to employ towns and cities, which were assigned the role of 'breakwaters' along the path of the attacking enemy, as fortresses. According to Directive No. 11, 'Fortresses must carry out the same tasks as the fortresses of old. They must prevent the enemy from seizing places of significance from the operational point of view. They must allow themselves to be surrounded and thus tie down as many enemy forces as possible.'[1] As opposed to preceding campaigns, the locations for the fortresses were selected in advance and headed by a commander chosen for his personal qualities. According to Directive No. 11, the fortress commander was subordinated directly to the army group commander, and not the army commander, in the sector in which the given fortress was located.

One should emphasize that they assiduously avoided using the word 'fortresses'. The reasons for this were quite obvious – the name fortress, without permanent fortifications (the construction of which demanded time and expenditure of materiel) appeared ridiculous. The more delicate formula of 'fortified place' (*Festung Platz*) was employed. The impossibility of maintaining large forces in a fortress forced them to adopt a compromise. Directive No. 11 called for the presence of a 'security garrison' and a 'full garrison'. The former was permanently located in the fortress and prepared it for defence, while the latter occupied its positions immediately before the attack on the fortress by the Red Army. The garrison's strength was determined by the army group command, depending upon the size of the fortress.

It should be noted that the subsequent fate of a fortress after its encirclement was not laid out in Hitler's directive. Later practice showed that they tried to relieve some fortresses from the outside. It was vaguely assumed that the isolated garrisons would be relieved following the overall stabilization of the situation at the front. There were precedents for this in the relief of the garrisons of Kholm, Demyansk and Sukhinichi in 1942, after the situation stabilized. At the same time, one should stress that a deep attack was required for relieving the above-mentioned cities.

The new concept was tested by the Germans not long after the publication of Directive No. 11. The Ukrainian cities of Proskurov, Ternopol' and Kovel' were destined to become the first fortresses. All of these were important road junctions, the retention of which would make the supply situation of the Red Army's forces attacking westward more difficult. It is very interesting to note that the status of fortress could be removed due to military necessity. For example, the status of fortress, which had been awarded earlier, was removed from the city of Proskurov at 13.00 on 24 March 1944.[2] This was done in accordance with the overall retreat by the First Panzer Army's forces under the threat of encirclement. That is, there was an element of military expediency in according the status of fortress and one should not exaggerate the 'thick-headedness' of the German command in this regard.

Chapter 1

Ternopol': The First Attempt

The struggle for the city of Ternopol' was, on the one hand, a peripheral one as regards the offensive toward the Dnestr River. On the other hand, fairly large forces were engaged in the fight for this major road junction in western Ukraine. Thus a description of the combat actions which led to the formation of the 'Hube[1] Pocket' would be incomplete without a description of the battle for Ternopol'. Following the breakout from the bridgehead over the Goryn' River, I.D. Chernyakhovskii's[2] 60th Army was in a very favourable position. The tank and mechanized corps of V.M. Badanov's[3] and P.S. Rybalko's[4] tank armies, which had moved ahead into the breach, had tied down the small German reserves, thus allowing the infantry behind them to follow in their tracks. Aside from the attack behind the tank armies, the 60th Army also had the task of securing the First Ukrainian Front's western flank. The situation here was also quite favourable, as the Germans lacked a continuous front along this axis. The army's right-flank formations were moving on Zbarazh and Ternopol'.

The tanks of the 4th Guards Tank Corps moved forward. For the 60th Army's rifle formations, the brigades of P.P. Poluboyarov's corps were like a 'needle', behind which they moved as the 'thread', while developing the tank troops' success. In this case, the phrase 'the tanks were moving' is not a figure of speech and should be understood literally. Tanks, with infantry riding on them, moved forward, while sometimes also loaded with canisters of fuel.

It was precisely such a cavalcade of ten tanks (eight vehicles from the 14th Guards Tank Brigade and two from corps headquarters), with infantry riding on them, that on the evening of 5 March reached the town of Zbarazh from the east. Poluboyarov, who was not above being personally at the spearhead of the attack, was in one of the headquarters tanks. It was quiet in the town and lights were on in the buildings, while the garrison's soldiers, who consisted of a regiment of the SS 'Galicia' Division,[5] were peacefully watching a movie. The 'Galicia' Division evidently had some serious problems, insofar as the tanks broke into Zbarazh quite unexpectedly, causing panic and a commotion among the garrison's soldiers. The T-34s,[6] along with their mounted infantry, passed through the whole town, firing in all directions, and took up defensive positions, not even on the southern outskirts, but on the Chernikhovtsy crossing to the south-west of the town. Not knowing this, the motor vehicle drivers in Zbarazh gathered themselves into a column and attempted to escape to Ternopol'. Upon colliding with a screen of Soviet tanks, the column's drivers abandoned their vehicles and scattered across the fields, while keeping up a disorderly fire. There was shooting all night in Zbarazh between Soviet infantrymen and small, isolated groups of Germans and Ukrainian SS troops.

However, a tank-borne assault by sixty men prevented them from clearing the town of the 'Galicia' Division's soldiers and small German subunits which had holed up in the buildings. The situation was exacerbated by the fact that intelligence had revealed large German forces, backed by armour, on the approaches to the town. Moreover, the German Armoured Train No. 71 was rendering support to the garrison of Zbarazh. It was an assault party from the train that pulled the headquarters of the Ukrainian SS troops out of the town.

General Poluboyarov immediately turned to the commander of the 60th Army, I.D. Chernyakhovskii, with a request to free up the 13th Guards Tank Brigade, which had earlier been directed to Vishnevets, as a forward detachment. The corps' other units were being brought up at the same time. A brigade of motorized riflemen arrived at Zbarazh on the night of 5/6 March, having only light infantry weapons. However, this was quite sufficient for clearing the town of scattered groups of the enemy. By midday on 6 March the 13th Guards Tank Brigade had arrived at the town and got into a fight for the Zbarazh station from the march. The infantry and armoured train became the brigade's enemy. Two SU-85s[7] were detailed to fight the latter and they quickly put the armoured train out of commission. This was confirmed by German data, and in the report by Armoured Train No. 71 it is pointed out that 'The locomotive received several direct hits and was unable to move'. However, at that moment the Germans managed to avoid the complete loss of the armoured train: they uncoupled the train's undamaged part and towed it away and, at night, with the assistance of three locomotives, evacuated the damaged part. Armoured Train No. 71 went in for repairs. After putting the armoured train out of action, the 13th Guards Tank Brigade occupied Zbarazh station and took up defensive positions, cutting the roads leading to the town. The brigade simultaneously carried out reconnaissance of the possible routes to Ternopol'.

German reserves with tanks and assault guns presented the greatest danger to the 4th Guards Tank Corps' brigades. Throughout 6 March Zbarazh was counterattacked several times by ten or eleven 'tanks' (according to Soviet data). According to German data, seven assault guns were operating in this area. However, one cannot of course exclude the employment of the 7th Panzer Division's tanks arriving from the west, which were advancing to link up with the division's main forces in Volochisk. Also, according to the scanty information available, Dr Major I. Erasmus, from the 7th Panzer Division, led the counter-attacking group.

Meanwhile, the *front* command demanded of Chernyakhovskii that he take Ternopol' as early as the evening of 7 March. Essentially, at that moment a race was underway on both sides of the front, with a very small divide separating success from failure. The German side was striving to restore the integrity of the front through the arrival of fresh formations, which were subordinated to the headquarters of the XLVIII Panzer Corps. These were the recently formed 357th and 359th Infantry Divisions, which had been unloading since 7 March in the Ternopol' area. It was specially noted in the Fourth Panzer Army's war diary, that 'One should make fewer demands on both divisions than on the rest, insofar as two-thirds of the rank and file were born in 1926'. The divisions were up to authorized strength in men, but were short of communications equipment and other gear.

The German command was trying to win time for deploying the arriving formations through counter-attacks in the Zbarazh area. The 4th Guards Tank Corps' brigades suffered appreciable losses in these battles and there remained only nineteen T-34s and six SU-85s in line.[8] One should add that as early as 7 March Poluboyarov attempted to develop the offensive in the direction of Ternopol', but it soon came up against the blown-up crossing near Chernikhovtsy. The Germans, in turn, threw a prefabricated metal bridge across the river alongside the blown-up crossing, and continued their counter-attacks on Zbarazh. At that moment Poluboyarov showed himself to be an intelligent tank commander. Upon putting out a screen in the southern part of Zbarazh, he gather together a shock group (the 12th Guards Tank Brigade with a battalion of motorized riflemen), which turned the enemy flank and attacked Chernikhovtsy along the other bank of the river. This manoeuvre forced the counter-attacking group to hurriedly fall back on Ternopol'. The road to the city was clear. Only the absence of fuel, which was traditional in the March fighting, held up the brigades of General Poluboyarov's corps, which at that moment had only 0.2–0.3 refills of fuel.

A serious obstacle to the advance of the Soviet forces became the washed-out dirt roads. The attacking 60th Army's motor transport became bogged down, forming enormous traffic jams of several hundred vehicles. In order to avoid vehicle losses, motor transport was even gathered into individual shelters, where it remained under guard until the roads could be restored. Motorized and horse-drawn artillery also became bogged down and advanced with great difficulty. They literally pushed the horse carts forward by hand. In one of the Soviet reports on the results of the March and April fighting, the conditions of the offensive were described in a few short but weighty phrases: 'The infantry units advanced up to their knees in the mud and the conditions for manoeuvre and feeding the fighting with ammunition were exceptionally difficult.'

By the evening of 7 March units of the 15th Rifle Corps began to approach the Zbarazh area. At this time the corps was commanded by Major General I.I. Lyudnikov, a veteran of Stalingrad who had become famous for the defence of 'Lyudnikov's Island'. It should be mentioned that at that moment the rifle units of Lyudnikov's corps were experiencing the *front*'s general problems with movement in conditions of washed-out roads. In a report by the 322nd Rifle Division on the results of the fighting, it was noted that on 8 March its regiments were advancing, 'having an insufficient amount of ammunition, while lacking artillery altogether, because the latter had gotten bogged down due to the very bad roads'.[9] Army commander Chernyakhovskii assigned the 4th Guards Tank Corps the task of capturing Ternopol' on 8 March, in conjunction with rifle units, and consolidating there while securely holding the approaches to the city. In order to achieve the thrust on Ternopol', titanic efforts were undertaken to restore the tanks' manoeuvrability. With the aid of a pair of U-2[10] liaison aircraft, 400kg of fuel each per flight was transported by air. Also, a column of trucks, with diesel fuel and oil, set out from the Yampol' area, accompanied by five tanks (not so much for protection as for towing out bogged-down vehicles). By this time oil had become a matter of life and death for supporting the tanks' combat capability, as the engines of the T-34s, which had become worn out in the preceding fighting, used up more of it. A certain amount of fuel was located in Zbarazh itself. All of this enabled them to refuel the tanks and raise the supply of fuel in them to 0.7–0.8 of a refill.

Just as was the case along the other sectors of the front, all of the 4th Guards Tank Corps' artillery had fallen behind on the flooded roads. Anti-tank artillery, in the form of both 57mm and 85mm guns, was completely absent,

Table 1.1: The Strength of the 4th Guards Tank Corps' Tank Park on 8 March 1944[11]

Unit	T-34	SU-85
12th Guards Tank Bde	11	7
13th Guards Tank Bde	12	4
14th Guards Tank Bde	12	4
3rd Guards Motorized Rifle Bde	–	4

which significantly reduced the opportunities for opposing the new types of German tanks. There were only twelve 120mm mortars and three rocket artillery platforms (*katyushas*).[12]

The shortest route to Ternopol' was the Zbarazh–Ternopol' road. However, the greatest enemy resistance was expected here. According to Poluboyarov's plan, it was planned to break through to the city by a turning movement through the village of Dubovtsy with the forces of the 12th and 13th Guards Tank Brigades, while simultaneously tying down the enemy from the front with the forces of the 14th Guards Tank Brigade. According to this plan, the first to enter the city from the north was to be the 13th Guards Tank Brigade, with the infantry in its wake, while breaking through to the southern outskirts, where it was supposed to take up defensive positions. In this manner the city was to be isolated from the arrival of reinforcements. This method, one might say, was the 'essence' of Poluboyarov's tactics for taking cities. In this way not only would the arrival of reinforcements be blocked, but the illusion of being encircled created as well. After this, the assault would begin by the motorized riflemen and infantry. Everything was built upon a surprise attack, insofar as the units that had arrived at the approaches to Ternopol' disposed of only light artillery and had limited supplies of ammunition. All wheeled transport had stalled and ammunition was being delivered by U-2s.

The start of the offensive was delayed by the late arrival of the 15th Rifle Corps' infantry at their jumping-off positions. As a result, the attack began when it was dark, at 05.15 on 9 March. As early as 06.00 the 13th Guards Tank Brigade's tanks and self-propelled artillery had reached the north-eastern outskirts of Ternopol' and entered the city. Upon breaking into the streets, the tanks crushed cars, carts and scurrying German soldiers, causing a panic. Immediately upon entering the city, the T-34s broke the illumination and communications lines. The bet on surprise proved justified to a significant degree: there was no organized resistance until sunrise, only isolated small-arms fire. However, it was precisely in the northern part of the city that the

'Demba' Fusilier Battalion, which had been formed from an NCO school and which had been dispatched to Ternopol', was located. The 'Demba' Battalion's elements did not give way to panic and took up an all-round defence, while claiming to have shot up two Soviet SU-85s, which had passed within 50m. It was also precisely the 'Demba' Battalion that was blocking the infantry's entrance into the city behind the tanks.

As a result, the tanks' breakthrough into the city was not supported by the infantry. The infantrymen, upon encountering rifle and machine-gun fire, took cover. To be fair, it should be pointed out that one of the reasons for this was the above-mentioned absence of artillery capable of suppressing the enemy's fire. Meanwhile, a pinning group, consisting of the 14th Guards Tank Brigade, had arrived at the approaches to Ternopol'. As Poluboyarov had expected, the bridge on the Zbarazh–Ternopol' road had been blown up. Seven hours of sustained labour by the engineers were required to restore it. As a result, the tank brigade's first three T-34s only arrived at Ternopol' at 07.30 on 9 March. Here they were halted by fire from tanks and assault guns.

Thus the attempt to take Ternopol' from the march was not successful and a planned assault began. On 10 March, having brought up their artillery, the rifle units became involved in street fighting. Two of the 322nd Rifle Division's regiments advanced through the city blocks in the north-eastern and eastern part of Ternopol', while approaching to within 600m of the station. The division's losses in two days of fighting were 50 men killed and 188 wounded. Elements of the 336th Rifle Division reached Ternopol' from the south-east. The enemy's data also testifies to the fact that the crisis with artillery support for the 15th Rifle Corps' infantry attack had been overcome. Major Erasmus, an officer who had been dispatched to Ternopol' from the headquarters of XLVIII Panzer Corps, wrote in his report that 'The city was under the enemy's massed artillery and mortar bombardment. The commandant and his attached 144th Artillery Command (Colonel Schrepler and his staff), were in the basement of the former command post, because all of the glass had been knocked out in the upper storeys by the bombardment.'

The first reports from Ternopol' caused a good deal of concern in General Erhard Rauss's[13] headquarters. At one moment they considered the city to have been all but lost and were thinking of how to minimize the consequences of it. It was seriously believed that the unloading of fresh formations arriving in the Ternopol' area was in danger of being aborted. It was noted in the Fourth Panzer Army's war diary that

Insofar as there is the danger that the enemy's tanks will break through Ternopol' onto the road leading to the west and will interfere with the unloading of troops in Yezerna and to the west, following a discussion of the situation, an order was issued by radio at 09.41 by the army commander and his chief of staff to cover the Yezerna–Ternopol' road with the aid of anti-tank weapons and to dispatch reconnaissance to Ternopol'.[14]

It was precisely for the purpose of clarifying and stabilizing the situation in Ternopol' that Major Erasmus was dispatched from the XLVIII Panzer Corps' headquarters.

Erasmus immediately set about preparing a counterblow for the purpose of throwing out the Soviet units that had penetrated into the city. The counterblow's main shock force was a tank group of two Panther[15] tanks, two armoured personnel carriers and a battery of assault guns (seven vehicles). They considered the north-eastern axis, where food stores were located, to be the most important. The German offensive began on the morning of 11 March. Erasmus wrote of the early morning hours, but according to Soviet data the counterblow followed at about 11.00 and was estimated in the 322nd Rifle Division's operational report at '600 infantry, supported by 17 heavy tanks and eight armoured vehicles'. Three battalions from 322nd Rifle Division's 1085th and 1089th Rifle Regiments were cut off by the counterblow and the remaining elements of these two regiments were thrown back to the suburbs. The 4th Guards Tank Corps' 3rd Motorized Rifle Brigade also came under attack.

The counterblow made the situation of the 13th Guards Tank Brigade's tanks and assault parties, which had broken into the city, entirely hopeless. They waged an isolated battle in the city for two and a half days. After expending its ammunition, the detachment broke out of the city on the three most combat-capable tanks and linked up with the corps' remaining units on 11 March. On this day elements of the fresh German 949th Infantry Regiment arrived in the city and took up defensive positions along the outskirts of Ternopol'. The opportunity of taking the city from the march had been lost.

It was precisely at this moment that the city of Ternopol' became the proving ground for testing one of the German army's most controversial concepts of the latter half of the war – the so-called fortresses. Hitler himself is considered its author. Strictly speaking, during the early stages of the war the Wehrmacht[16] also employed tactics quite close to those of the fortresses.

Units and formations that had ended up isolated had occupied an all-round defence and sought to hold out, awaiting a relief attack from without. It is sufficient to recall Kholm, Demyansk and Sukhinichi (von Gilsa's group) in the 1941–2 winter campaign, and Millerovo and Chertkovo in the winter of 1942–3. However, in 1944–5 the concept was taken to its logical conclusion and formalized in a series of orders. The key moment in its formation became the *Führer*'s Directive No. 11 of 8 March 1944 on 'fortified places' (*Festung Platz*). It was pointed out as early as the introductory part of the order that 'The fortresses are supposed to carry out the same tasks as the fortresses of the past. They must prevent the enemy seizing places important from the operational point of view. They should allow themselves to be surrounded and thus tie down as many large enemy forces as possible. In this manner they must create the prerequisites for successful counterblows.'[17]

One must note that they assiduously avoided using the word 'fortress' in the text of the directive. The reasons for this were quite obvious – the name 'fortress', without permanent fortifications, appeared ridiculous. It was planned to employ cities as fortresses, which were assigned the role of 'breakwaters' along the path of the attacking enemy. The 'fortified places' were supposed to tie down significant numbers of the advancing forces, diverting them to the siege instead of continuing the offensive. The necessity of freeing up a road junction was supposed to force the Red Army to storm the fortress. In this sense, Ternopol' was practically an ideal choice: all the roads, railways and communications lines came together in the city.

Ternopol' was declared a fortress on 10 March by an order from Army Group South, to be operationally subordinated to the Fourth Panzer Army command (the subordinating of the fortress to corps was clearly forbidden by Directive No. 11). The chief problem of Fortress Ternopol' was the absence of a permanent garrison made up of combat-capable troops, which should have been the equivalent of at least a division in strength. As of 11 March 1944 the garrison numbered 94 officers, 682 NCOs and 3,952 enlisted men.[18] Elements of the 949th Grenadier Regiment – 47 officers, 364 NCOs and 1,868 enlisted men – formed the most numerous group. The remaining elements comprised a very colourful company. The so-called 'Demba' Fusilier Battalion (nearly 700 men), which had been formed from an NCO school, later showed a high level of combat capability. It was not named after its commander, but for the place where it was formed (in Poland). Aside from this, the garrison also included a shock group from the 154th Reserve Division (244 men), a reinforcement battalion from the 7th Panzer Division, and the remnants of the 543rd Rear Security Battalion (134 men). The latter consisted of non-combatants with physical shortcomings and since the end of 1941 had been guarding military sites in Ternopol'. The garrison also included engineer subunits from the 7th Panzer and 359th Infantry Divisions. The so-called 'Group Fischer' was separate. The 500th Penal Battalion numbered 236 men. It included servicemen from the Kriegsmarine,[19] Luftwaffe[20] and panzer units. Nor did they do without 'eastern volunteers'. The remnants of a battalion from the 'Galicia' Division, which had fallen back into the city, numbered 153 men. The command element of the 'Galicia' Division, down to section commanders, was German. Aside from the infantry and engineers, there were a number of scattered artillery units in Ternopol', including an anti-tank battalion and a battalion of self-propelled 150mm heavy infantry guns from the *Leibstandarte* Division.[21] The armoured forces were represented by two Panthers and two armoured personnel carriers from the 7th Panzer Division, and a battery of *Sturmgeschützen*[22] from the recently-formed 301st Assault Gun Brigade.

Directive No. 11 devoted particular attention to the role and place of the fortress commander, stating that 'The "fortress" commander must be a soldier with a strong will, specially found for this position, if possible, at the rank of general'. Major General Egon von Neindorff, who had previously commanded the 36th Infantry Division in the Bobruisk area, was selected as the 'strong soldier' for Ternopol'. However, he arrived at Ternopol' nearly two weeks after his appointment as fortress commander and was able to do little before the city's encirclement. Before the autumn of 1943, von Neindorff had not commanded so much as a regiment or division on the Eastern Front, having only combat experience in the West and the Balkans. In 1941–3 he commanded units and formations in France. This was a shortcoming on the one hand, while on the other he had no experience of defeats and retreats (the situation in Army Group Centre during the winter of 1943–4 was relatively stable).

Meanwhile, the fighting for Ternopol' continued. One should not think that the 4th Guards Tank Corps' units fighting in Ternopol' had been left to their fate by the command. In order to turn the situation around, they attempted to move up units of the 4th Tank Army, which were in the Skalata area, to help Poluboyarov's tank troops. At 15.15 on 15 March the commander of the 6th Guards Mechanized Corps was ordered to put out a screen in the Skalata area, consisting of one brigade, and to move on Ternopol' with his remaining forces. The 63rd Tank Brigade, with a battalion from the 61st Guards Tank Brigade, was additionally attached to the corps, for a strength of 32 T-34s, two SU-85s, and 289 automatic riflemen.[23] However, it proved nearly impossible to rapidly pull the corps out of the fighting around Skalat, so they dispatched a forward detachment and the reinforced 63rd Guards Tank Brigade. The latter was finally halted around Romanuvka by the start of the German counteroffensive.

So why was Ternopol' not taken from the march? Later, under interrogation in Soviet captivity, one of the officers of the Ternopol' garrison, a Lieutenant Colonel Keienburg,[24] in reply to a question as to the reasons for the fortress's prolonged resistance, stated: 'I believe that the NCO training command [the 'Demba' Fusilier Battalion] played a very significant role in this, if not the decisive one.'[25] In a report by the 4th Tank Corps, it was noted with vexation: 'The first attempt to capture Ternopol' through a surprise tank attack in conjunction with infantry, while it enjoyed great initial success, subsequently ended in failure due to the infantry's slow actions.'[26] One must say that the German side confirms the data by the 4th Tank Corps command as to the infantry's passive behaviour during the first storming of Ternopol'. There is the following entry in the Fourth Panzer Army's war diary: 'The commandant rates the combat value of the enemy infantry before Ternopol' as insignificant and that of the tank troops as good.'[27] To be fair, one must say that the Soviet infantry in the beginning phase of the battle around Ternopol' had suffered significant losses. From 7 to 13 March the 322nd Rifle Division lost 185 men killed, 250 missing in action and 872 men wounded, for a total of 1,307 men.[28]

Within the framework of the First Ukrainian Front's overall offensive, the 60th Army's 15th Rifle Corps (322nd, 336th, 148th, and 340th Rifle Divisions, 1st Guards Artillery Division, 7th Anti-Tank Brigade, 98th Mortar Regiment, and two combat engineer battalions) was assigned the task of capturing Ternopol', in conjunction with the 4th Guards Tank Corps. At this time the corps occupied a 30km front. The 15th Rifle Corps' strength is characterized by the following figures (see table).

As is clear from the figures given opposite, the formations were considerably below their authorized strength. One should also note that the shortage concerned not only the rank and file, but the artillery as well. The latter, to be sure, was compensated to a significant degree by the presence of the 1st Guards Artillery Division, with 152mm, 122mm and 76mm guns.

Table 1.2: The Numerical Strength of the 15th Rifle Corps' Divisions as of 20 March 1944[29]

Unit	Men	Mortars		
		120mm	*82mm*	*50mm*
322nd Rifle	5,312	16	42	–
336th Rifle	4,129	17	20	3
148th Rifle	4,652	16	21	–
340th Rifle	5,940	4	37	–

Unit	Guns				Anti-Tank Rifles
	122mm	*76mm (Divisional)*	*76mm (Regimental)*	*45mm*	
322nd Rifle	6	12	7	21	57
336th Rifle	11	11	4	12	73
148th Rifle	11	13	3	4	35
340th Rifle	1	9	5	7	26

The 15th Rifle Corps' main task was to secure the commitment of the 1st Tank Army into the breach and to cover its right flank. This task determined the choice of the direction of the main attack. It was decided to launch it along the corps' left flank with the forces of the 336th, 148th and 340th Rifle Divisions. Following the crushing of the enemy's defences, it was planned to deploy to the west and to bypass Ternopol' from the south, with a simultaneous arrival at the Vosushka River and the formation of an external encirclement front around Ternopol'.

By the start of the Soviet offensive on 4 March 1944, the Ternopol' garrison numbered 4,422 men, including 97 officers, 714 NCOs and 3,611 enlisted men.[30] Aside from rifles, the garrison disposed of 330 automatic rifles, 182 light machine guns, 45 heavy machine guns, 24 81mm mortars, 18 120mm mortars, nine 37mm anti-tank guns, a 50mm anti-tank gun, seven 75mm anti-tank guns, four 75mm regimental guns, two 150mm regimental guns and six 150mm self-propelled regimental guns. The garrison also disposed of three 1eFH16 105mm light field howitzers and seven s.FH18 150mm heavy field howitzers (including one *Hummel*[31]). There were six *Sturmgeschützen*, one StuH assault howitzer[32] and one armoured personnel carrier. Overall, it would be difficult to call the garrison defenceless.

The distribution of forces along the defensive sectors was as follows (if one may speak of the defensive core of each sector). The 500th Penal

Battalion and elements of the 'Galicia' Division (10 officers, 68 NCOs and 510 enlisted men) defended the northern sector along a 2.5km front. Captain Fischer, the commander of the penal battalion, was in charge of the sector. The 949th Infantry Regiment (seven officers, 76 NCOs and 505 enlisted men) defended the eastern sector along a 3.6km front. It was commanded by the regimental commander, Colonel von Schonfeld. The so-called 'Becker Group' (eight officers, 62 NCOs and 358 enlisted men) defended the southern sector along a 2.1km front. Finally, the 543rd Security Battalion (six officers, 73 NCOs and 379 enlisted men) defended the western sector (the Zagrobelya area). Major Lentz, the battalion commander, commanded here.

Each of the defensive sectors consisted of field positions along the approaches to the city. Full-scale trenches had been dug and wooden stands for the machine guns had been put up in the machine-gun nests. There were covered dugouts with a layer of logs in the communications trenches. A much weaker second trench line, consisting of unfinished trenches, had been prepared, with gaps of 70–100m. The city of Ternopol' itself was almost completely unprepared and its buildings had not been configured for defence. The defenders fired from windows and, in some cases, from holes caused by exploding shells. In this Ternopol' sharply differed from the later German fortresses of 1945, with their barricades across the streets and windows blocked up with bricks, leaving only narrow embrasures.

The defence of the Ternopol' fortress relied on propping up the perimeter of the defensive front with a powerful reserve, which was the 'Demba' Fusilier Battalion. On 20 March 1944 it numbered 11 officers, 116 NCOs and 511 enlisted men, armed with 100 sub-machine guns, 42 light machine guns, 11 heavy machine guns, one 81mm mortar, eight 120mm mortars, two 75mm anti-tank guns and one 50mm anti-tank gun.[33] There was also the 'Schtiller Armoured Group' (named after its commander, Captain Schtiller), in which all the *Sturmgeschützen* and *Grille*[34] guns were included. The garrison's headquarters consisted of 10 officers, 4 office workers, 20 NCOs and 68 enlisted men.[35]

The city of Ternopol' could boast of no fortified structures. The majority of the city's buildings were made of brick, from one to two storeys in the outskirts and from one to four storeys in the city centre. The majority of blocks had from one to three buildings of three to four storeys, which formed the core of the block and around which were grouped smaller one to two-storey buildings with outbuildings. However, the buildings in the centre of Ternopol' were quite sturdy, with walls up to a metre thick. The streets were fairly narrow, with streets 20–30m wide predominating, with only the L'vov highway having a width up to 50m. A railway lines cut the city from north to south, with a large number of branch lines in the area of the station. There were no squares in the city, with the exception of the market.

The German command placed its hopes on stabilizing the situation in the Ternopol' area on the 507th Panzer Battalion (with Tigers),[36] which had unloaded from trains on 21 March, the day of the start of the Soviet offensive. The battalion was subordinated to the XLVIII Panzer Corps. However, it was decided to employ the Tiger battalion to the north of Ternopol', quite far from the axis of the Soviet forces' main attack, probably for the purpose of attacking deep into the flank and rear of the attacking Soviet units. The underestimation of the enemy would mean this plan was doomed from the start. As a result, on 23 March the 507th Panzer Battalion received orders to 'rout the tanks the enemy has crossed over the Seret River along the 357th Infantry Division's sector'. The 60th Army, reinforced by anti-tank units and the 59th Independent Tank Regiment (twelve T-34s on 22 March), was attacking here to bypass Ternopol' from the north. On 22 March the regiment occupied the village of Kurovtse and on the morning of the following day arrived at the Ternopol'–L'vov road. The regiment was to support the infantry of the 60th Army's 28th Rifle Corps, or more exactly Major General A.Ya. Kiselyov's[37] 140th Rifle Division and Major General P.M. Bezhko's 107th Rifle Division.

According to Soviet data, the 140th Rifle Division's 96th Rifle Regiment was attacked by five tanks and a battalion of infantry. The Tigers broke into the depth of the position of one of the regiment's battalions, but the infantrymen did not run away, but, while letting the tanks pass, began to cut them off from the infantry. As a result, the counter-attacking Germans took cover before the forward edge and the tanks turned back. The same division's 283rd Rifle Regiment was subjected to yet another attack. According to Soviet data, it was carried out 'primarily by tanks', but was later repeated by seven tanks and a battalion of infantry. Later the form of attack changed once again: three tanks fired from stationary positions while supporting the actions of their infantry. An armoured train also operated against the 140th Rifle Division's 283rd Rifle Regiment. As a result, the 283rd Rifle Regiment fell back during the second half of the day and consolidated, and its attack on Yezerna was halted.

However, the most effective opposition to the Tigers proved to be on the 140th Rifle Division's left flank. At 08.00 on 23 March the 59th Tank Regiment's

T-34s, advancing from Kurovtse, reached the L'vov highway. It was here that their collision with the newly-arrived Tigers, which were moving from Yezerna, took place. The outcome of the fighting was more than predictable: the 59th Tank Regiment lost eight T-34s knocked out and burned[38] and fell back to Kurovtse. The Germans claimed seven Soviet tanks destroyed and two 'knocked out' by the Tigers.[39] The infantry, which the 59th Tank Regiment's tanks were supposed to support, advanced, while being held by the enemy's artillery and machine-gun fire. In the Kurovtse area, the 140th Rifle Division's 285th Rifle Regiment, as noted in the division's operational report, 'engaged in a firefight with the enemy's 12 tanks', but the presence of tanks forced them to order the regiment to go over to the defensive. Even the 107th Rifle Division, which had been subordinated to Chernyakhovskii from the 13th Army and which had been moved to the Yezerna area following a march (its units had managed to get some rest), came under attack by the Tigers. As indicated in the neighbouring 140th Rifle Division's operational report, German tanks attacked Tsebruv and 'sowed panic in elements of the 107th Rifle Division that were occupying this place'. The situation in Tsebruv was restored by 16.00. On the evening of 24 March yet another attack, with the support of Tiger tanks, followed, this time against the 140th Rifle Division's 96th Rifle Regiment (five vehicles, according to Soviet data), and two 45mm guns were knocked out. At the same time, the formation's losses were moderate: according to the results for 23 March, the 140th Rifle Division lost 109 men killed and 140 wounded.[40] On the whole, one must admit that with the commitment of the Tigers into the fighting the Germans managed not to halt, but only to contain the Soviet units' offensive on Yezerna and around it. However, the Tigers' partial success was absolutely pointless, as it in no way effected the advance of the Soviet tank armies to the Dnestr or even the 4th Guards Tank Corps bypassing Ternopol' from the south.

On 24 March the 507th Panzer Battalion once again attacked to support the infantry units. This time the attack fell upon the 140th Rifle Division's 96th and 283rd Rifle Regiments, which were trying to bypass Yezerna from the north. The Tigers once again cut into the 96th Rifle Regiment's positions. However, this time this did not take place without cost for the heavy German tanks. According to Soviet data, 'three enemy Tiger tanks were knocked out, of which the enemy recovered two tanks during the night'. According to German data, the 507th Panzer Battalion irretrievably lost two Tigers. One tank (chassis no. 250682) was destroyed by an engine fire and the explosion of

its ammunition 700m to the north-east of Yezerna, and the second (chassis no. 250827) was put out of action by artillery fire 500m to the west of Nesterovtsy and burned.[41] It is interesting to note that the 28th Rifle Corps' infantry dealt with the enemy's heavy tanks entirely on its own. Furthermore, having survived the Tiger counter-attack on the evening of 24 March, the Soviet infantrymen resumed the offensive on the night of 24/25 March. The 140th Rifle Division's losses for 24 March were sixty-four men killed and forty-three wounded.

Essentially, the German defence in the area to the west of Ternopol' was saved from collapse only by the Tigers. The strength of the 357th Infantry Division's combat elements at this time numbered 1,859 men, and those of the 359th Infantry Division 1,863 men, not including the 949th Grenadier Regiment encircled in Ternopol'. One should mention that the Army Group South command reacted with great displeasure to the news that the newly-arrived 68th, 357th and 359th Infantry Divisions ended up being routed within a few days. In response, General Fangor, the chief of staff of the Fourth Panzer Army, wrote:

This should come as no surprise. The divisions consist primarily of 18-year-olds. Having barely begun their training, they ended up being drawn into a large-scale battle against large enemy tank forces. With all will in the world, the young people were not able to withstand this, either physically or spiritually, which the poor condition of the roads and terrain contributed to in no small degree. Today these soldiers are in a state of apathy and completely exhausted.[42]

As of 24 March, out of fifty-one Tigers in the 507th Panzer Battalion, only twenty-six vehicles were ready for combat, with sixteen listed as in short-term repair, seven in major repair and two listed as irretrievably lost.[43] Subsequently, the 507th Panzer Battalion's heavy tanks propped up the infantry for a time, and then were included in Friebe's group. The so-called 'Group Mittelmeer', from the 503rd Panzer Battalion (three combat-ready Tigers and six in short-term repair as of 23 March),[44] was also dispatched here to the 359th Infantry Division. Thus, while disposing of quite impressive Tiger forces, the XLVIII Panzer Corps was unable to bring them to bear in time to repel the Soviet offensive. One should also note that at that moment the 60th Army's anti-tank weapons had been concentrated in the area to the south and south-west of Ternopol' to cover the offensive flank of M.Ye. Katukov's[45] tank army.

On the night of 23/24 March and the morning of 24 March the 15th Rifle Corps' forces attacked to envelop the city from the north and south. The 322nd Rifle Division attacked the village of Yanuvka to the west of Ternopol', through Pronyatin, in order to bypass the city from the north. The 148th Rifle Division moved on Yanuvka from the west and south-west, attacking through Berezovitsa. At midday on 24 March the divisions linked up in the area of Height 361.0, to the west of Zagrobelya, and completed the encirclement of Ternopol'. At the time of the encirclement, the garrison's ration strength was 4,602 men (103 officers, including office personnel, 745 NCOs and 3,764 enlisted men).[46] In accordance with one of the later reports, this was not the combat strength, but rather the overall ration strength.[47] Most likely, the increase since 20 March took place as a result of the retirement into Ternopol' of various units, or by including among the garrison's number elements which were already in the city but which were not formally subordinated to the commandant.

The Soviet units sought to consolidate the encirclement by attacking into the rear of Ternopol', against Zagrobelya. However, a scouting party, consisting of three tanks from the 13th Guards Tank Brigade, which was dispatched to Zagrobelya, was unsuccessful and all three vehicles were burned by fire from enemy tanks in the city. The beast which had fallen into the trap was still strong. But at this moment hardly anyone thought that the siege of Ternopol' would continue for another three long weeks.

The German command's next step in the Ternopol' area was an action which might be called a 'raid'. On 24 March the fortress commandant received a radiogram from the Fourth Panzer Army's headquarters: 'On the morning of 25.3 the formation will attack from Yezerna along the Yezerna–Ternopol' road, in order to bring a supply convoy into Ternopol' and to rout the enemy west of Ternopol'.' One might have assumed that Ternopol' would be relieved, or that a corridor would be punched through to the city in order to extract the garrison from the encirclement. However, an addition to the radiogram left no doubts as to the task of the group dispatched to Ternopol': 'The tank formation has the task of easing the garrison's situation, not to bring it out. The fortress is to be held in accordance with the *Führer*'s order.' The commandant was also ordered to carry out preparations for receiving supplies and shipping out the wounded with tanks, in order to shorten the wait time of the combat group in the city and to enable it to head back as quickly as possible.

The reserve, which the Fourth Panzer Army command was preparing to employ for accompanying the supply convoy into Ternopol', became the so-

called 'Friebe Panzer Formation' (*Panzerverband* Friebe), which took its name from its commander, Colonel Werner Friebe. One should note that here the term *verband* was used, and not 'battle group'. The tank formation was gathered together from units that had arrived as reinforcements. First of all, this was a battalion of Panthers (the 11th Panzer Regiment's 1st Battalion), which had been returned to the Eastern Front following its rearmament with new equipment, and which had initially belonged to the 6th Panzer Division. Secondly, these were the first battalions of the 8th and 74th Motorized Infantry Regiments in armoured personnel carriers, which had earlier belonged to the 8th and 19th Panzer Divisions. Colonel Friebe himself was not a tank commander, having only staff experience, albeit at a panzer corps headquarters. Overall, the formation consisted of two battalions of motorized infantry in armoured personnel carriers, a battalion of Panthers, an artillery battalion, an engineer company, a signals company, a heavy bridge command, and a battalion of armoured rocket artillery. The latter, however, was only able to enter the fighting on 26 March and did not take part in the raid of 25 March. Signals and medical subunits had been attached to the formation and it could operate independently apart from the corps' and army's main forces. The strength of 'Friebe's Formation' was about 5,000 men (5,089-man ration strength as of 26 March). On the whole, this was a very valuable resource, particularly when taking into account the catastrophic situation of the encircled First Panzer Army and the XIII Army Corps' critical situation around Brody. Nevertheless, the formation was activated in the interests of the Ternopol' fortress.

At a conference between the commander of the XLVIII Panzer Corps, General Balck,[48] and Colonel Friebe (army commander Rauss took part in the conversation by telephone), the following plan was adopted for 25 March:

> At 04.30 the offensive by the units of the 507th Battalion of 'Panzers' in Yezerna, followed by Friebe's formation. The destruction of the enemy a bit east of Yezerna by the 507th Battalion. The rout of the expected flank threat from the north and south, a turn to the south and the destruction of the enemy in Pokropivna. At 04.45 the attack by Friebe's formation along the road to the east, toward Ternopol'. Establish contact with the fortress and secure the passage of the supply convoy.[49]

Friebe attempted to postpone the raid by a day, but was unsuccessful. He tried to justify this by the necessity of giving the troops a rest following their march from the Brody area and to familiarize themselves with the terrain, to at least repair six Panthers, to await the arrival of the rocket launchers and, finally, to recharge the radio batteries (which would have improved command and control). But he was turned down. Moreover, the 507th Panzer Battalion, with Tigers, was not directly subordinated to him. As was noted in the report by the staff of the XLVIII Panzer Corps, which was written after the raid, 'This would have required the concentration of the battalion in Yezerna and the resulting complete baring of the front. This, in turn, would most likely have led to the crushing of the 357th Infantry Division's front, which, as experience shows, is incapable of overcoming a crisis.' That is, having transformed the Tigers into a prop for the poorly-trained infantry, Balck's headquarters did not want to part with them and transfer them to Friebe. Moreover, even the army headquarters' direct and unambiguous instructions, which followed at 22.40 on 24 March, were ignored: 'The 507th Battalion of Tigers must be subordinated to Friebe's tank formation.' The pretext became the late arrival of the order to resubordinate the battalion, which prevented them from issuing the corresponding orders to the units. As a result, the 507th Panzer Battalion attacked, while remaining subordinated to Balck's headquarters. On the whole, one sees here Balck striving to employ the subordinated formation, first of all, in the interests of restoring his own corps' front. In its turn, the Fourth Panzer Army command sought to 'push through' a munitions convoy into Ternopol' and to avoid being accused of poorly preparing the city as a fortress. After all, there had been an entire week of relative calm in which to carry out the *Führer*'s will.

According to a report on the condition of the XLVIII Panzer Corps' armour of 25 March,[50] there were twenty-two combat-ready Panthers and two *Hummel* self-propelled guns (plus about 120 armoured personnel carriers, judging from later reports) in Friebe's group, and twenty-six Tigers in the 507th Panzer Battalion. It's of interest to note that Friebe, in his report on the results of the raid, wrote about the 507th Panzer Battalion's fifteen combat-ready Tigers. This forces one to suppose that on 25 March the battalion was not operating at full strength and that a part of the vehicles could have been 'held back'. The convoy, which it was planned to take into Ternopol', consisted of motor vehicles with 40 tonnes of ammunition and five medical vehicles. The convoy was prepared in great haste, left L'vov and was unable to arrive earlier than 08.00 on 25 March. However, the decision was made to begin the offensive, without waiting for it.

The main opponent of the German raid remained the 60th Army's rifle units. At this time the retention of one of a division's rifle regiments on the approaches to Ternopol' and the movement of the remaining two to the west had become the standard scheme for Chernyakhovskii's army. Two regiments from the 322nd Rifle Division were along the approaches to Yezerna and, to the south, near Pokropivna, there were two regiments from the 107th Rifle Division, and even further to the south were two regiments from the 148th Rifle Division. Moreover, the 107th Rifle Division's 516th Rifle Regiment bestrode the Yezerna–Ternopol' road in the area of Height 363, occupying a perimeter defence and forming an anti-tank strongpoint standing right in the path of the German raid toward Ternopol'. This decision seems quite logical: to cut the road along the path of a possible relief attack. Only the 140th Rifle Division was located in its entirety around Yezerna and to the north.

However, the main surprise for Group Friebe's Panthers and Tigers was still only moving up to the battlefield. As early as 23 March, when Friebe's formation was still located in the Brody area, the First Ukrainian Front's artillery commander resubordinated Colonel N.D. Chevola's 8th Guards Independent Anti-Tank Brigade to the 60th Army. One of the heroes of the Kursk salient and the fighting around Korsun', at this time he had been nominated to be made a Hero of the Soviet Union, which he would be in the summer of 1944. Chevola's brigade received orders to move up to the Yankovtsy (to the north-east of Yezerna and north of Ternopol' along the Seret River) area for the purpose of covering the crossing over the Seret. The 8th Guards Independent Anti-Tank Artillery Brigade was moving to the crossing as early as the evening of 24 March. At that moment it disposed of forty ZIS-3s[51] and nineteen ZIS-2s,[52] which was a powerful argument against Friebe's detachment. The anti-tank brigade was still located away from the road to Ternopol', but its mobility enabled it to quickly move up to the threatened axis. The overwhelming majority of the brigade's motor transport consisted of Lend-Lease[53] Studebakers, Dodge ¾s and Willys Jeeps, capable of overcoming difficult road conditions.

The German raid on Ternopol' began early in the morning of 25 March with an attack by Tigers from Yezerna. In essence, the idea of keeping the 507th Panzer Battalion subordinated to the corps was simple – to keep it on a 'short leash'. The battalion was given the task of attacking from the bridgehead near Yezerna and to punch a path for Friebe's tank formation, and to then 'cover it'. The Tigers were supposed to 'patrol approximately as far as the halfway point on the road to Ternopol' and to keep the road open both for the tank formation and for the convoy'. The 'leash' thus remained quite short, only as far as the halfway point. If they had subordinated the Tiger battalion to Friebe, then he would have placed it in the front as a ram and followed it all the way to Ternopol'. Friebe essentially wrote this openly later in his report. Such a scenario for the valuable Tigers evidently did not suit Balck.

Nonetheless, five Tigers was quite a serious argument. Elements of the 140th Rifle Division's 283rd Rifle Regiment were thrown back from Yezerna by the tanks' attack, while on the one hand part of the infantrymen remained in the buildings they occupied on the eastern outskirts of the town (even having telephone communications with the command), while part fell back to the east without reporting this. According to the results of an investigation, that was instigated by divisional commander A.Ya. Kiselyov, Captain V.F. Rzhevskii, the 22-year-old commander of a battalion in the 283rd Rifle Regiment, was dispatched to a penal battalion,[54] while the regimental commander Gusev was warned that he was not fully up to his job. The elements of two of the 322nd Rifle Division's regiments, which had been attacked by German heavy tanks, were thrown out of their positions and retreated. Friebe's formation moved behind the Tigers. The tank battalion moved forward as a ram, while the infantry moved behind it in armoured personnel carriers – one battalion to the left of the road and one to the right, the road itself having been mined. However, the most serious problem became the Soviet artillery. As Friebe later wrote in his report on the raid, 'Large forces of light and heavy artillery waged well-aimed and concentrated fire from the south, east and north'. On the one hand, Friebe's detachment, which consisted of armoured vehicles, did not have to fear artillery. The armoured personnel carriers' and tanks' armour defended them against mortar and shell fragments. On the other hand, not having any artillery of its own, Friebe's detachment could put up nothing to oppose this bombardment. The Tigers could not do anything against fire from guns in hidden positions. In these conditions, it was impossible for the ammunition convoy to accompany the attack. Under bombardment it would simply have been converted into an enormous fireworks display.

In the meantime, having received information on the enemy's advance on Ternopol', Colonel Chevola moved up the 322nd and 323rd Guards Independent Anti-Tank Artillery Regiments (ZIS-3 guns) to head them off. At around midday the anti-tank troops of the 322nd Guards Independent Anti-Tank Artillery Regiment reached the road and took up positions from the march, while reinforcing the 107th Rifle Division's regiment's anti-tank defence. As a result, Friebe's group ran into stubborn resistance 4km from Zagrobelya, literally within a few paces of the fortress. Besides the anti-tank artillery, several tanks from the 4th Guards Tank Corps' 13th and 14th Guards Tank Brigades became an obstacle. Also according to German data, the armoured personnel carriers and tanks of Friebe's group were subjected to attacks from the air by Soviet ground-attack aircraft. Actually, according to Soviet data, despite the unfavourable weather conditions, the 5th Fighter Corps' 227th Assault Air Division, in groups of two to four Il-2[55] aircraft, without fighter cover, attacked the enemy's vehicles in the Yezerna area. Breaking through this well-prepared strongpoint could have resulted in heavy losses of tanks and armoured personnel carriers. If the relief of the garrison and its extrication to link up with the XLVIII Panzer Corps' main forces had been required, then these losses would have been justified. But given the impossibility of getting the trucks into the fortress under fire, breaking through into Ternopol' made no sense. The situation was exacerbated by the great expenditure of fuel by the tanks and armoured personnel carriers on the washed-out roads.

As a result, at 13.00 on 25 March Friebe made the decision to cut short the operation and, having evacuated as many vehicles as possible, fall back to his starting position. Fresh on the tail of these events, Friebe reported to the chief of staff of the XLVIII Panzer Corps:

> A very difficult day and the enemy were quite different from what we had expected. He had organized his anti-tank defensive positions along the line of the heights and mined the road. We had to clear out all of the hollows in the grove west of Ternopol'. I wanted to bypass the road from the south and regrouped. There were very powerful positions before the heights near Height 361 (1.5km north of Yanovka). There was particularly heavy artillery fire against the jumping-off positions. Following the loss of commanders and communications equipment, as well as in light of the absence of an order to liberate those besieged, I made the decision to withdraw. The withdrawal was very difficult, and we managed to carry it out only under the cover of smokescreens.

According to Soviet data, elements of the 322nd Rifle Division's 1087th Rifle Regiment were defending on Height 361. By 'the grove west of Ternopol'', we should probably understand the Chakhary woods, to which units of the 322nd Rifle Division fell back.

Only eleven Panthers (although twenty-five were counted during the march) remained in fighting condition in Friebe's group immediately following the raid. On the morning of 26 March three Panthers and three armoured personnel carriers were listed as irretrievably lost.[56] At the same time the Germans claimed to have destroyed twenty-five anti-tank positions and three tanks, but the 322nd Guards Anti-Tank Artillery Regiment lost only one of its guns. One should state that the claims by Chevola's anti-tank troops were more modest and more realistic – three armoured personnel carriers, one fuel tanker and one medium tank. The 107th Rifle Division claimed to have knocked out nine enemy tanks, including three Tigers, four armoured personnel carriers and three motor vehicles.[57]

A breakthrough to Ternopol' and the retreat back after a few hours would most likely have resulted in the massacre of Friebe's detachment. By evening the 322nd Guards Anti-Tank Artillery Regiment had reached its positions astride the road. Correspondingly, even having crushed one regiment of Colonel Chevola's brigade, the Germans would have had to face a second regiment on the return journey. Moreover, the Soviet command disposed of sufficient forces in the area of the road to form a dense infantry screen for several hours. Correspondingly, in case of a breakthrough to Ternopol', Friebe's group stood a good chance of staying locked up in the fortress. On the whole, one may state that in this episode the power of artillery had been clearly demonstrated. It remained the god of the 'war of engines' of 1941–5. Despite the presence of a powerful tank fist and motorized infantry in armoured personnel carriers, the absence of proper artillery support (up to 210mm inclusively, as had been the practice earlier among the German panzer forces), deprived Friebe's group of the opportunity to even resolve tasks limited in time and space.

One should note that the commandant of Ternopol' found out about the attempt to push through a supply convoy to the fortress after 16.00 (having received a telegram: 'The escort of the supply convoy is impossible today. Await further orders'). At 14.00, when Friebe's tank formation had already set out on its return journey, von Neindorff was still just making inquiries about its location. They simply forgot about him, while the corps and army headquarters were thinking about their own tasks.

However, the activity of Friebe's group as part of the XLVIII Panzer Corps was not limited to the unsuccessful raid on Ternopol'. The corps command sought to take maximum advantage of the shock capabilities of Friebe's tanks and motorized infantry for stabilizing the front. An order arrived on the following morning (that is, 26 March) to attack south of the road on Kozlov, in order to destroy 'the powerful enemy forces that have crossed the Vosushka to the west' and to clear the Yezerna–Kozlov–Plaucha Mala–Zborov area. This time, Balck's corps subordinated the Tigers in the Yezerna area to Friebe without hesitation. Besides this, the XLVIII Panzer Corps command put the 359th Infantry Division into the counteroffensive, which was supposed to attack from Taurov to Kozlov, supported by five Tigers and one Panther (it's unclear where the latter came from, as it suddenly appeared in the latest report, so it's possible that the vehicle was from Friebe's group).

According to the report on the state of its equipment as of 08.00 on 26 March,[58] Friebe's group disposed of thirty-eight combat-ready Panthers (including fourteen on the march from the Brody area), four combat-ready command tanks, twenty-eight combat tanks and two command Panthers in short-term repair and four in long-term repair. Aside from this, there were 127 combat-ready armoured personnel carriers.

At 05.00 on 26 March Friebe's formation went over to the offensive in two combat groups along both banks of the Vosushka. The right combat group (the Tigers from the 507th Battalion and a battalion of infantry in armoured personnel carriers) attacked Kozlov from the area 2km west of Yezerna. Elements of the 148th Rifle Division had actually crossed the creek in this area. The left combat group of Friebe's detachment (a battalion of Panthers and an infantry battalion in armoured personnel carriers) was advancing to the east, from Yezerna along the eastern bank of the Vosushka toward Kozlov. Units of the 107th Rifle Division were located along the immediate approaches to Yezerna. One must say that Balck was an experienced commander and understood the possibilities of a tank attack against an attacking enemy. Units having offensive tasks were more vulnerable than those that had gone over to the defensive. On the morning of 26 March the 107th Rifle Division's 504th Rifle Regiment attacked Yezerna. The attack by Friebe's Panthers and armoured personnel carriers was an unpleasant surprise for it. As noted in the formation's operational report, 'The 1st and 3rd/504th Rifle Regiment ... were scattered and partially destroyed following a short battle'.[59] Yet another battalion from the 504th Rifle Regiment, which was covering the flank near Pokropivna, was also attacked by tanks and 'scattered'. The regimental headquarters in Pokropivna came under tank attack as well. The 107th Rifle Division's 522nd Rifle Regiment, which was attacking to the west, also came under attack by tanks from different directions and, quoting the operational report, 'having suffered losses, was scattered'.[60] At the same time, the consequences of the attack for the 107th Rifle Division should not be overstated. The division's losses were listed as 38 men killed and 115 wounded in the 28th Rifle Corps' evening operational report.[61] Nor is there any indication of an epic rout in the German operational documents – a report by Friebe's group to the corps headquarters mentions only forty prisoners.[62] The negative consequences of the attack were significantly mitigated by the fact that this was once again a raid, and not a counterblow for the purpose of occupying a particular line. As Colonel Friebe wrote in his report on the results of the fighting, 'The left combat group fell back along the undamaged bridge in the Kozlov area to the western bank of the stream, in order to prepare the formation west of Kozlov in accordance with the corps' order on further operations'. Actually, the mass of tanks and armoured personnel carriers, having attacked from Yezerna and 'scattered' Soviet elements near Pokropivna, did not halt and did not consolidate, but returned to the west, allowing the Soviet infantry to come to and ask itself the question 'What was that?'

The second combat group of Friebe's formation, together with the Tigers, advanced more slowly, while trying to throw even small groups of Soviet infantry out of the farms. Elements of the 148th Rifle Division faced this combat group, but there was not an apocalyptic picture of loss of control and subunits scattered by tanks in its operational reports. According to a preliminary evening report, the division lost nineteen men killed and thirty-seven wounded. At the same time, the period of active operations ended as early as the morning and by 09.00 Berlin time Friebe's right combat group had reached Kozlov, which at this moment had already been taken by an attack by Tigers and the 359th Infantry Division's infantry.

Upon receiving reports about the quite rapid achievement of the assigned tasks, Balck attempted to squeeze everything he could out of the Panthers and mechanized infantry temporarily assigned to him. He ordered that the success be developed further to the south and to immediately attack to the south-east with all forces and destroy the enemy in Slobodka and Gorodishche. That is, the armoured groups were supposed to pass with fire and sword along the entire front of the XLVIII Panzer Corps and stabilize the situation. However, it was already problematical whether an offensive that ran counter to the initial plans could be realized. By 17.00 Friebe had managed to gather a battalion of mechanized infantry and all the operational Panthers. The group began to advance to the south, but encountered stubborn resistance near Slobodka. The

135th Rifle Division's subunits, supported by the artillery of the 60th Army's 106th Rifle Corps, held out in Slobodka. As Friebe wrote later in his report, 'Heavy fighting developed with the enemy in Slobodka. Before long the entire inhabited locale was burning brightly and the terrain was illuminated as if by daylight. Powerful mortar fire, by all appearances primarily from the eastern bank of the stream, fell upon the attacking group. It was impossible to enter the inhabited locale. One may assume that the enemy can no longer be in the place.' However, this was an attempt to turn wish into reality. The gathering twilight forced them to discontinue the fight for Slobodka until the next morning. As early as nightfall Friebe's formation was removed from the XLVIII Panzer Corps for a new operation to stabilize the situation in the Brody area. General Balck soberly evaluated the time Friebe's formation would be subordinated to him and sought to get the most out of its tanks and infantry. He managed to do this to a certain extent, but one cannot but note that Chernyakhovskii's headquarters did not abandon offensive operations as a consequence. During the following days the 60th Army's right-flank formations sought to advance to the west.

On the day after the unsuccessful attempt to break into Ternopol' with the forces of Friebe's group, the Soviet command issued an ultimatum to the garrison to lay down its arms, which was rejected by von Neindorff. After this, Soviet forces began preparing to storm Ternopol'. The 302nd Rifle Division (it numbered 4,780 men[63] by the start of the fighting for Ternopol' and arrived on 31 March) was transferred to the 15th Rifle Corps and the 94th Rifle Corps, which included the 117th Guards and 99th Rifle Divisions, was also being brought up to the city. Units of the 94th Rifle Corps carried out a march on 26–27 March and moved to their jumping-off positions for the offensive.

The rank and file of the divisions brought in for the assault was quite small. The average strength of the companies in the 15th Rifle Corps' units was thirty men and even less in the 94th Rifle Corps – twenty-five men.[64] The divisions' strength in 'active bayonets' is shown in the table.

Table 1.3: Strength of the Divisions Assaulting Ternopol'.

	336th Rifle Div.[65]	*117th Gds Rifle Div.*
Active bayonets	1,200	1,161
Average Company Strength	30	43

	302nd Rifle Div.	*99th Rifle Div.*	*Total*
Active bayonets	845	459	3,665
Average Company Strength	35	17	–

Combat operations from 24 to 31 March primarily involved destroying the enemy along the external line of Ternopol's field defences. During this period the main attack was launched from the south-east by the forces of the 336th and 99th Rifle Divisions. The 336th Rifle Division's task at this time was 'to cut Ternopol' into two parts with two rifle regiments'.[66] The offensive's first goal became the capture of the main strongpoint of the enemy's external defensive line – the height with the quarry and brick factory. The height dominated the surrounding terrain and enabled the enemy to control the approaches to the city from the south and south-east. It had been transformed into a powerful strongpoint with a well-developed trench system, supported by artillery and mortar fire from the rear.

The 15th and 94th Rifle Corps' command, attaching great significance to this height, concentrated their forces for its storming. About 25,000 shells of various calibres were discharged against it. The garrison's problem was the fact that a battalion from the 949th Infantry Regiment, which consisted of recruits born in 1926, was defending along this very important sector. The two-hour artillery and aviation preparation caused heavy losses. The combat capability of this regiment's young rank and file was practically suppressed. The previously-mentioned Lieutenant Colonel Keienburg expressed himself on this matter as follows: 'As concerns the 949th Infantry Regiment, then it, if one may express oneself thusly, ruined the entire deal for us. The combat capability of the soldiers from 1926 was particularly low.'[67] As a result of a concentrated attack, the key height was captured by 28 March and Soviet units reached the outskirts of Ternopol'.

Only the artillery kept the defence of the fortress from collapsing. However, the Ternopol' garrison's artillery was not in a condition to constantly withstand the Soviet attacks. As was mentioned in one of the reports, two more days of such intensive fighting as on 28 March and the garrison's artillery would have had to cease fire. The 'air bridge' to Ternopol' did not even come close to supplying the defence's minimal needs. Only 44 containers, containing 144 high-explosive shells for the leIG18 infantry guns, 111 for the tank guns, 25 for the 75mm anti-tank guns, and 112 for the leFH18 light field howitzers made it to the garrison in five days of encirclement. The fortress commander reported to the commander of the Fourth Panzer Army: 'The amount of munitions delivered by air is completely insufficient and, in the majority of cases, unsuitable. The containers have been scattered about the entire town and one cannot find them between the buildings in conditions of enemy bombardment.

Part of them falls into enemy hands and part in the water, such as a case of medical supplies.' It was even impossible to reach the containers that had fallen on the roofs. Konstantin Simonov,[68] who spent time in Ternopol', later recalled: 'There were even some kinds of red spots on the roofs. I didn't understand this immediately and asked what this meant. It turns out that they're parachutes. The Germans drop ammunition with them and many of them fall in our lines. A lot of them get stuck on the roofs and we prevent them from retrieving them. We keep these roofs under fire day and night.' The contents of the containers were also an indirect indication of the state of the defence. P.N. Lashchenko, the commander of the 332nd Rifle Division, later recalled: 'The cargo often fell into our lines and were able to easily determine by their contents just what the enemy was particularly short of.'[69] However, one should note that the task of supplying the garrison by air was eased to a great extent by the large food stores available in Ternopol'. An officer of the garrison, Lieutenant Colonel Dirich, noted during interrogation in Soviet captivity that 'We had a sufficient supply of food and it was not dropped by aircraft.'[70]

However, the Soviet offensive slowed down with its arrival at the city blocks. The attacks of 29–30 March were unsuccessful. The main idea of the new assault on the city, as the commander of the 15th Rifle Corps, I.I. Lyudnikov, planned it, was an attack by the 302nd Rifle Division against the central part of the city with the task of splitting the garrison into two isolated parts, this time the northern and southern. It was then planned to destroy the enemy's northern and southern groups in detail in conjunction with units of the 4th Guards Tank Corps attacking from the north-east, and the 99th and 336th Rifle Divisions attacking from the south-east. Essentially, this was a classic elimination of an encircled group of forces – splitting it into parts, with their subsequent crushing in detail.

The assault began with a powerful working-over of the enemy's forward line by artillery and aviation at 15.00 on 31 March. Events developed most dramatically along the 12th Guards Tank Brigade's (of Poluboyarov's corps) offensive sector in the northern part of Ternopol'. On the morning of 31 March the brigade numbered sixteen T-34s and four SU-85s. The infantry did not follow the tanks, but Poluboyarov insisted on continuing the attack. Its results were predictable: the brigade lost four tanks burnt, three knocked out and two which blew up on mines, for no result. The 12th Guards Tank Brigade's remnants (seven T-34s and two SU-85s) were subordinated to the 302nd Rifle Division.

By the morning of 31 March the 302nd Rifle Division reached Ternopol', following a forced march. At 14.30, preceded by an artillery preparation, the newly-arrived formation joined in the assault on Ternopol'. Simultaneously, on 31 March two air raids were launched against the 'fortress' by the forces of the 2nd Air Army. Twenty-six Pe-2s,[71] eighty-three Il-2s and forty-one fighters took part in the first attack, and twenty-seven Il-2s and thirty-four fighters in the second, for a total of 211 sorties, and dropped 45 tonnes of bombs. The attack by a fresh formation along a new axis and massed attacks from the air brought success and the blocks along the city's outskirts were captured. On the night of 31 March/1 April the division's 827th Rifle Regiment broke into Ternopol' station. The Germans managed to avoid a catastrophe and the fall of the fortress by throwing in the crews of their field howitzers (they were in any event nearly out of ammunition) into the fighting as infantry.

By 1 April the capabilities of the Ternopol' garrison had already been reduced to a significant degree. Losses for the ten-day period from 20 March through 1 April 1944 were 2,325 men, with 2,097 remaining in line.[72] At the same time, equipment losses remained moderate, as only two *Sturmgeschützen* had been put out of commission, and with three StuG III[73] assault guns and one StuH 42[74] remaining in action.

According to another report, the following amount of armour was in the Ternopol' fortress as of 30 March:[75]

Four *Sturmgeschützen* (with another two out of commission);
Six *Grille*;
One *Hummel*;
One Panzer IV[76] (with another one out of commission);
One armoured car.

Later, following the capture of Ternopol', the Soviet responded with scepticism to the figures put forward by the garrison's captured officers as to the amount of armour, pointing to a larger number of captured armoured vehicles. There is some truth to these words. For example, according to one of the reports from the 503rd Heavy Tank Battalion, one Tiger (serial number 250896) was listed as 'having been left in Ternopol".[77] However, it is doubtful that this tank was capable of combat during any of the fighting for the city. The number of combat-ready tanks and self-propelled guns at the disposal of the Ternopol' garrison was not large. There was almost 25m³ of fuel for all of it, which more than covered requirements.

One should say that there was no unanimity regarding further actions at the headquarters of the garrison of Ternopol'. According to testimony in captivity from Lieutenant Colonel Dirich, von Neindorff's deputy, the commander of the 949th Infantry Regiment, Colonel Schönfeld, as early as the beginning of the encirclement, 'considered the defence of the city hopeless and said that he did not wish to perish senselessly'. Thus Schönfeld planned a break-out for 1–2 April, under the cover of a heavy snowfall. However, von Neindorff categorically opposed this plan and it was buried without ever having been born.

The End of the Ternopol' Fortress

Despite the fact that by 4 April the advance by Soviet forces in Ternopol' had essentially halted, the commandant of the 'Ternopol' fortress' evaluated his situation without enthusiasm. On this day General von Neindorff radioed the following to the headquarters of the Fourth Panzer Army and Army Group: 'Given the continuation of the enemy's attacks with fresh reinforcements, the carrying out of the commander-in-chief's demand of 2320 of 1.4.44 to hold out for a few more days is impossible. We have crowded into a tight space and there is no delivery of ammunition and the units are in poor condition.' The reply from Army Group headquarters proved to be unexpected: 'The relief operations have begun successfully today. Hold on.' This reply was unexpected because no kind of relief operations had even begun. This declaration in the radiogram to von Neindorff was an outright lie. Of course, one could argue that the offensive toward the First Panzer Army was the beginning of the effort to relieve Ternopol', but this is obviously stretching things.

The planning of offensive operations in the direction of Ternopol' began only on 5 April, the day after the false radiogram, when Rauss's and Model's[78] staffs began to discuss 'when it would be possible to launch an attack to ease Ternopol's situation'. At this juncture the relief of the Ternopol' garrison had greater morale and political significance than military necessity. The garrison's losses from 20 March through 6 April were 2,764 men, with only 1,658 remaining in line.[79] That is, the strength of the garrison, if it had been possible to save it, would have been unlikely to significantly reinforce Fourth Panzer Army. The losses in a relief attack might have been comparable to the strength of the garrison.

Despite the declaration about 'honourable duty' regarding Ternopol', the task of establishing communications with Hube's army of course had the greatest priority. Only when it became clear that the relief of the First Panzer Army was proceeding successfully did their gaze turn toward the ill-starred fortress. During the course of discussions, Fangor, the chief of staff of the First Panzer Army, assumed that the 10th SS Panzer Division would be able to establish communications with the First Panzer Army on its own and proposed employing the 9th SS *Hohenstaufen* Panzer Division for an attack on Ternopol'. The events of 6 April confirmed this assumption. The *Frundsberg* Division[80] really did successfully advance as far as Buchach on its own and establish communications with the First Panzer Army's forward units. Because of this, Model, although still cautiously, ordered the main mass of the SS 9th Panzer Division to remain at its jumping-off positions behind the XLVIII Panzer Corps, dispatching only individual elements of the *Hohenstaufen* Division to Kozova, with the task of attacking to the south-east, 'in order to operate in conjunction with the 10th SS Panzer Division on that bank of the Strypa'.

Yet another step in the direction of preparing to relieve Ternopol' was the return of Friebe's formation to the XLVIII Panzer Corps' sector. On 7 April Friebe's formation was pulled out of the fighting and into the Fourth Panzer Army's reserve. The army command turned down the request by the headquarters of the XIII Army Corps the following day, on the pretext of the necessity of carrying out urgent repair work. However, they did not return Friebe's formation to the Brody area in the days that followed. On 10 April 1944, according to the regular report on the availability of armour (*Bestandmeldung*), the condition of the Panthers in Friebe's detachment was described as follows.[81]

Table 1.4: The Condition of Group Friebe's Tank Park on 10 April 1944.

	Panthers	*Command Tanks*	*Bergepanthers*[82]
Available	69	6	2
Combat-Ready	20	3	1
Up to 14 Days in Repair	32	3	1
More than 14 Days in Repair	14	–	–
K-Werk[83]	3	–	–

It can clearly be seen that Friebe's detachment, while sufficiently strong overall, could only put twenty line Panthers into the fighting. That is, on the one hand, the words from Rauss's headquarters on the necessity of urgent repair were not dissembling. On the other hand, the Fourth Panzer Army command was clearly ready to accept territorial losses in the Brody area for the sake of an attack on Ternopol'.

Also, as was traditional, the Tigers of the 507th Panzer Battalion, which had previously carried out tasks for propping up the infantry units' front, was to be transferred to Friebe's group. As of 9 April, the battalion was subordinated to the 349th Infantry Division on the corps' left flank. Of course, the role of 'fire brigade' for the infantry did not tell in the best way on the combat capability of the recently full-strength battalion of Tigers. The overall strength of the XLVIII Panzer Corps' units' and formations' armour along the Ternopol' axis at this time is indicated in the following table.

Table 1.5: The Strength and Condition of the XLVIII Panzer Corps' Armour on the Evening of 10 April 1944.[84]

Unit	Muster Strength	In Service	Short-Term Repair	Long-Term Repair
311th Assault Gun Bn	19 StuG, 1 Pz IV, 1 Pz III[85]	11 StuG, 1 Pz IV, 1 Pz III	4 StuG	3 StuG
359th Infantry Div. (507th Heavy Panzer Bn)	26 Pz VI	5 Pz VI[86]	8 Pz VI	13 Pz.VI
Friebe's Group	6 Pz VI (from the 507th Panzer Bn), 22 Pz V (Panthers)			
SS 9th Panzer Div.	32 Pz IVs, 31 assault guns			

The decisions made by Model were soon formulated into an order and dispatched to Rauss's headquarters on 10 April. The essence of the operational plan was reflected in it by the following words: 'The XLVIII Panzer Corps, to which the 9th SS Panzer Division and Friebe's formation are attached, is to launch a concentrated attack on 11 April from the Kozlov area and to the south, in order to relieve the garrison of Ternopol'. Ternopol' itself, following the pullout of the troops located there, is to be surrendered.' The *Hohenstaufen* Division was to be transferred from Hausser's corps and from 09.00 on 4 April subordinated to the XLVIII Panzer Corps. However, the XLVIII Panzer Corps was not to be subordinated to Balck in its entirety, because in the order the formulation 'minus subunits activated in another place' was employed. Two battalions and an artillery battalion from the *Hohenstaufen* Division were to be subordinated to the First Panzer Army and did not take part in the offensive.

The plan, which was prepared by the headquarters of the Fourth Panzer Army, was quite simple and logical. It was planned to attack with the SS 9th Panzer Division, which had been attached to the army, from the Gorodishche area, and with Friebe's formation from the Kozlov area, where both bridges remained intact. Upon getting across the Vosushka River, the units activated for the operation were supposed to jointly attack along the opposite bank on Ternopol'. If one formation could not break through the Soviet defences, it was planned to throw it across the river into the rear of its more successful neighbour. Aside from the mobile formations, it was planned to employ the infantry in the breakthrough to Ternopol'. As was noted in the Fourth Panzer Army's Order No. 65 of 10 April, 'We should activate all of the units at the disposal of the 359th Infantry Division in the relief offensive. We are, first of all, speaking of employing the main mass of the division's artillery for preparing the offensive and supporting its beginning phase.' This was perhaps the plan's weakest point. The support for the German *blitzkrieg* in the beginning of the war was the combat-capable infantry divisions, which followed on the heels of the mobile formations. They covered the flanks and occupied territory. In 1944–5 the Germans were no longer able to do this, as the result of which offensives by massed armour failed. A typical example of this, of course, is Lake Balaton in 1945.

Formally, the plan provided for saving the numerous wounded among the garrison of the fortress. The Fourth Panzer Army's order declared: 'After the entire garrison and all the wounded link up with the relief group and the transport of those who cannot move on their own is assured, it will be necessary to fall back in stages to the Strypa.' Von Neindorff, in light of the destruction of the fortress's transport on the streets of Ternopol', was promised motor vehicles for evacuating the wounded. However, at the same time an alternative plan was under study, in which they could not secure a 'corridor' for the evacuation of everyone from Ternopol': 'If we cannot directly reach the fortress's defensive line, the garrison must try to break out.' The XLVIII Panzer Corps had the right to order a break-out.

As one might have expected, the road conditions in the spring of 1944 became the first test of the plan for breaking through to Ternopol'. The regrouping of the *Hohenstaufen* Division from the SS II Panzer Corps' right flank to the XLVIII Panzer Corps' sector was carried out with great difficulty and had not been completed by the close of 10 April. The motorized infantry subunits were concentrating before dawn on 11 April, while only the self-propelled artillery had arrived from among the artillery subunits. Friebe's group was even moving up to its jumping-off positions along ruined roads on the night of 10/11 April. It is usually indicated in the literature that Friebe's group went over to the attack with 24 Panthers, 9 Tigers and 101 armoured personnel carriers, but this looks more like a report on the group's condition on the night of 10/11 April (eight Tigers and twenty-four Panthers).[87] There were fewer combat-ready tanks available on the evening of 10 April (see above). The number of vehicles in line following the march must have inevitably decreased. Thus it appears that the actual attack capabilities of Friebe's group on 11 April were small and significantly less than during the raid of 25 March.

The Soviet command, in turn, was aware of the threat to relieve Ternopol' and distributed its available forces accordingly. For example, the experienced anti-tank gunners of N.D. Chevola's 8th Guards Anti-Tank Artillery Brigade were directed to cover the Kozova–Ternopol' road. The 28th Anti-Tank Artillery Brigade was located directly around Gorodishche. The Soviet command's most weighty argument on the approaches to Ternopol' became the High Command Reserve's 1st Guards Artillery Division (see table).

Table 1.6: The Condition and Ammunition Supply of the High Command Reserve's 1st Guards Artillery Division[88]

Unit	Equipment	Number at Firing Points	Provisioning (% of unit of fire)
1st Gds Anti-Tank Corps Artillery Bde	1937 model 152mm howitzer	31	0.3
169th Gds Howitzer Artillery Rgt	1938 model 122mm howitzer	20	0.2
203rd Gds Howitzer Artillery Rgt	1938 model 122mm howitzer	15	1.2
399th Gds Howitzer Artillery Rgt	1938 model 122mm howitzer	18	0.5
167th Gds Light Corps Artillery Rgt	1942 model 76mm gun	24	0.7
200th Gds Light Corps Artillery Rgt	1939 model 76mm gun	9	0.6
206th Gds Light Corps Artillery Rgt	1942 model 76mm gun	24	0.8

Aside from the expected opposition, an unexpected enemy for the Germans was moving up to the Ternopol' area. This was the 6th Guards Tank Corps from P.S. Rybalko's army, which included the 52nd and 53rd Guards Tank

Brigades. The former received thirty tanks from the 7th Guards Tank Corps and the latter forty new tanks at Dubno station. By the evening of 9 April the corps had reached the area to the south-east of Ternopol' and could easily be moved up to prevent attempts to relieve the fortress.

At the same time, one must admit that the capabilities of the 106th Rifle Corps' 135th Rifle Division, which was located directly along the path of the SS forces' main attack near Gorodishche, were not exactly impressive. It numbered 6,204 men on 31 March.[89] By the start of the German offensive the composition and grouping of the 106th Rifle Corps' artillery was as follows (see table).

Table 1.7: The 106th Rifle Corps' Artillery's Quantitative and Qualitative Composition by 11 April 1944.

Unit	45mm Gun	76mm Regimental Gun	76mm Divisional Gun
135th Rifle Div.	27	4	9
340th Rifle Div.	2	7	13
Total	29	11	22

Unit	122mm Gun	82mm Mortar	120mm Mortar
135th Rifle Div.	4	39	8
340th Rifle Div.	10	45	9
Total	14	84	17

Besides this, the 340th Rifle Division's artillery was supported by the 1156th Artillery Regiment, which had been attached to it, consisting of twelve 152mm gun-howitzers. The corps had been reinforced by the 1st Guards Artillery Division, consisting of the 1st Artillery Brigade (thirty-one 152mm gun-howitzers), the 200th Howitzer Artillery Brigade (fifty-one 122mm howitzers) and the 28th Anti-Tank Artillery Brigade, consisting of the 1840th and 1842nd Anti-Tank Artillery Regiments. All of this was augmented by a battalion of '*katyushas*' (six launchers). The 135th Rifle Division's artillery was chiefly for firing over open sights in anti-tank strongpoints. Three 76mm divisional guns and ten 122mm howitzers were in concealed positions.

Six anti-tank strongpoints were created in the 135th Rifle Division's sector, with five of them along the forward edge of the defence from Slobodka to Denisuv station:

Table 1.8: The 135th Rifle Division's Anti-Tank Strongpoints.

Unit	45mm Gun	76mm Regimental Gun	76mm Divisional Gun
Strongpoint 1	8	1	–
Strongpoint 2	4	1	2
Strongpoint 3	2	–	1
Strongpoint 4	3	–	–
Strongpoint 5	4	1	–
Total	21	3	3

Anti-Tank Strongpoint No. 6, consisting of six 45mm guns, was located in the depth. All of the anti-tank strongpoints in the 135th Rifle Division's sector had fire coordination. Such anti-tank defence would not have been bad for 1941–2, but it was still a weak defence against Tigers. Yet another negative feature of the organization of the anti-tank defence was the insufficient number of minefields along the approaches to the strongpoints.

The 148th Rifle Division (5,160 men as of 31 March), which had been proven in the fighting of 25 March, lay along the path of Group Friebe's offensive around Kozlov.

The offensive began in the early morning of 11 April. All of Friebe's attempts to break through the 148th Rifle Division's defence near Kozlov were unsuccessful. As was noted in the XLVIII Panzer Corps' report on the results of the fighting, 'The third attack by Friebe's tank formation against the eastern part of Kozlov once again broke down under powerful artillery and mortar fire'. The German's own powerful artillery fire is also noted in Soviet reports. However, this artillery duel was won by the Soviet side. The 148th Rifle Division's losses in this battle, according to the division's reports, were moderate: eight men killed and twenty men wounded.[90]

Having begun their offensive in the early morning, the SS forces occupied Gorodishche, but the bridgehead occupied by them on the eastern bank of the Vosushka was not held. Moreover, as a result the commander of the *Hohenstaufen* Division was accused of not reporting the loss of the bridgehead to Balck's headquarters (meaning he made a decision on the basis that this bridgehead was still in German hands). South of Gorodishche, near the village of Mlynets, a bridgehead was nevertheless occupied and the Germans even managed to seize the commanding Height 367. But the bridging equipment got bogged down on the bottomless roads and they were able to drag it out of the mud only late in the evening, with the help of assault guns. It was already clear by morning that because of the terrain conditions it was not possible to lay a bridge near Mlynets. The offensive was at a dead end.

One should mention that according to the results of the offensive's first day, Balck was by no means ecstatic over the performance of his SS formation. As he noted, 'The command of the SS 9th Panzer Division thinks in a very heavy-handed and schematic way'. Subsequently, the headquarters of the XLVIII Panzer Corps noted the SS division's 'horrifying lack of tactical skill, particularly among the mid-level commanders', the result of which was 'even the failure to carry out the orders issued for the attack'. Aside from this, the SS forces displayed insufficient skill in cooperating with artillery and aircraft. In the post-war historiography the SS forces are traditionally pictured as the elite of the Third Reich's armed forces, but the reality was somewhat more complex than this stereotype.

Meanwhile, the XLVIII Panzer Corps command was planning an offensive, based upon the availability of the already non-existent bridgehead near the road bridge near Gorodishche. On the morning of 12 April Balck ordered the commander of the SS 9th Panzer Division, *Obergruppenführer*[91] Bittrich, 'To expand the bridgehead in such a way that we can lay a bridge down outside the zone of the enemy's direct fire. For this, you need to take Slobodka and Height 330, north of Slobodka.' Simultaneously, Friebe's formation was pulled out of the fighting and thrown to the south to force the river near Slobodka, which it was planned to capture. To be sure, the relief of Friebe's formation only took place the following day. Actually, the day of 12 April was lost for nothing. The SS forces were unable to regroup for the attack on Slobodka, and as a result as early as evening had renounced their planned offensive. The 135th Rifle Division's losses in these battles may be considered moderate: during 11 and 12 April it lost 154 killed and 444 wounded.

The fighting for Slobodka unfolded on 13 April, in which, aside from *Hohenstaufen*'s units, Friebe's formation took part. Only by evening did it become clear that 'The army found out about the loss of the small bridgehead, which had decisive significance for the continuation of the offensive, only at 19.00 on 13.4'. Thus the seizure of Slobodka no longer made any sense, as this location was valuable only for securing the bridgehead against bombardment. The experienced commander of the mechanized infantry regiment in Friebe's group spoke directly to the XLVIII Panzer Corps' chief of staff regarding the offensive from Slobodka to the east on Ternopol': 'An attack against Heights 363 and 330 on the eastern bank of the Vosushka has no chance of success.'

Thus two days were lost with nothing to show for them. As strange as it sounds, the presence of army group commander Model at *Hohenstaufen*'s command post played a role in the failure to inform Balck's headquarters. Model was accustomed to leading from the front and heard the report on the loss of the bridgehead shortly afterwards, but this information did not go any further. That is to say, there was a lack of coordination among the German command at various levels.

The delay at the crossing had fatal consequences for the garrison of Ternopol'. At 13.00 on 12 April, following a destructive three-hour artillery preparation, units of the 15th Rifle Corps renewed the assault. One of the prerequisites for this was receiving reinforcements. At 22.00 on the evening of 12 April the 302nd Rifle Division received 1,200 reinforcements, with the 302nd Rifle Division's 823rd Rifle Regiment immediately receiving 470 men. Another 1,045 men were received the following day, although the 302nd Rifle Division no longer had weapons for them.

Meanwhile, the offensive by the relief group was at last speeding up. Engineer reconnaissance discovered a suitable place for a bridge south-west of Gorodishche, and one was laid on the night of 13/14 April and *Hohenstaufen*'s tanks and self-propelled guns rolled across it. At about 10.00 (Berlin time) several Tigers from Friebe's formation moved across the bridge. One should say that a compromise decision had been made: Friebe's group was subordinated to *Hohenstaufen*, but with the simultaneous subordination of all of the SS division's armour to Friebe himself.

The attack by the Tigers proved to be a serious test for the 135th Rifle Division's infantry. The anti-tank strongpoints, which consisted primarily of 45mm guns, were swept aside, which in turn forced the rifle elements to fall back. As was later noted in the 7th Guards Anti-tank Artillery Brigade's report, 'Units of the 135th Rifle Division began to fall back in disorder on Khodachkuv Vel'ki, where they were halted due to measures taken and occupied defensive positions. The 1840th Anti-Tank Artillery Regiment took the entire brunt of the tank attack, fighting in encirclement in the majority of cases.'[92] The anti-tank crews were not the only ones to end up in a difficult situation. The SS 9th Panzer Division's and Group Friebe's armour broke through as far as the positions of the 1st Guards Artillery Division's 399th Howitzer Artillery Regiment. As was stated directly in the report, the German tanks 'began to flatten the regiment's equipment and shoot its rank and file'. As a result, in the fighting on 14 April the 399th Howitzer Artillery Regiment immediately lost seventeen guns, of which eight remained on the battlefield occupied by the enemy.

The 'revelation' by the Germans of their bridgehead near Gorodishche and the breakthrough to the road to Ternopol' forced Chernyakhovskii to move up all of his available reserves to meet the attackers. The first of these were the 52nd and 53rd Guards Tank Brigades, with the attached 11th Guards Heavy Tank Regiment. The 53rd Guards Tank Brigade moved out in the early morning of 15 April directly on Khodachkuv Vel'ki. One cannot say that the fighting near Khodachkuv Vel'ki went well for V.S. Arkhipov's 53rd Guards Tank Brigade. Arkhipov himself described this battle in great detail in his memoirs, presenting it as quite successful. However, according to documents, the results of the day were the brigade's loss of eighteen tanks knocked out and burned.[93] Moreover, very sharp words were addressed to Arkhipov in the 6th Guards Tank Corps' report on the results of the fighting: 'The 53rd Guards Tank Brigade lost 30 tanks due to the lack of reconnaissance, observation, the poor employment of the terrain for tank actions in ambushes, and the poor masking and digging in of tanks.'[94] Aside from the tanks, a regiment of 76.2mm ZIS-3s from Colonel Chevola's 8th Guards Independent Anti-Tank Artillery Brigade was thrown into the Khodachkuv Vel'ki area. The regiment got into heavy fighting and immediately lost seven guns that day. The 68th Guards Rifle Division was the infantry core of the Soviet defence near Khodachkuv Vel'ki. Despite the efficient arrival of reserves, they were unable to immediately halt the enemy. By the evening of 15 April Khodachkuv Vel'ki had been lost.

Meanwhile the penetration into the part of Ternopol' on the eastern bank of the Seret remaining under the control of the fortress's garrison forced von Neindorff on the night of 14/15 April to pull his forces from this bridgehead into the Zagrobelya suburb of Ternopol'. This immediately sharply worsened the supply situation as the food stores remained on the eastern bank. Just a few hours remained for the existence of fortress Ternopol'. However, it would have been a big mistake to consider the elements of the fortress's garrison that fell back to Zagrobelya as completely demoralized and hardly capable of combat. During the course of the attack on Zagrobelya on 15 April, four T-34s and two self-propelled guns were set on fire by two assault guns (these are described as 'Ferdinands'[95] in Soviet documents).[96]

Yet another turning point in the fate of the 'fortress' was the death of Major General von Neindorff on 15 April. Colonel von Schönfeld, the commander of the 949th Infantry Regiment, took command of the remnants of the garrison holed up in Zagrobelya. He no longer waited for the relief column or even the XLVIII Panzer Corps' order (as was called for in the plan). At 22.00 on 15 April, at a conference of garrison officers, Colonel von Schönfeld ordered a break-out. One of the mysteries of the Ternopol' fortress is connected with the organization of the break-out. The German researcher G. Fricke writes: 'This order was only known to the officers, of whom not a single one made it to the German positions. As a result, it is unknown how the break-out was organized, insofar as the testimony of those soldiers who broke out differs.'[97]

The solution to the riddle is probably quite simple. At 03.00 on 16 April the assault on the Zagrobelya suburb began by two regiments from the 336th Rifle Division and a regiment from the 117th Guards Rifle Division from the north-west and south. Actually, this offensive (which coincided exactly with the start of the break-out) became the impulse for the practically hopeless attempt. The break-out actually began at 02.00 on 16 April by two groups of 700 men apiece, including the walking wounded. Fairly large groups of those surrounded managed to break through the defence along the Zagrobelya perimeter and reach the positions of the 1st Guards Artillery Division's gun brigade (152mm ML-20 gun-howitzers). The gun crews scattered the attacking German infantry with their personal weapons. One encounters affirmations that those surrounded nearly overran the artillery crews' positions, but documents do not confirm this. The 1st Corps Artillery Brigade's rank and file losses were comparatively light: seventeen men killed and five wounded.[98] At the same time, the artillerymen counted 408 prisoners taken.[99]

However, the matter was not limited to an attack on the positions of the 1st Guards Artillery Division. The Soviet command had prepared a surprise for the fortress's garrison in the form of the 9th Guards Anti-Tank Artillery Brigade, which had been moved up from the reserve and had still not been committed into the fighting. It was during the night of 15/16 April that the brigade's anti-tank artillery regiments took up position with their front facing east in the Ternopol' area, and the groups breaking out of the fortress collided with them. They opened fire on the Germans with high explosive shells and even case shot from ZIS-2 guns. The gun crews even took up rifles, automatic rifles and machine guns. According to the night's results, the anti-tank gunners of the 9th Anti-Tank Artillery Brigade counted 200 German officers and men killed and 70 captured.[100] Their own losses were five men killed and twenty-three wounded.[101]

In view of the increasing chaos and the failure to receive an order to break out, not all of the German units abandoned Zagrobelya. Some of them had already been tied down by fighting since the start of the Soviet forces' night attack. By 07.00 the resistance by the remnants of the Zagrobelya garrison had been crushed. As a result of the fighting in Zagrobelya, 1,223 prisoners were taken, including 15 officers. The epic of the storming of the Ternopol' fortress was over.

Despite the fact that the Ternopol' garrison had already been scattered during the night of 15/16 April and was trying to break out in small groups to link up with German units outside, combat operations continued around Khodachkuv Vel'ki and Gorodishche. In the early morning of 16 April Friebe's formation, with the support of *Hohenstaufen's* motorized infantry, attempted to break through to the east. At this time Friebe's formation was at its maximum strength for the period of the operation – twelve Tigers and twenty-six Panthers.[102] This was evidently the result of the return of tanks from the repair shops. However, the German tanks encountered stubborn resistance from the 60th Army's rifle, artillery and tank units that had been brought up to Khodachkuv Vel'ki. As was noted in the report by the XLVIII Panzer Corps' headquarters on the results of the fighting: 'The enemy is putting up stubborn resistance, with the support of major artillery forces and anti-tank defence, and is constantly counter-attacking with the support of tanks.' On this day the 53rd Guards Tank Brigade lost three tanks burned and seven knocked out, the 52nd Guards Tank Brigade six burned and four knocked out, and the 11th Guards Heavy Tank Regiment four ISs[103] burned and three knocked out. One must say that the fighting against the German tanks around Khodachkuv Vel'ki cost the 6th Guards Tank Corps dearly. During 15–18 April fifty-two tanks were irretrievably lost (including four IS-122s[104]), while another twenty-three vehicles were listed as knocked out.[105]

The growing resistance around Khodachkuv Vel'ki and the arrival of the first soldiers from Ternopol' at the positions of Friebe's group led to the effective curtailment of the XLVIII Panzer Corps' offensive as early as 17 April. The relief operation had essentially ended in failure. In all, fifty-five men from the garrison made their way to the German units.[106] Moreover, the bulk of them did not arrive at the positions of the SS troops and Friebe's group, but by a roundabout route in the Yezerna area. Group 'Demba' demonstrated quite a high level of survivability, and fourteen men made it out. It was perhaps only the SS troops from *Leibstandarte* that demonstrated greater survivability – two men from a platoon and two men from the crews of six *Grille* self-propelled guns. Only 0.5 per cent of the men from the 949th Infantry Regiment made it out, or 14 men out of more than 2,000. The last commander of the 'fortress', von Schönfeld, was killed during the break-out.

What did the unsuccessful attempt to break through to the fortress cost the Germans? According to a report of 19 April, the SS 9th Panzer Division numbered sixteen Panzer IVs and eight assault guns in line, while Friebe's tank group reported eight Tigers and twenty Panthers.[107] That is, the number of the SS 9th Panzer Division's combat vehicles fell considerably compared to the beginning of the operation, while the strength of Friebe's group remained relatively stable. On 19 April the XLVIII Panzer Corps reported the irreparable loss of only three Panthers from Friebe's group and four Panzer IVs and two *Sturmgeschützen* from the 9th SS Panzer Division during the course of the attempt to relieve Ternopol'.[108] However, this is obviously an understatement. According to a report by the 507th Panzer Battalion on 20 April, a Tiger (serial number 250974) was irretrievably lost 800m south of Khodachkuv Vel'ki on 15 April, set on fire by fire by Soviet artillery.[109] Moreover, this vehicle even made its way into the 1st Guards Artillery Division's photographic report, and not in a good condition. The absence of an admission of this tank's loss makes one doubt the accuracy of the report altogether.

At the same time, one should not say that participation in the attempt to relieve Ternopol' led to heavy losses for the 507th Panzer Battalion, despite the collision with numerous Soviet anti-tank units around Khodachkuv Vel'ki. The 507th Panzer Battalion numbered only seven combat-ready line Tigers, while another eighteen vehicles were listed as being in short-term repair (plus three command Tigers), eight vehicles in long-term repair, and three vehicles in K-Werk as of 20 April.[110]

Losses among the Soviet forces which stormed Ternopol' were 2,876 men killed and 11,903 wounded. According to Soviet documents, losses in armour during the storming of Ternopol' were as follows:[111]

4th Guards Tank Corps – fifty-two T-34s and fifteen SU-85s;
1827th Self-Propelled Artillery Regiment – three SU-152s;[112]
1889th Self-Propelled Artillery Regiment – five SU-76s.[113]

In counting the armour losses in the fighting for Ternopol' it is necessary to take into account a tank company from the 6th Guards Tank Corps' 52nd Guards

Tank Brigade from Rybalko's army. The company, numbering ten tanks, took part in the fighting along with the 336th Rifle Division and lost two tanks burned and three tanks knocked out.[114]

In toting up the results of the struggle for Ternopol', one may draw the following conclusions. One can say that Ternopol', as one of the trial fortresses, was extremely unlucky. There were major anti-tank artillery forces within the 60th Army which stormed the city. As of 1 April 1944 the entire First Ukrainian Front disposed of seven anti-tank brigades, of which four ended up being drawn into the fighting at Ternopol': the 7th, 8th and 9th Guards and the 28th Anti-Tank Artillery Brigades. All of them had something to do and the 60th Army fired off 2,918 57mm gun rounds during April.[115] Such a mass of anti-tank artillery, along with the 1st Guards Artillery Division's howitzers, doomed the relief attack to failure.

In order to relieve Ternopol', the German command gathered a tank group that was even more numerous than that which broke through to Buchach to meet the First Panzer Army. However, the plan for breaking through to the 'fortress' and the evacuation of the garrison's remnants and the wounded, which was so important from the morale and political point of view, did not work out. If such a thing had taken place, then Goebbels's[116] propaganda would probably have trumpeted the news to the entire world, thus supporting the fortress concept. But everything turned out just the opposite. The break-out of only fifty-five defenders of Ternopol' by no means inspired the garrisons of future fortresses. Thus fortresses were a difficult matter in the summer of 1944, and their garrisons rapidly abandoned Vitebsk and Bobruisk.

Nevertheless, Ternopol' was defended longer than one could have expected. The resilience of the garrison of fortress Ternopol' was supported in no small degree by the presence of a mobile reserve in the commandant's hands, which is what the 'Demba' Battalion was. An officer from the Ternopol' garrison, Lieutenant Colonel Keienburg, who was interrogated on 17 April 1944, stated that the 'Demba' Battalion was thrown company by company into the most important sectors of the front and had a very high combat capability.[117] However, on the whole, the combat capability of a garrison that had been thrown together from various elements was not high.

A powerful argument for the 'fortress', besides the 'Demba' Battalion, was the mobile reserve of *Sturmgeschützen* and the 150mm self-propelled guns. In a report on the actions of the 94th Rifle Corps' artillery on the results of the fighting for Ternopol', it was noted that 'It is especially necessary to note the successful actions of the enemy's self-propelled guns, which while skilfully manoeuvring, inflicted significant losses on our units'.[118] The corps even created special groups of scouts which hunted German self-propelled guns and, upon finding them, would call down fire from heavy guns.

One of the features of the last year or year-and-a-half of the war was the Germans' active employment of snipers. If during the *blitzkrieg* period the experience of the Kaiser's snipers from the First World War had been forgotten by the Wehrmacht, then having learned a bitter lesson from the 'Voroshilov riflemen',[119] the Germans began to revive the tradition. In the 60th Army's war diary on the results of the fighting for Ternopol', it was noted as a shortcoming in their troops' operations, 'The absence of our snipers and hunters, which could fight the enemy's snipers and destroy important targets, on which in many cases depended the outcome of a fight for a house or building'.[120]

Yet another means of supporting the resilience of the fortress's defence were hand-held anti-tank weapons. As was noted in a report summarizing the First Ukrainian Front's combat experience for March, 'The enemy is conducting the fight against tanks in inhabited locales with the aid of *Raketenwerfer*[121] anti-tank rocket launchers. The effectiveness of its employment within a distance of 200m is quite high. The majority of our tanks, of those destroyed in the street fighting in the city of Ternopol', was destroyed precisely by this kind of weapon.'[122] This evidently refers to the rocket-powered *Ofenrohren*[123] with the 'fortress's' garrison. About 200 'Faust-1' and 'Faust-2' *Faustpatronen*[124] were delivered to the garrison as early as April, at the very end of the siege, in parachute containers. Thus the Ternopol' garrison became the precursor of the German fortresses of 1945, this time on German territory.

Chapter 2

Kovel': An Exception to the Rule

There were inherent defects in the very concept of the 'fortress' that manifested themselves quite clearly during the course of the fighting for Ternopol'. First of all, there was depriving the garrison of artillery as a means of fighting (due to the rapid expenditure of ammunition and the doubtful possibility of its delivery from outside). A second factor was the very uncertain prospects for the garrison's survival. However, this depended heavily on circumstances. If Ternopol' was completely unlucky in the fact that the First Ukrainian Front put into play significant tank and artillery forces against its relief, then someone else must eventually draw the winning ticket. This was the garrison of the city of Kovel'.

The Soviet forces' limited successes during the course of the 1943–4 winter campaign in Belorussia, on the one hand, and their significant successes on the Ukrainian right bank on the other, resulted by the middle of February 1944 in the formation of a significant gap between the *fronts* along the western and south-western strategic directions in the area of the basin of the Pripyat' River. Along this direction, following the loss of the city of Sarny and the Red Army's attacks on Rovno and Lutsk, the Germans fell back to the line of the Stokhod River, that is, to the German army's old positions dating back to 1915–16. Pillboxes from the time of the First World War could still be found here and there along this line. The railway bridge over the Stokhod along the Kovel'–Sarny road had been blown up on 2 March 1944, thus sharing the fate of many other bridges methodically demolished by the Germans during their retreat to the west. The entire enormous space along the boundary between the *fronts* was for a time controlled on the Soviet side by separate cordons from Colonel M.M. Zaikin's 143rd Rifle Division.

It was entirely to be expected that they decided to do something about this. According to *Stavka*[1] Directive No. 220027 of 17 February 1944, a new *front* was formed along the junction of the Belorussian and First Ukrainian Fronts, which was named the Second Belorussian Front (K.K. Rokossovskii's[2] Belorussian Front was according renamed the First Belorussian Front).

According to the *Stavka* directive, a new *front* headquarters was not formed from scratch, but was activated from the freed-up reserves following the abolition of the Northwestern Front in November 1943. It was ordered to 'transfer itself to the Rokitno area' from Rybinsk by 20 February. P.A. Kurochkin,[3] who had formerly commanded the Northwestern Front (he was deputy commander of the First Ukrainian Front at the time of his appointment), was appointed *front* commander, with Lieutenant General F.Ye. Bokov[4] the member of the military council, and Lieutenant General V.Ya. Kolpachki[5] (following his relief as commander of the 63rd Army) as chief of staff.

The Second Belorussian Front comprised the following units:

Lieutenant General P.A. Belov's[6] 61st Army (transferred from the First Belorussian Front);

Major General N.I. Ivanov's 77th Rifle Corps, consisting of three rifle divisions, and the headquarters of Lieutenant General Polenov's[7] 47th Army;

Lieutenant General I.F. Nikolayev's 70th Army consisting of four rifle divisions (transferred from the *Stavka* reserve), Major General's 125th Rifle Corps, and Lieutenant General of Aviation F.P. Polynin's[8] 6th Air Army, Captain First Rank V.V. Grigor'yev's Dnepr Military Flotilla, and artillery and engineer units.

The 6th Air Army had previously been subordinated to the abolished Northwestern Front. As its chief of staff, Major General Storozhenko, noted ironically at the meeting for the transfer to Sarny, 'we're moving from one set of swamps to another'.

In all, the Second Belorussian Front received (actually available as of 14 March): twenty-two rifle divisions (eighteen rifle divisions on hand as of 14 March), six cavalry divisions (three cavalry divisions, plus another three in the *front* reserve), and three air divisions, one tank brigade, five independent tank regiments (one independent tank regiment, plus another in the *front* reserve), up to twenty artillery (mortar) regiments, and other units. *Stavka*, having allotted significant forces to the new formation, assigned Kurochkin an ambitious task on 4 March 1944: 'To prepare a *front* offensive operation, with the direction of the main attack on Kovel'. The immediate task is to take the line Lyubeshov–Kamen'-Kashirskii–Kovel'. The *front* is to subsequently attack with the task of capturing Brest and reach the Western Bug River along the Brest–Gorodlo sector ...'[9]

The *front*'s attack sector was more than 350km. Moreover, Moscow ordered it to begin the attack during 12–15 March, 'without expecting the complete concentration of all of the *front*'s forces'. It was essentially planned to cut Army Group Centre's communications near Brest by the Second Belorussian Front's offensive and to contribute to the collapse of the 'Belorussian Balcony' as early as the spring of 1944. We should point out that in March 1944 the Western Front also continued to attack. This took place against the background of the newly-begun offensive by three Ukrainian fronts through the spring mud (a successful offensive, as opposed to that of their neighbours).

However, the first target was nevertheless an important road junction in the Poles'ye[10]–Kovel'. The 47th Army was to be aimed at the city, while the 70th Army, which was to be inserted between the 61st and 47th Armies, received orders to attack Brest. The 60th Army, in turn, received orders to eliminate the enemy's bridgehead along the southern bank of the Pripyat' River. The first target of the Second Belorussian Front's offensive was definitely Kovel'. A road (running parallel to the front), which was very important for the Germans and which connected Army Group Centre's and Army Group South's flanks, ran through it. In the event of its loss, an equivalent road lay 100–150km to the west. The Red Army's capture of Kovel' would bring the Soviet forces to the approaches to Brest and would open up opportunities for operating in relatively favourable terrain.

The Poles'ye was, from the point of view of conducting offensive operations, no picnic, to put it mildly. A particularly difficult area was precisely the wooded and swampy sector lying between the Styr' and Tur'ya rivers (that is, right up to Kovel'), which is cut by the north-south flowing Stokhod River and its numerous tributaries. The abundance of swamps, small rivers, lakes and continuous forested areas, given the sandy soil and the complete absence of improved roads, narrowed the troops' scope for manoeuvre. This was exacerbated by the heavy snowfalls in February, which by March had created drifts a metre high and which had begun to melt in the spring. The daytime melting and the nighttime freezing made the roads almost impassable for the greater part of the day.

Another operational factor for the Soviet rear in the spring of 1944 in the Poles'ye was the presence of armed groups of nationalist rebels. As was noted in a report by the headquarters of the 143rd Rifle Division on the fighting for Kovel', 'During this time Bul'ba[11]–Bandera[12] bands operated quite openly in support of the enemy. The presence of nationalist bands hostile to the Red

Army increased the employment of troops for convoying supplies and cut down the pace of their movement, forcing transport to halt at nightfall.'

Despite the fact that the *Stavka* directive, with its tasks for the new *front*, was issued on 4 March, as early as 2 March the commander of the 47th Army issued orders for the 143rd Rifle Division to prepare to attack Kovel'. The division, while covering the deployment of the corps' and army's main forces, reached the Stokhod River by 5 March and took up defensive positions along a broad front. By the start of the offensive the 143rd Rifle Division had gradually turned over its extensive sector to the arriving units of the 47th and 61st Armies and headed for the line of the Tur'ya River.

The divisions that had prepared for the advance toward Kovel' were in good condition for the middle of the war and at the tail end of a winter campaign. By 14 March the 143rd Rifle Division numbered 6,206 rank and file and the 260th Rifle Division 7,001. At the same time, the latter was better outfitted with automatic weapons, disposing of 1,849 Shpagin[13] sub-machine guns, and 244 light and 81 heavy machine guns, as opposed to the 143rd Rifle Division's 1,046 Shpagins, 170 DP[14] and 68 heavy machine guns. But the 143rd Rifle Division, which had been educated by the experience of fighting in the Poles'ye, had the important advantage of possessing 1,370 horses, as opposed to the 807 in the 260th Rifle Division. All the artillery of Colonel M.M. Zaikin's division had already been made horse-drawn.

On 12 March the 143rd Rifle Division received orders to reach the line of the Tur'ya River to the north of Kovel'. One regiment was delayed in turning over its sector, while the other two reached the Tur'ya River after a 36–40km march and forced the crossing with the aid of previously-assembled assault bridges. One has to note the high level of command and control: communications between the 143rd Rifle Division's headquarters with its regiments was carried out by radio. The division attacked with open flanks. There was simply no neighbour to the left, while the gap between it and the 260th Rifle Division reached 25km. For this reason, it was necessary to dispatch powerful flank detachments in the direction of the open flanks. Reconnaissance was also conducted in a very original fashion, by a single divisional cavalry group, numbering about seventy men, into which all of the regiments' cavalry platoons had been gathered. The enemy's weak resistance favoured the advance in this situation. The Germans had been abandoning their strongpoints to the north-east and east of Kovel' and were hurriedly falling back to the city.

Since 4 March von dem Bach's[15] battle group had been directly subordinated to the Fourth Panzer Army command. The Soviet forces' assumption of active operations along the Kovel' axis was noticed by the enemy before long, including the names of the attacking formations. On that score, there is the following entry in the Fourth Panzer Army's war diary for 12 March:

At 20.00 *Obergruppenführer* von dem Bach reported to the commander on the appearance of the Soviet 260th Rifle Division, from the known army, along his sector. In this case, the situation of the group, which had previously been fighting only bands[16] and cavalry formations, has significantly worsened. The *Obergruppenführer* doubts that he can hold the enemy with the forces available to him. The commander replied that at the present moment the army cannot spare him a single soldier, insofar as all available forces have been concentrated along the southern flank, where a decisive battle is being fought. The commander does not see a particular threat in the sector of the XIII Army Corps and that of von dem Bach's group, insofar as overall the enemy is on the defensive here, while employing shock formation in the south. If a danger to Kovel' should arise, the combat group must pull back all of its forces there as, according to data supplied by the *Obergruppenführer*, who is simultaneously the fortress commander, positions for an all-round defence are being constructed there.[17]

To be honest, Kovel' was an extra headache for the Fourth Panzer Army's headquarters against the overall unfavourable backdrop of the major Soviet offensive involving tank armies (on 4 March the Proskurov–Chernovtsy operation began). This undoubtedly told on the quality of the command situation in the Kovel' area.

On 13 March the attacking Soviet units were building bridges over the overflowing Tur'ya River. Despite the complete destruction of the bridges by the enemy, they were restored by the engineers in little more than a day, thanks to the employment of the local population. In two days of fighting following the forcing of the Tur'ya River, units of the 143rd Rifle Division, while advancing to the west and bypassing Kovel' from the north, cut the railway line and roads leading from the city to Brest and Lyuboml'. As was noted in a report, the 143rd Rifle Division's 487th Rifle Regiment, having reached Myzovo station, 'routed its garrison of Magyars,[18] of which twenty were killed and three captured'. Forty railway trucks were captured at Myzovo station.

Many prisoners were taken on 16 March at Koshary station. A great stroke of luck was the capture of prisoners from the SS *Wiking* Division. They divulged the following extremely important information: 'The SS *Wiking* Division, following its defeat in the Korsun'-Shevchenkovskii area, is reforming in the Chelm [that is, along the opposite bank of the Bug River] and Lyuboml' area and has orders to reinforce the Kovel' garrison in the next few days.' However, the prisoners understated the strength of *Wiking's* armoured park ('up to 20 tanks and self-propelled guns'). Actually, the SS *Wiking* Division was being reformed in the Lublin and Chelm area and received orders in the beginning of March to move to the Kovel' area.

In the light of this, the desire to take Kovel' by storm, before the garrison could be reinforced by reserves, becomes quite understandable. On 16 March there followed an order from the 47th Army's headquarters to attack it. It was planned to attack the city, which had already been outflanked by the 77th Rifle Corps' offensive, from the north-west and south (by the 125th Rifle Corps moving up from the east). Two of the 77th Rifle Corps' divisions and one of the 125th Rifle Corps' divisions (175th Rifle Division) were directed against Kovel'. The 77th Rifle Corps was to be reinforced by two tank regiments and the 18th Assault Engineer Brigade. The 125th Rifle Corps received one tank regiment as reinforcements. The encirclement and siege of the city was not planned by the Soviet command. The assigned task was quite clear: 'To destroy the enemy's Kovel' group of forces and to prevent its withdrawal to the west.' The 47th Army's 77th Rifle Corps was ordered to cover the army's rear against Brest (a threat from the west was evidently not taken into account) with a single regiment.

The commander of the 77th Rifle Corps somewhat modified the army commander's instructions and ordered his forces to attack Kovel' with all three formations at his disposal. The 143rd Rifle Division was to attack the north-western outskirts of Kovel', the 60th Rifle Division the northern outskirts, and the 260th Rifle Division the eastern outskirts. The strength of the formations deployed by the 47th Army in the fight for Kovel' is shown in the table overleaf.

Table 2.1: The Numerical Strength of the 47th Army's Formations on 16 March 1944.

Unit	Men	Horses	Motor Vehicles
60th Rifle Div.	6,888	971	112
143rd Rifle Div.	6,185	1,370	90
260th Rifle Div.	6,463	806	75
76th Rifle Div.	6,929	881	116
175th Rifle Div.	7,016	841	74
328th Rifle Div.	5,182	962	85
18th Assault-Engineer Bde	2,161	205	73

Unit	Rifles	Shpagin SMGs	Light Machine Guns	Heavy Machine Guns
60th Rifle Div.	3,837	1,794	262	81
143rd Rifle Div.	2,538	1,046	170	68
260th Rifle Div.	4,000	1,849	224	81
76th Rifle Div.	4,124	1,857	244	81
175th Rifle Div.	4,166	1,720	246	81
328th Rifle Div.	2,725	1,746	164	52
18th Assault-Engineer Bde	138	1,704	106	–

It is obvious that the 143rd Rifle Division was distinguished from the 47th Army's other formations by the number of its horses. At the same time, the 47th Army's formations were about equally supplied with motor vehicles.

The divisions which had arrived at the 47th Army had a full complement of mortars and artillery (eighteen 120mm mortars and fifty-four 82mm and 50mm mortars, twelve 122mm howitzers, thirty-two 76mm regimental guns, twelve 76mm divisional guns and thirty-six 45mm anti-tank guns). Those units that had been previously in combat did not have the full complement. For example, the 143rd Rifle Division disposed of only eighteen 76mm regimental guns, nine 76mm divisional guns, twenty-four 45mm guns and eleven 120mm mortars. Only in 122mm howitzers did the 143rd Rifle Division have as many as the newly-arrived divisions – twelve. The 328th Rifle Division disposed of only seven 122mm howitzers, eight regimental and five divisional 76mm guns and eighteen 45mm guns. The new divisions also disposed of a large number of sub-machine guns, reflecting the Red Army's tendency for arming its infantry with Shpagins in increasing numbers toward the end of the war,

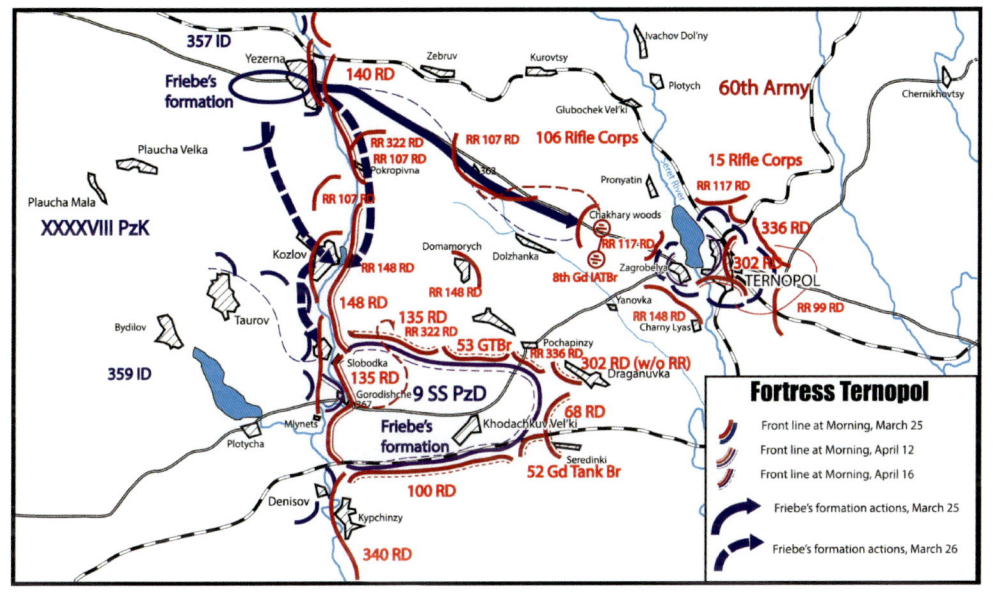

Fortress Ternopol

357 ID
Yezerna
Zebruv
Kurovtsy
Ivachov Dol'ny
Plotych
60th Army
Chernikhovtsy
140 RD
Friebe's formation
Glubochek Vel'ki
Plaucha Velka
RR 322 RD
RR 107 RD
RR 107 RD
106 Rifle Corps
15 Rifle Corps
RR 117 RD
Pokropivna
Pronyatin
RR 107 RD
Chakhary woods
336 RD
Plaucha Mala
XXXXVIII PzK
RR 117 RD
302 RD
Kozlov
Domamorych
Dolzhanka
8th Gd IATBr
Zagrobelya
TERNOPOL
RR 148 RD
148 RD
RR 148 RD
Yanovka
RR 148 RD
RR 99 RD
Bydilov
Taurov
135 RD
RR 322 RD
Charny Lyas
359 ID
53 GTBr
Pochapinzy
RR 336 RD
302 RD (w/o RR)
Slobodka
Draganuvka
135 RD
Gorodishche
9 SS PzD
Mlynets
Khodachkuv Vel'ki
68 RD
Plotycha
Friebe's formation
Seredinki
52 Gd Tank Br
Denisov
100 RD
Kypchinzy
340 RD

Front line at Morning, March 25
Front line at Morning, April 12
Front line at Morning, April 16
Friebe's formation actions, March 25
Friebe's formation actions, March 26

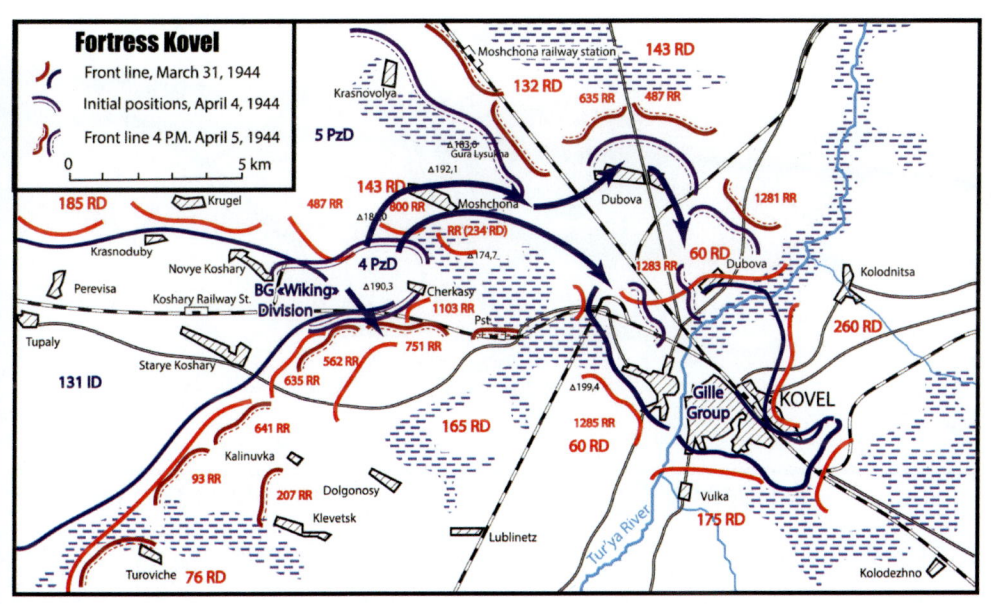

Fortress Kovel

Front line, March 31, 1944
Initial positions, April 4, 1944
Front line 4 P.M. April 5, 1944
0   5 km

Moshchona railway station
143 RD
132 RD
635 RR
487 RR
Krasnovolya
5 PzD
Gura Lysucha
143 RD
1281 RR
185 RD
Krugel
487 RR
800 RR
Moshchona
Krasnoduby
RR (234 RD)
60 RD
Dubova
Novye Koshary
4 PzD
Dubova
Kolodnitsa
Perevisa
Cherkasy
1283 RR
Koshary Railway St.
BG «Wiking» Division
1103 RR
Pst
260 RD
Tupaly
751 RR
KOVEL
131 ID
Starye Koshary
562 RR
Gille Group
635 RR
165 RD
1285 RR
641 RR
60 RD
Kalinuvka
Vulka
93 RR
207 RR
Dolgonosy
175 RD
Klevetsk
Lublinetz
Tur'ya River
Turoviche
76 RD
Kolodezhno

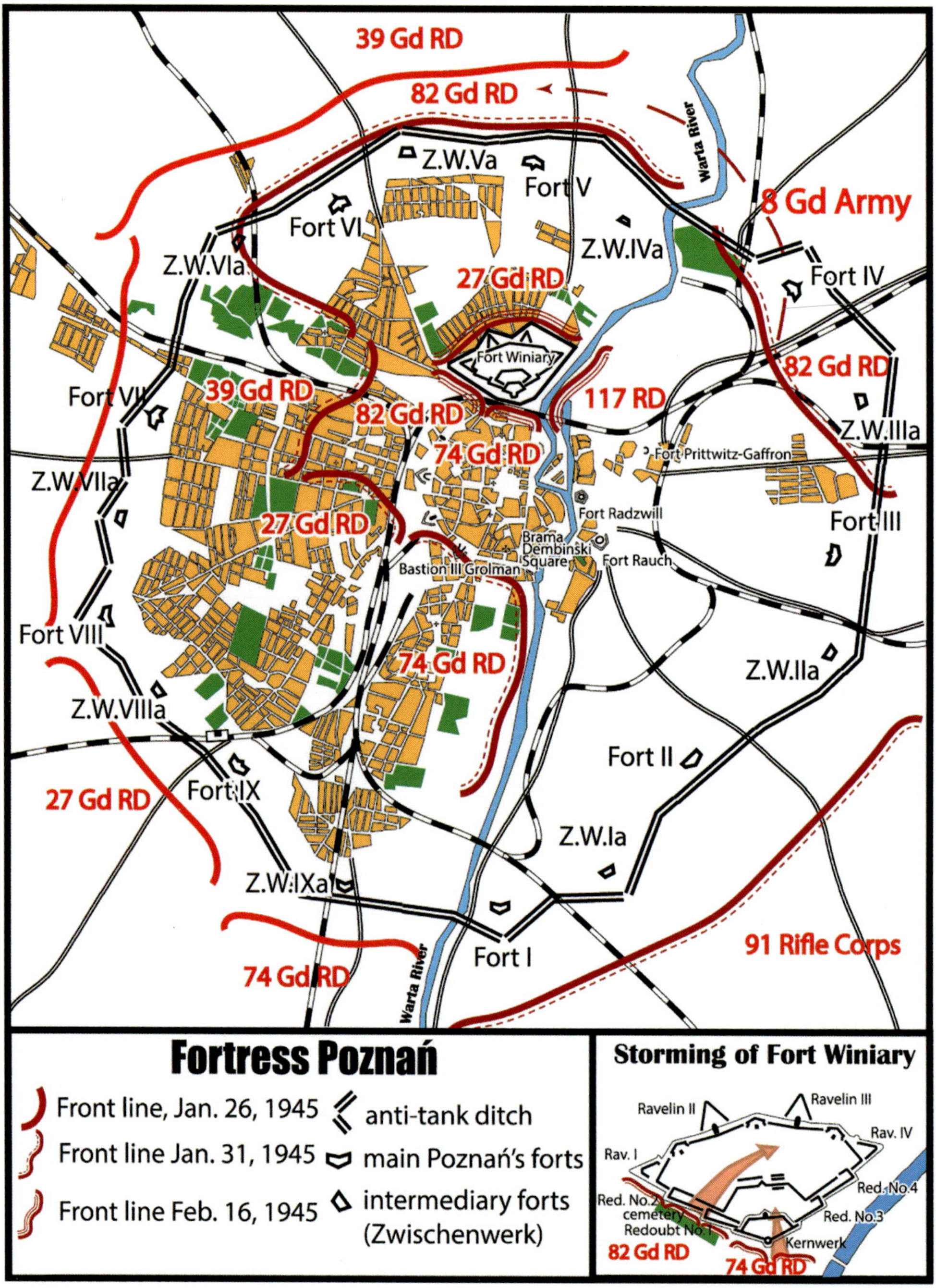

39 Gd RD
82 Gd RD
Warta River
Z.W.Va
Fort V
8 Gd Army
Fort VI
Z.W.IVa
Z.W.VIa
Fort IV
27 Gd RD
Fort Winiary
82 Gd RD
Fort VII
39 Gd RD
117 RD
82 Gd RD
Z.W.IIIa
74 Gd RD
Fort Prittwitz-Gaffron
Z.W.VIIa
Fort Radzwill
Fort III
27 Gd RD
Brama Dembinski
Square
Fort Rauch
Bastion III Grolman
Fort VIII
74 Gd RD
Z.W.IIa
Z.W.VIIIa
Fort II
27 Gd RD
Fort IX
Z.W.Ia
Z.W.IXa
91 Rifle Corps
Fort I
74 Gd RD
Warta River
Fortress Poznań
Front line, Jan. 26, 1945
anti-tank ditch
Front line Jan. 31, 1945
main Poznań's forts
Front line Feb. 16, 1945
intermediary forts (Zwischenwerk)
Storming of Fort Winiary
Ravelin II
Ravelin III
Rav. IV
Rav. I
Red. No.4
Red. No.2
cemetery
Redoubt No.1
Red. No.3
Kernwerk
82 Gd RD
74 Gd RD

Pen and Sword Books
c/o Casemate Publishers
1950 Lawrence Road
Havertown, PA 19083

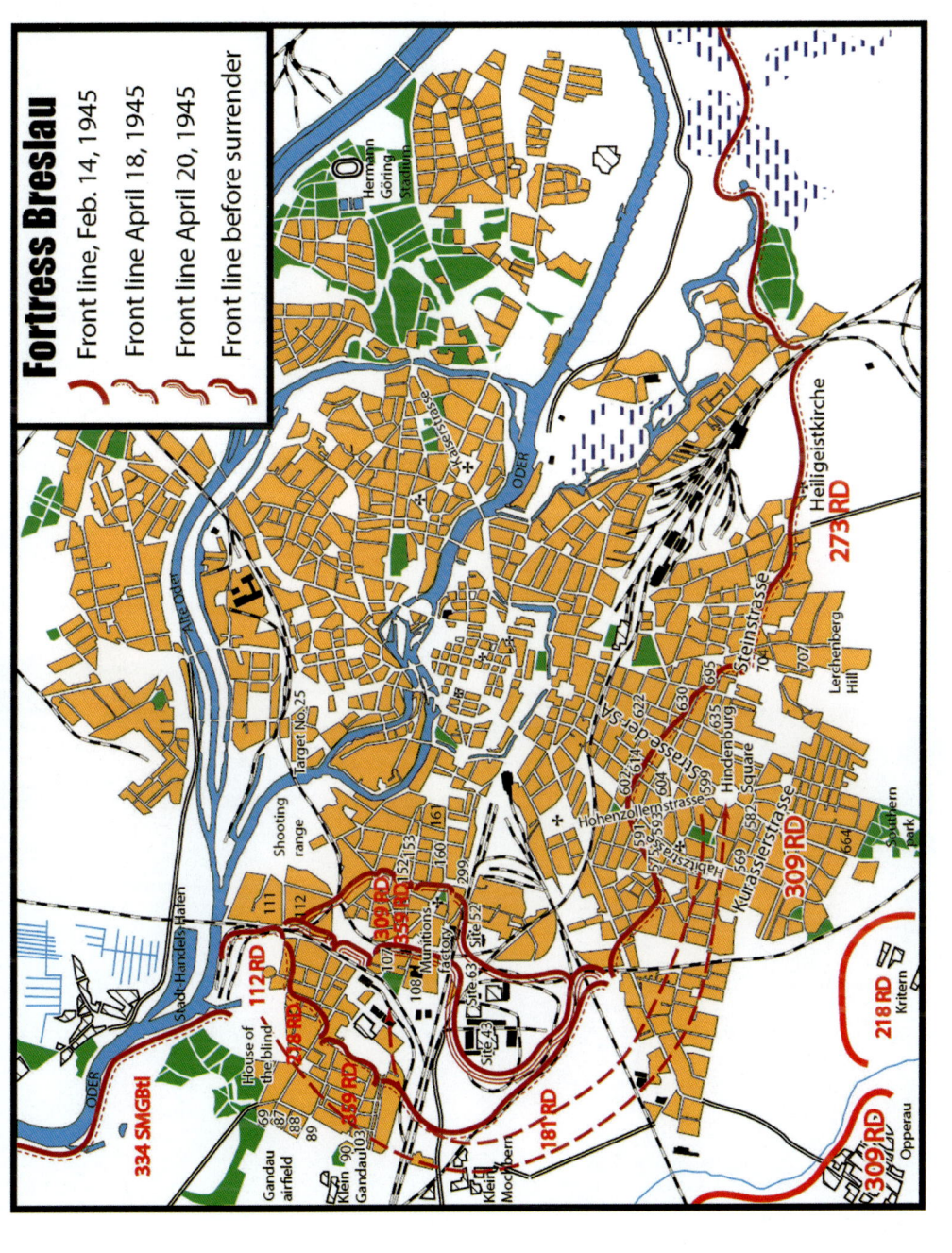

Fortress Breslau

- Front line, Feb. 14, 1945
- Front line April 18, 1945
- Front line April 20, 1945
- Front line before surrender

334 SMGBtl

Gandau airfield

House of the blind

Stadt-Handels-Hafen

112 RD

176 RD

259 RD

Klein Gandau

Shooting range

Target No.25

111

12

107

108

309 RD

259 RD

152 153

160 161

299

Munitions-factory

Site 63

Site 43

Site 52

181 RD

Klein Mochbern

ODER

Alte Oder

Kaiserstrasse

ODER

Hermann Göring Stadion

Hohenzollernstrasse

Strasse der SA

602 614

605 593

599 604

622

630

635

695

707

Hindenburg Square

Habitzstrasse

Kürassierstrasse

Steinstrasse

309 RD

273 RD

Helligeistkirche

Lerchenberg Hill

569 582

664

Südpark

218 RD

Kritern

309 RD

Opperau

1. The commander of a motorized battalion of automatic riflemen, Captain G.T. Dobrunov (in the centre) with comrades next to a BA-64 armoured car. 4th Guards Tank Corps, 60th Army.

2. I.D. Chernyakhovskii, commander of the 60th Army, photographed in the summer of 1944. In his command post as commander of the Third Belorussian Front, after being promoted to general and receiving his second star (Hero of the Soviet Union) (29 July 1944).

3. I.I. Lyudnikov, commander of the 15th Rifle Corps. The successful storming of Ternopol' would facilitate his appointment as an army commander in Belorussia.

4. An abandoned Panther from the 7th Panzer Division on the street in Ternopol'. (*TsAMO*)

5. A knocked-out *Sturmgeschütz* assault gun on the street in Ternopol'. (*TsAMO*)

6. A knocked-out SU-152 self-propelled gun in Ternopol'. (*TsAMO*)

7. A parachute-dropped supply container on the roof of one of the buildings in Ternopol' (from a newsreel clip).

8. A burnt-out transport glider on the street in Ternopol'. (*TsAMO*)

9. Soviet infantry in the street fighting for Ternopol'.

10. The railway station in Ternopol'. (*TsAMO*)

11. A Maxim machine gun team putting its weapon in order.

12. A panoramic view of the approaches to Kovel' from the roof of the railway station.

13. The Catholic church in Kovel'. An enormous structure built in the 1930s.

in numbers according to authorized strength and in reality. The 18th Assault Engineer Brigade was armed predominantly with automatic weaponry, but this was to be expected in view of the specific nature of its combat role.

At the same time, one should note that the reinforcement and outfitting of the formations sent to the Second Belorussian Front was carried out at a rapid pace. For example, Colonel A.V. Bogoyavlenskii's 60th Rifle Division had been pulled out of the fighting around Kalinkovichi with a strength of 2,712 men and was unloaded at Kursk during 16–17 February. Already by 26 February the division's strength had been raised to 7,203 men, and on 27 February it began loading onto trains. During 2–4 March it had already suffered its first losses from air strikes against the railway around Sarny (79 men killed, including a regimental commander, and 250 wounded). Of course, the reinforcements that had arrived at the division had a couple of months of training, but the subunits were formed in haste. Training was not conducted in the formed subunits. The reinforcements consisted of 1,934 Russians, 656 Ukrainians, 83 Belorussians and 947 men from Central Asia. It's difficult to call this a solid formation, but the existing core of soldiers and commanders with combat experience gave hope for its success in combat.

In light of the specific terrain conditions, the 47th Army did not receive a tank corps or even a tank brigade, but tank regiments with an authorized strength of twenty-one tanks. It was those regiments, outfitted with Valentine[19] and Sherman[20] tanks received through Lend-Lease,[21] that took part in the fighting around Kovel'.

Meanwhile, the commander of the SS *Wiking* Division, SS *Gruppenführer*[22] Herbert Gille, arrived in Kovel' in a Fieseler Storch[23] light aircraft together with his assistant operations officer SS *Hauptsturmführer*[24] Westphal. The plane had been fired upon during the approach to Kovel', which immediately indicated a crisis situation around the city. An acquaintance with the city's garrison could hardly have aroused any enthusiasm. At that moment the German units in the Kovel' area were divided into two battle groups. The first was commanded by Colonel von Bissing and its core was the SS 17th Cavalry Regiment and several independent battalions, including two *Landwehr*[25] ones made up of older soldiers. The group's overall combat strength (*Gefechtsstaerke*)[26] was 2,214 men.[27] The second group was commanded by Lieutenant Colonel of the *Schutzpolizei*[28] H. Holtz. It included engineer, security and police units, a battalion from the 213th Security Division, and also Armoured Train No. 10. The overall strength of the group was 1,457 men.[29] The strength of the garrison's combat units was therefore 3,671 men. Besides this, the Kovel' garrison included an artillery battalion with 105mm howitzers, an anti-aircraft battalion, and rear and support units. The units blockaded in Kovel' disposed of the following heavy weapons:[30]

Eight 1eFH18 10.5cm light field howitzers;
Eight 1eIG18 7.5cm light infantry guns;
Two captured Polish 75mm guns;
Three PAK-38 50mm anti-tank guns;
Three captured Soviet 45mm anti-tank guns;
Two 37mm anti-tank guns ('door knockers');
Twelve 37mm and seventeen 20mm anti-aircraft guns;
Thirty-seven 81mm mortars and nineteen 50mm mortars;
Forty-eight heavy machine guns (type not indicated).

It is sometimes claimed that there were no anti-tank guns at all with the units blockaded in Kovel'. As we see, this was not the case. Three 50mm guns are not so few, when taking into account the 47th Army's limited tank park, while the 37mm and 45mm guns were quite suitable against light vehicles. According to indirect data, there was at least one 88mm gun, which was actively employed by the Germans during the *blitzkrieg* period as an anti-tank gun. However, improvements in the tactics of the Allies' tank troops gradually led to the withdrawal of these AA guns as ground-combat weapons. The *Faustpatronen*, which were appearing in ever-increasing numbers, had not yet been sufficiently mastered by the troops. The garrison's trump card, as subsequent events will show, was holder of the Knight's Cross Major H. Heisler's 662nd Engineer Battalion (150 men). This experienced commander, who had led the battalion since 1941, was able to compensate for the shortage of anti-tank weapons through engineer means.

In an order by the Fourth Panzer Army at 22.50 on 16 March, Gille was appointed commander of the defence of Kovel'. At 01.30 the next morning, a radiogram arrived from the commander of Army Group South, Erich von Manstein,[31] which reminded Gille of *Führer* Order No. 11 about fortresses, according to which he now had to operate. The von dem Bach battle group, which was responsible for the defence of the Kovel' fortress, was renamed Battle Group Gille.

A coordinated attack on Kovel' from different directions, as planned by the 47th Army's headquarters, could not be carried out. The 143rd Rifle Division was closest to the city. At 07.00 the division's forward detachment (a battalion from the 635th Rifle Regiment) completed the envelopment of the Kovel' group of forces by cutting the Kovel'–Vladimir-Volynskii railway line in the Lyublinets area to the south-west of the city and reached the Tur'ya River south of the flour-milling factory. However, the tanks of the 223rd Tank Regiment, which had been allotted for the attack on Kovel', were late due to problems with crossings and the poor condition of the roads. The planned attack at 10.00 was postponed. Moreover, by 12.00 only the 223rd Tank Regiment's nine Valentines had reached the Kovel' area. At that moment the Shermans (twelve vehicles) were still far behind, waiting to cross the Stokhod River and Tur'ya River (to the north of Kovel'). According to the 143rd Rifle Division's report, the commander of the 223rd Tank Regiment did not arrive with his headquarters and nine tanks until 15.00. However, the corps commander hurried the attack along and they nevertheless decided to carry it out closer to evening. At 18.30 the tanks were concentrating in the Lyublinets area. One should say that that axis of attack was chosen quite intelligently – from the jumping-off positions along the south-western outskirts. It was justifiably expected that the defence of the Kovel' fortress would be weaker from the rear.

Thus the attempt to storm Kovel' on 17 March nevertheless took place. The 223rd Tank Regiment, with the engines of its Valentines droning, broke into the city at 20.00, when it was already twilight, from the direction of the flour-milling factory. Going against all the training manuals, the tanks moved in column along the road, pouring fire in all directions from their guns and machine guns. The terrain conditions prevented them from moving off the road. The tank regiment's report particularly noted the good command and control of the tanks by radio. They broke into the city in column formation and panic broke out, but the attack was not supported by the infantry. As a result, as early as 21.30, the tanks returned to their jumping-off positions. One Valentine was knocked out, but was quickly recovered. One should note that there is a discrepancy between the description of events by the headquarters of the 143rd Rifle Division and that of the tank battalion, but the 223rd Tank Regiment's report dovetails with the latest action reports. The 143rd Rifle Division's 800th Rifle Regiment, which was attacking Kovel' from the north, was halted under heavy fire 500m from the railway bridge over the Tur'ya River.

The 60th Rifle Division, contrary to the entry in the 47th Army's war diary, did not take part in the offensive of 17 March. The division's subunits, which were worn out by the lengthy 200km march and having only 0.3 of a unit of fire, did not attack on this day. The 260th Rifle Division's attack on Kovel' from the most heavily-fortified direction, that is, from the east, got only as far as the close approaches to the city, the village of Belin. At the same time, the division sustained quite significant losses: 89 men killed and 286 wounded. It was announced, however, that the enemy left more than 200 corpses on the battlefield. The 125th Rifle Corps' 175th Rifle Division also failed to reach Kovel' and on 17 March was fighting (successfully) for the villages to the south-east of the city.

Soviet units along the Kovel' siege perimeter observed aircraft dropping supply containers from practically the first day of blockading the city. There was no landing strip for aircraft within the fortress, which put the garrison in an unfavourable position from the very beginning. However, parachute containers were dropped, some of which fell among the Soviet positions.

A genuinely coordinated assault took place the following day, 18 March, in the early morning and from the very same positions as the previous day. The 223rd Tank Regiment's Valentines, along with the infantry from a battalion of the 635th Rifle Regiment, attacked the enemy. However, the experience of the tank breakthrough on the evening of 17 March had forced the enemy to adopt countermeasures during the night and this time the road leading into the city was mined. Two Valentines were knocked out and the movement in column became impossible. The tanks exchanged fire with the Germans in place. As a result, the attempt to break through into the city failed. Meanwhile, the Soviet forces along the perimeter of the Kovel' siege were being reinforced. The 230th Tank Regiment (eleven Valentines and ten Shermans) was arriving from the east.

The shortage of ammunition in the 77th Rifle Corps' units could not be fully compensated for by air strikes. As F.P. Polynin, the commander of the 6th Air Army, recalled: 'By 18 March only eighteen Il-2s, fourteen Yak-9s,[32] five Pe-2s, and eighty-five Po-2s[33] had managed to fly to their new fields. The remaining planes sat as if anchored on their former airfields.'[34] That is, about 70 per cent of the 6th Air Army's combat aircraft (122 planes out of 181) arrived in the Sarny area from Nevel'. Judging by the 6th Air Army's reports to the *front* headquarters, even the *Shturmoviks*[35] that had already rebased to new airfields were not carrying out combat sorties. The 6th Air Army's aircraft only flew reconnaissance missions on 17–18 March, including U-2 night aircraft.

However, for a while no one believed that prolonged fighting for the fortress lay ahead. The mood in the 47th Army's headquarters at that time may be characterized by a phrase from the memoirs of M.Kh. Kalashnik, the chief of the army's political section: 'All of us were sure that just a day or two more, five at most, and the encircled garrison of Kovel' would capitulate and the city would be taken.'[36]

During the night of 18/19 March the engineers cleared some of the mines on the road near Lyublinets to the south-west of Kovel', but they were unable to drive a real passage through the minefield. On the morning of 19 March another two Valentines were knocked out by mines on the road. However, this time the tank troops and infantry had a 'Plan B'. The 143rd Rifle Division, which had been reinforced with a battalion by the commander, repeated its attack by a circuitous route, through Height 199.4, directly to the west from Kovel'. Valentines from both tank regiments attached to the 143rd Rifle Division took part in the attack. As a result, as early as 10.00 on 19 March elements of the 635th Rifle Regiment occupied the flour-milling factory on the outskirts of Kovel'. Fighting began for the city blocks.

At that moment the 230th and 223rd Tank Regiments' Shermans arrived from the crossings over the Stokhod and Tur'ya. The commander of the 143rd Rifle Regiment decided to employ all twenty-one M4A2s[37] (ten and eleven from the two tank regiments, respectively) massed on the 800th Rifle Regiment's attack sector. But the attack by the American tanks in a single column along the Brest road on 19 March ended in a fiasco. Two M4A2s were knocked out by mines (one from each regiment). Some of the tanks attempted to move off the road and bogged down in a swamp. Further on, as Zhitnik, the 143rd Rifle Division's chief of staff, elegantly put it: 'Those following in the column's wake were knocked out.' Most likely, they became victims of 50mm anti-tank guns.

In the evening Gille summed up the result of the day in a radiogram to the Fourth Panzer Army: 'Powerful attacks with the overall support of 18 tanks along all fronts. In the western part we managed to throw back the enemy who had broken through with several counter-attacks, while two tanks were destroyed in close fighting. Both the enemy and we suffered heavy losses. 29 prisoners were taken.'[38]

As early as sunset the 223rd Tank Regiment's tanks were once again sent into battle and even broke into the city, but returned after losing three vehicles. These could have been knocked out by either anti-tank guns firing point-blank in the streets, or by *Faustpatronen*. As a result, the presence of an engineer battalion (even two) in Kovel' and the terrain conditions enabled the Germans to compensate for the weakness of the garrison's anti-tank weapons. By 20 March only three combat-ready Shermans remained in line in the 230th Tank Regiment, and four in the 223rd Tank Regiment by 22 March.

However, on 19 March the 60th Rifle Division achieved a significant success and its units managed to crush the Germans' resistance in the village of Dubova on the northern approaches to Kovel'. Moreover, the Germans falling back into the city in disorder came under flanking fire from a battalion of the 143rd Rifle Division's 800th Rifle Regiment, which was occupying defensive positions facing east. The Germans were mowed down by machine guns and 76mm guns. The results of the fighting were declared as 150 officers and men killed. However, as a result, the commander of the 800th Rifle Regiment received a dressing-down for his lack of initiative. It was believed that the moment of the enemy's retreat could have been employed for breaking into the city on his heels. According to reports from the 800th Rifle Regiment and the 60th Rifle Division, they were met by heavy enemy fire on the approaches to the city. The 260th and 175th Rifle Divisions also achieved a relative success on 19 March, when one regiment from each reached the south-eastern and southern outskirts of Kovel'.

One of the prerequisites of the successes of 19 March was the activities of the Soviet air force. On this day the 6th Air Army actively attacked the garrison of Kovel' from the air. The Il-2 *Shturmoviks*, escorted by Yak-9 fighters, attacked the Kovel' railway station in groups of from three to seven planes. As was noted in the 6th Air Army's daily report, 'As a result of bombing the Kovel' station, an explosion of enormous force took place, with flame and clouds of black smoke, which rose to a height of 800m (presumably an ammunition depot was blown up).'[39]

The resumption of the assault on 20 March brought no appreciable success. The infantrymen attempting to break into Kovel' were met with dense fire from the area of the railway station. The 800th Rifle Regiment's attacking subunits were also hit by machine-gun fire on the right from the embankment on the loop of the railway tracks to the west of the station, which were surrounded by swamps. Thus a large part of Colonel Zaikin's division's losses were suffered by the 800th Rifle Regiment, which attacked Kovel' along the Brest road. From 15 through 20 March the regiment lost 88 men killed and 458 wounded, while the 143rd Rifle Division as a whole lost 128 men killed and 589 wounded.

Units of the 60th Rifle Division, which attacked from the north and along the road from Kolodnitsa to Kovel', encountered fire from Armoured Train No. 10. The railway tracks in the north of the city and in the area of the station ran close to what were then outskirts of the city, enabling the armoured train to engage the attackers. As was noted in the division's operational report for 20 March, the 1285th Rifle Regiment, 'under heavy fire from an armoured train, artillery, mortars, and flanking fire from machine guns from the southern outskirts of Verbka[40] and the northern outskirts of the city of Kovel', advanced only 800m and lay down before a water-filled ditch 4–5m wide'. An anti-tank ditch had actually been dug along the approaches to the city from the east and had been transformed by the spring rains into an obstacle tested since the Middle Ages. In order to flesh out the picture of the fighting, one must add the features of Kovel' at night. The actions of engineers and infantry attacking at night were complicated by the 'continuous illumination of the terrain by the enemy's rockets'. This was probably an impressive sight: the illumination by rocket flares and the trails of machine-gun bursts along the perimeter of a city lost in the woods and swamps.

A summary radiogram from Gille on the evening of 20 March to the headquarters of the Fourth Panzer Army stated: 'The enemy is carrying out heavy fire from artillery and mortars, mainly against the station area. Assault aviation is constantly attacking, dropping bombs and firing from its wing weapons. We have suffered heavy losses in men and materiel. Six tanks were destroyed during the day and eight men captured.'[41]

One could point to the shortage of ammunition as one of the chief reasons for the failure of the attempt to take the city from the march. From 16 through 20 March the 47th Army expended 2,645 45mm rounds, 681 76mm regimental artillery rounds, 2,140 76mm divisional artillery rounds, 374 122mm howitzer rounds and 40 152mm rounds. This expenditure includes the fighting along the external encirclement front and on the approaches to Kovel'. 203mm guns, which were traditionally employed for storming cities in the second half of the war, were absent from the 47th Army altogether.

Meanwhile, the intensity of the fighting was increasing along the Kovel' fortress's external encirclement front. On 20 March there was an attack by a German forward detachment against a screen that had been set up facing west by two of the 143rd Rifle Division's platoons. Having pushed aside the screen, the Germans attempted to develop the offensive along the railway, but were halted in the area of Koshary station. Colonel M.M. Zaikin, the commander of the 143rd Rifle Division, made the decision, which was confirmed by the 77th Rifle Corps' command, to pull one of his division's regiments out from the fighting for Kovel' and to deploy it to the external encirclement front of the fortress. The choice fell upon the 685th Rifle Regiment, which was removed from its positions on the night of 20/21 March.

The headquarters of the 47th Army gave its subordinate forces a dressing-down on the basis of the results of the first days of the fighting for Kovel'. One of these was a personal warning to the commander of the 60th Rifle Division, Colonel Bogoyavlenskii, that he was not fully suited for his job 'because of the poor organization of the battle on 17–19.3.44'. The army headquarters ordered that the garrison of Kovel' be split into several parts by attacks from the west and south. Moreover, judging by the toponyms employed, General V.S. Polenov's staff assigned the mission according to a large-scale map, and not according to a city map (on which there was no such toponym as 'manor houses'.

The activity of the Soviet air force was making life increasingly unpleasant for the units surrounded in Kovel'. Gille radioed the following to the Fourth Panzer Army: 'Constant attacks by the enemy's assault aviation against our positions and railway sites since the morning of 21.3. Armoured Train No. 10 was put out of action as the result of a direct hit. We desperately need fighter cover.'[42] The headquarters of the Fourth Panzer Army replied at 13.15: 'It is impossible at the present time to organize fighter cover due to the aircrafts' insufficient range and the waterlogged landing fields.' At 18.15 Gille once again radioed the army headquarters, this time with a description of the consequences of the air strikes: 'The enemy's assault air aviation attacked some 12 times. We suffered heavy losses and the city has been heavily damaged. Armoured Train No. 10 has been destroyed by a direct hit. There are 900 wounded in the fortress.'[43] Thus the *Shturmoviks* dealt with Armoured Train No. 10, which had made life difficult for the 60th Rifle Division's units attacking the city. Gille did not list the number of wounded for the day, but instead the growing number of wounded located in the fortress. A radiogram of 20 March indicated 750 wounded.

One cannot fail to note that at this time Kovel' was not a priority target for the 6th Air Army. The *Shturmoviks* were operating more intensely against the railway lines leading to Kovel' from the west, while attempting to prevent the concentration of German reserves. On 21 March thirty-three Il-2s were operating over Kovel' with sixty-five Il-2s against the railway stations. Moreover, the destruction of the armoured train by the *Shturmoviks* was not even claimed. The Germans' Armoured Train No. 10 really was put out of action and not repaired, despite the subsequent relief of Kovel'.

Just what exactly was taking place along the external encirclement front? What was forcing the Soviet command to devote more attention to strikes against the enemy's communications? The closing of the ring around Kovel' forced the German command to take emergency measures to relieve it by an attack from outside. They chose the headquarters of the XLII Army Corps as the command organ for the relief group of forces. On 4 March 1944 the headquarters of the XLII Army Corps, which had survived the Korsun'-Shevchenkovskii encirclement, had been pulled back to an area 50km from Peremyshlyany. The corps headquarters had lost its motor vehicles, communications equipment and a third of its rank and file in the 'cauldron'. The corps was commanded by the Knight's Cross holder 59-year-old General of Infantry Franz Mattenklott. The order to transfer the headquarters of the XLII Army Corps to the Chelm area, with the task of taking over the command of units arriving for the breakthrough to Kovel', followed on 18 March. As early as 19 March Mattenklott's headquarters arrived in Chelm and was subordinated to Army Group South's Fourth Panzer Army.

The first formations that came under the corps command were the Hungarian 7th Infantry Division and the German 131st Infantry Division. The latter, which consisted of two regiments (the third had been disbanded due to losses), had been arriving at Lyuboml' since 18 March from the crucible of the positional battles around Vitebsk. The 190th Assault Gun Brigade was transferred to the Kovel' area, along with the 131st Infantry Division from the Vitebsk area. Upon arriving, it received reinforcements in the form of self-propelled guns originally designated for the *Wiking* Division. Major General Weber commanded the 131st Infantry Division at this time. It was precisely the 131st Infantry Division's two regiments that were to begin the breakthrough to Kovel'. It was decided not to move the less-capable Hungarians to the first line. They were tasked with defending the 1941 boundary line along the Western Bug River in the corps' rear. Hungarian subunits were simultaneously placed under the XLII Army Corps, upon being activated for guarding the railway to the east of the Western Bug River. A combat group from the

SS *Wiking* Division, led by the commander of the artillery regiment, SS *Standartenführer*[44] Richter, was also transferred to the XLII Army Corps.

It is difficult to describe the SS *Wiking* Division's situation at this time as anything but peculiar. *De facto*, on 4 March 1944 the division numbered 4,242 'combat soldiers' (that is, those directly taking part in combat) and 9,245 'daytime soldiers' (that is, including rear units, training subunits and headquarters units).[45] However, there were only 825 98k carbines, 50 G.43 self-loading rifles, 135 *Sturmgewehren*,[46] 85 MP-38/40 sub-machine guns, and 140 light and heavy machine guns for this entire horde.[47] The formation had no howitzer artillery at all.

This led to a situation in which Mattenklott, in a 21 March conversation with Erhard Rauss, the commander of the Fourth Panzer Army, on 21 March stated the following: 'The SS *Wiking* Division is receiving weapons.' He requested that each soldier who received a weapon be dispatched to the front, 'so that these elements could at least operate against partisans before the arrival of their heavy weapons'.[48] Thus this elite formation initially played only a very minor role in the fighting for Kovel'.

The *Wiking* Division's component units were in approximately the same shape. One of the battalions of the *Wiking* Division's tank regiment had been rearmed with Panther tanks since 1943 and was being reformed and trained in Western Europe. This was part of an overall campaign, embracing the army's tank divisions and the SS tank divisions – the removal and rearming of the tank regiment with new Panther tanks. As a result, not all the battalions returned to their division. As of 12 March 1944, the SS 5th Panzer Regiment consisted of the following:[49]

Five Panzer IVs and three command Panthers in the regiment's headquarters;

Thirty-four Panthers and two 'Bergepanthers' available in the first battalion, with another thirty-nine Panthers and three command tanks en route;

Five Panzer IVs in the second battalion.

The SS 5th Panzer Regiment's Panther battalion received a total of seventy-three tanks. At the same time, there were only two 18-ton towing vehicles out of an authorized twelve, which reduced the ability to recover disabled Panthers from the battlefield. This was compensated to a certain extent by the presence of the 'Bergepanthers' – repair and recovery versions of the Panther. Not all of the tanks listed above could be immediately sent to the Kovel' area.

After the war, as part of a programme for analysing the experience of the fighting, the Americans questioned Mattenklott and the general wrote an essay for them about the operation to relieve Kovel'. He expressed himself as follows as regards the choice of action: 'The XLII Corps had the mission of relieving Kovel'. The corps realized that in light of the weakness of its forces success could be achieved by an offensive along a narrow front along the railway, while paying no attention to threats to the flank and rear. The corps thus hoped to defend the sole remaining railway as a supply line and to deceive the enemy as to its strength.'[50]

In accordance with the decision adopted, the 131st Infantry Division received orders to advance in a wedge along the railway line, with the 431st Infantry Regiment to the right and the 434th Infantry Regiment to the left. The formation's reconnaissance battalion would move behind the centre of the combat formation. *Wiking*'s combat group initially received orders to cover the flank. The unloading of the 131st Infantry Division's units was completed on the evening of 19 March, while the artillery arrived the following day, 20 March. The 131st Infantry Division's infantry went over to the offensive, without waiting for its complete concentration, and as early as 20 March was reporting the capture of Matseyuva.

According to the Soviet version of events (the report by the 143rd Rifle Division), 'On 20 March the enemy's forward detachment, consisting of a single infantry battalion and six tanks, reached Tupaly (east of Matseyuva), dislodged our screen, consisting of two rifle platoons, and began to operate in the direction of Koshary station'. The six tanks were evidently the 190th Assault Gun Brigade's assault guns. Mattenklott later told the Americans of the capture of numerous prisoners. They could not have been taken from the two platoons. The entire 487th Rifle Regiment (whose platoons were near Tupaly) reported a few dozen killed and wounded. It cannot be excluded, however, that in Matseyuva there could have been rear-area elements busy gathering captured equipment.

The increasing pressure from the west forced the Soviet command to reorient the 143rd Rifle Division to the west in its entirety. The first formation to move west was the 635th Rifle Regiment on 20–21 March. However, the relief of the positions near Kovel' took place gradually and continued until 23

March, which led to their being thrown into defensive positions piecemeal. The tank regiments were being deployed along with the 143rd Rifle Division to meet the offensive threat, but also in stages. The 230th Tank Regiment, with three Valentines, was the first to take up defensive positions near Starye Koshary, and near Koshary station with three Shermans.

The gradual movement of troops to the external encirclement front led to a situation in which the 131st Infantry Division, by taking advantage of its temporary superiority of force, successfully attacked Starye Koshary and Novye Koshary and Krugel'. As early as the evening of 21 March[51] the Germans managed to drive out the Soviet infantry (the 635th Rifle Regiment and a battalion from the 487th Rifle Regiment) and occupied these places. The 230th Tank Regiment's tanks remained in their positions and fought to the last in isolation. There was no miracle in the battle with the *Sturmgeschützen* and the day ended for the 230th Tank Regiment with the loss of two Valentines burned, while the remaining vehicles were damaged. To be fair, on the whole, the 143rd Rifle Division suffered quite appreciable losses for 21 March – 55 men killed and 168 wounded. That is, its units were thrown out of their positions following a serious fight. Four of the 223rd Tank Regiment's Shermans arrived at the battlefield after the infantry's withdrawal to the next defensive line, but were unable to change the course of the fighting in their favour. Meanwhile, the 223rd Tank Regiment's Valentines continued to fight on the outskirts of Kovel', while supporting the units assaulting the fortress. The measures adopted earlier by the Soviet units for preparing a defence, particularly planting mines, although they failed to stop the Germans, did inflict losses. The car of the commander of the 131st Infantry Division, General Weber, hit a mine; the general was wounded and the formation commander became one of the regimental commanders – Colonel G. Seegers.

Meanwhile, the main forces of the 143rd Rifle Division were gradually deploying to the west. The division, having been relieved of its positions near Kovel' by units of the 60th Rifle Division, took up the defence of the line astride the Chelm–Kovel' railway. The accumulation of forces enabled the Soviets to go over to launching counter-attacks. On the night of 23/24 March a battalion from the 143rd Rifle Division's 800th Rifle Regiment won back the village of Krugel', while claiming to have killed about 100 German infantrymen at the cost of insignificant losses (three killed and thirty-three wounded) to itself.

The remaining formations attached to the 47th Army were simultaneously arriving from the east. The 185th Rifle Division took up defensive positions in the Shaino area, to the right of the 143rd Rifle Division. The 125th Rifle Corps' 76th Rifle Division, having forced the Tur'ya River to the left, was approaching the front from Koshary to Torgovishche, with its front facing north-west. Before long it was subordinated to the 77th Rifle Corps. As a result, the 143rd Rifle Division's offensive sector shrank from 12km to 6km. The narrowing of the defensive front even allowed the Soviets to pull the 143rd Rifle Division's 800th Rifle Regiment into the reserve, thus forming the classical array of two regiments in the first line and one in reserve. The 223rd Tank Regiment took up the defence with three Shermans to the east of Starye Koshary and one Sherman in Cherkasy.

The 76th Rifle Division was not only holding its positions, but was also counter-attacking the right flank of the XLII Army Corps' shock group. One cannot say that it achieved great success in this undertaking, as a battalion from the 216th Rifle Regiment encountered a hurricane of fire from infantry weapons and 'tanks' (assault guns) in an attack on Milyanovichi. A battalion from the 185th Rifle Division counter-attacked the left flank of the wedge stretched toward Kovel', in the Paryduby–Krasnoduby area, but also without significant results. However, in light of the reinforcement of the screen along the railway and the growing pressure along the flanks, the 131st Infantry Division's forward advance toward Kovel' was doubtful. Now, even a single step forward threatened to close the Soviet counterblows' 'pincers' along the railway and to form a 'cauldron' to the west of Kovel'.

On 26 March the XLII Army Corps began a new attempt to break through the Soviet defence and to reach Kovel' along the railway. The attack affected only the 143rd Rifle Division's defensive sector, which bestrode the railway, occupied by the 487th and the 635th Rifle Regiments. What is curious is that the 143rd Rifle Division's documents note that they became aware of the approaching offensive 'through the testimony of a captured German' (a defector?). This enabled them to take countermeasures. One of the 487th Rifle Regiment's battalions abandoned its positions, which had already been registered by the enemy, during the night and dug in 200m in front of them. At 05.00 (Moscow time) on 26 March the artillery preparation began, falling only on the empty trenches. The first infantry attack followed at 06.30–07.00, supported by armour. The word 'tanks' figures in Soviet reports, but these were evidently assault guns. Following the failure of the first attack, a second followed at 11.00, but success was limited to an advance of 300–350m. The 223rd Tank Regiment (four Shermans and five Valentines on the morning of 26 March) took part in repelling the attack, claiming three enemy assault guns destroyed. Soviet losses for the day were two Shermans and two Valentines knocked out. On the whole, the repulse of the Germans' attack was a hard-fought battle and cost the 143rd Rifle Division's 587th Rifle Regiment alone 114 killed and wounded.

Mattenklott does not even mention this unsuccessful attempt to break through the Soviet forces' defence in his essay for the Americans, although it was reflected in both the Soviet and German documents. The Fourth Panzer Army's war diary contains the following remark: 'Our own losses are significant.'[52] The Fourth Panzer Army's headquarters estimated that at that time the strength of the 131st Infantry Division's infantry companies had fallen to between twenty-five and thirty men. Following the failure of 26 March, a lull set in for two days.

The plan for relieving the Kovel' fortress unexpectedly got a second wind. On the evening of 26 March Mattenklott was informed of an order subordinating his corps to Army Group Centre's Second Army. At this time the Germans' Fourth Panzer Army really had its hands full due to the encirclement of Hube's First Panzer Army at Kamenets-Podol'sk and the struggle for yet another fortress – Ternopol'. At a conference in Chelm, the chief of staff of the Second Army informed Mattenklott that the army had a plan to activate General Hossbach's LVI Panzer Corps, consisting of the 4th and 5th Panzer Divisions and a *jäger*[53] division, for relieving Kovel'. On the morning of 24 March the 4th Panzer Division's units received orders from the division commander about their transfer from the Bobruisk area to the Kobrin area. Wheeled transport was to move on its own, while the tracked and half-tracked vehicles were to be transported by rail.

The first relief attempt undertaken by the LVI Panzer Corps, an attack along the Brest–Kovel' road, suffered a defeat in the valley of the Pripyat' River near Ratno. The Germans' enemy here was the left-flank units of the Second Belorussian Front's 70th Army. All attempts by the 5th *Jäger* Division to break through over the Pripyat' River and its tributaries and to open a road for the 4th Panzer Division were unsuccessful. Attempts at turning manoeuvres were also unsuccessful. As a result, on 2 April the LVI Panzer Corps gave up trying to advance further along this axis.

As the intensity of the fighting for Kovel' increased and the enemies brought up fresh forces, a true front line gradually began to form. The 234th Rifle Division arrived after reforming, numbering 7,113 men (as of 25 March) and armed with 3,654 rifles, 1,916 Shpagin sub-machine guns, and 244 light and 81 heavy machine guns. Such a high percentage of automatic weaponry was quite typical of fresh formations. The division received orders to cover the Kovel' area from the north, while striding the Brest–Kovel' railway with two regiments. One of the 234th Rifle Division's was pulled into the 77th Rifle Corps reserve. It was precisely the arrival of the 234th Rifle Division's two regiments that enabled the Soviets to hold off the pressure from the LVI Panzer Corps' 5th *Jäger* Division. The latter, following the failures around Ratno, was put in to cover the flank of a new relief attack.

The arrival of an anti-tank brigade was a significant fillip for the 47th Army. This was the 3rd Anti-Tank Artillery Brigade, consisting of three regiments, armed with forty-eight 76mm guns and twenty 57mm ZIS-2s. By 25 March 1944 the brigade had concentrated in the Kovel' area. This reserve, if employed intelligently, could have greatly complicated the Germans' relief attack.

Meanwhile, due to the enemy's activity along the external encirclement front and the failures to storm the fortress, the resubordination of the 47th Army's divisions took place according to their various tasks. The storming of Kovel' was entrusted to the 125th Rifle Corps, to which was transferred the 77th Rifle Corps' 60th and 260th Rifle Divisions. The 77th Rifle Corps, in turn, became responsible for repelling attacks from the west. To be sure, the 328th Rifle Division, which was along the external encirclement front, remained subordinated to the 125th Rifle Corps, although along a secondary axis around Torgovishche. Due to the departure of the 143rd Rifle Division, the regrouping of forces and the doubtful successes of the initial phase of the assault, the attacks on Kovel' were temporarily halted. The 125th Rifle Corps was allotted the 123rd Artillery Regiment and the 1939th Regiment with light anti-aircraft guns to support the assault. The 123rd Artillery Regiment took up positions near Belin, to the east of the city. However, on 23 March there were only 248 152mm rounds in the regiment.

The new plan by the 47th Army's headquarters, in Order No. 006, was that 'the main attack while assaulting the city be launched by the forces of two rifle divisions from the east and south, reinforced by all the artillery and engineer units'.[54] Here one can detect the study of the map of the city, as an attack from the west required the crossing of the Tur'ya River and did not promise rapid success. Here one could only count on defeating the garrison's units forced to hold their positions for meeting the relief group of forces.

Order No. 006 ordered the troops to form assault groups, 'including in them the necessary artillery calibres, up to heavy guns, inclusively, for firing over open sights, as well as engineer and sapper units'. The army commander ordered that 'The detachments are to be supplied with axes, crowbars, grenades, and explosives for blowing up individual structures and the enemy's firing points'.

Aside from all of this, the 125th Rifle Corps conducted an analysis of the reasons for the failure of the attempt to take the city from the march with the forces of the 175th Rifle Division. The shortage of ammunition headed the list: 'By the start of the offensive the artillery's firing positions had 15–20 rounds apiece per tube. The same amount of rounds existed for the mortars.'[55] There was at least ammunition for the divisional artillery, although at different depots, although its delivery was made more difficult by the shortage of fuel. The picture of the city was quite vague. The battalions had no large-scale maps of Kovel'. Among other reasons listed were 'the absence of assault groups consisting of sappers and infantry'. The assault-engineer brigade's sappers had been detailed to restore bridges and for laying down tank routes, which was also necessary, but as a result the 18th Assault Engineer Brigade, which had been attached to the 47th Army, did not take part in the fighting for the city.

The 125th Rifle Corps' divisions prepared for a few days to attack the city, forming assault groups and setting up the artillery for firing over open sights. The commanders reconnoitred their objectives. Each gun detailed to support an assault group was assigned specific targets. The preparation for the assault was completed by 25 March. Now, small assault groups, in close cooperation with artillery, were to test the resilience of the enemy's defence. In the 60th Rifle Division's 1285th Rifle Regiment they prepared five assault groups, with sixty-five men in each, while the 1283rd Rifle Regiment had six groups of fifty men each, and the 1281st Rifle Regiment had three groups of fifty to sixty apiece. Ammunition was brought up, using the local population's horses and wagons.

The 175th Rifle Division was the first to go over to the offensive on Kovel' from the south at 14.00 on 25 March. All of the formation's three rifle regiments managed to break into the city. However, the attack was not further developed and was met with powerful enemy fire. Casualties proved to be quite heavy and the 175th Rifle Division lost during this day 127 killed and

367 wounded. On the following day, 26 March, the corps' two other divisions joined the 175th Rifle Division. The offensive began at 13.15, following a short 20-minute artillery preparation. The 60th Rifle Division's assault groups managed to advance 100–150m and captured several buildings, but were subsequently halted by enemy fire. The division lost twenty-six men killed and seventy-six wounded on this day. In the 260th Rifle Division's sector the attack which immediately followed the artillery preparation did not bring success. However, following an additional working-over of the enemy's positions by the artillery, the division's centre (1030th Rifle Regiment) was able to immediately advance 1,000–1,300m. However, during the days that followed he 1030th Rifle Regiment collided with a reclamation canal, which it only managed to overcome on 29 March, through a neighbouring regiment's sector.

They were unable to achieve even this result along the other sectors. As indicated in an entry in the 60th Rifle Division's war diary for 28 March, 'an insignificant success was achieved, which was expressed in the capture of individual buildings'. The 300–400m advance in the city on 27 March cost the 175th Rifle Division 55 killed and 122 wounded. The expenditure of ammunition rose, while the troops fired off more than 100 152mm shells for the gun-howitzers. However, this was by no means the limit for dreams of storming a city with sturdy structures. The attackers' losses at this time are shown by the following figures (see table).

Table 2.2: Losses in the 47th Army's Formations During the Assault on the City of Kovel', 19–28 March 1944.[56]

Unit	Killed	Missing in Action	Total
60th Rifle Division	377	7	1,769
175th Rifle Division	291	15	1,368
260th Rifle Division	437	16	2,026

However, the garrison's situation was far more serious than it might seem from the besiegers' trenches. On 27 March Gille radioed the following: 'Artillery ammunition has practically been expended. There are constant air strikes at strafing level.' He reported the following day that 'The situation is serious. The artillery's ammunition has been used up. We immediately need a delivery of shells for the light field howitzers.'[57] Given the absence of landing strips for Ju-52s,[58] this was almost a pointless request. Technically, of course, they could have dropped parachute containers with 105mm rounds, but a regular supply of ammunition could not be maintained in this manner.

Before the LVI Panzer Corps launched its attack, the Germans undertook yet another attempt to break through to Kovel' along the railway from Chelm. The arrival of the *Wiking* Division's fresh forces favoured this new offensive. These were, first of all, the 5th Panzer Regiment, to which the Panther battalion returned following its rearmament. Beginning on 24 March, the tank companies of the Panther battalion were unloading in Chelm for the purpose of their further transfer to the east. The first train from Chelm to the east left at 00.30 on 27 March. This carried the 8th Company, which arrived at Matseyuv at 05.30. SS *Obersturmführer*[59] Nicolussi-Leck commanded the 8th Company. The actions of his company became one of the most famous parts of the struggle for Kovel' and were practically a legend in the history of the *Wiking* Division. However, if one examines it closely, this was quite a strange undertaking.

It all began on 25 March when Gille, still subordinated to the Fourth Panzer Army, radioed the following from Kovel' to E. Rauss, with a copy to Himmler:[60] 'Due to heavy losses and the poor weather, we will be able to hold Kovel' only if the *Wiking* Division's Panther battalion breaks through to us, reinforces the defensive front and attacks the enemy facing the 131st Infantry Division from the east.'[61] Gille's idea looked fresh, but doubtful, because fuel was required for tank activities (even more so for Panthers) in Kovel'. Thus the headquarters of the Fourth Panzer Army delicately replied to the commander of the Kovel' garrison that there was as yet only a company of tanks and that 'a request has been transmitted to higher authority for employing this company in accordance with what has been proposed'.

Gille's proposal looks doubly doubtful if you look at the terrain. The enemy's intention to carry out a relief attack was quite obvious to the Soviet command, as was the fact that the attack would come along the railway line. It is precisely the latter fact that arouses some amazement. As was pointed out in the 143rd Rifle Division's report on the results of the fighting, 'the enemy's ignorance of the fact that the area east of the "Pst" site was impassable for tanks and hardly passable for infantry' had been noted. The 'Pst' site was the railway halt along the railway line running to Kovel' from the west. On a small-scale map the space to the east of the 'Pst' to the outskirts of Kovel' really does look like a continuous swamp. The 143rd Rifle Division's chief of staff, Guards Colonel A.A. Zhitnik, had seen it with his own eyes and obviously knew what he was talking about. Taking into account the fact that the Germans had already occupied Kovel' for a few years, then such a choice appears very strange. Nobody corrected General Mattenklott regarding the route of the relief attack, including the officers of the city's garrison (Gille, for understandable reasons, also had only a vague notion of the geography around the city).

The first target of the 8th Company's attack was the Soviet positions along the perimeter of the wedge made in the 47th Army's defence by the XLII Army Corps. At 13.30 on 28 March the Panthers supported an attack on Torgovishche (the 328th Rifle Division's right-flank positions) and forced the Soviet infantry to fall back. Such an attack should have forced them to go over to the defensive, at least temporarily. Later, the Panthers advanced further on along the railway to the east, to the 131st Infantry Division's forward positions.

The Panther company received orders to support the 131st Infantry Division's 434th Infantry Regiment's thrust on Kovel' the following morning. A battalion from the SS *Deutschland* Regiment, with ten assault guns, was even brought in for the offensive. A battalion from the 434th Infantry Regiment, with seven assault guns, was entrusted with covering the shock group's flank from the north. The first objective was the village of Cherkasy. Thus the Germans managed to gather considerable armoured forces for the 29 March offensive.

The 143rd Rifle Division's 487th Rifle Regiment occupied positions along the axis of the SS troops' planned attack north of the railway, with the same division's 635th Rifle Regiment south of it, and with the 800th Rifle Regiment (in reality, just one battalion) in the second echelon. By 25 March 1944 the 143rd Rifle Division had already fallen considerably in strength to 4,860 men and had suffered tangible losses on 26 March. The 223rd Tank Regiment numbered two Shermans and four Valentines in line as of the evening of 28 March.

The German offensive of 29 March began with a series of air strikes between 11.20 and 13.30. The weather had suddenly deteriorated and snow began to fall. According to Soviet reports, the first attack by tanks carrying infantry followed only at 14.20, with the defenders estimating the enemy's strength at up to fifty armoured vehicles. At 16.15 six German tanks, identified as Tigers (they were evidently speaking of Panthers), launched an attack which led to the breakthrough of the 487th Rifle Regiment's defence. As was noted in the 143rd Rifle Division's report, the attackers, 'having crushed three divisional 76mm guns, broke through to the height at Mark 190.3 and by 17.15, had flattened and crushed our infantry with his tanks'. Having broken through the 487th Rifle Regiment's defence, the Panthers cut the 800th Rifle Regiment in half from the second echelon and captured Cherkasy. At 17.15 (18.15 Moscow time), Nicolussi-Leck reported by radio on the capture of Cherkasy and reported on the condition of his company's Panthers: eight vehicles in line and eight put out of action. The 143rd Rifle Division claimed to have destroyed twenty-three enemy armoured vehicles on 29 March, including the 131st Infantry Division's assault guns.

A battalion of the 143rd Rifle Division's 800th Rifle Regiment fell back to the north and consolidated in Moshchona. The 635th Rifle Regiment was cut off from the 143rd Rifle Division's main forces but was commanded by radio (it was, after all, 1944). Afterwards, the 635th Rifle Regiment, having uncovered the absence of a continuous front, broke through to its division. Having seized Cherkasy, the Germans decided not to move further. The snowfall covered the surrounding terrain and no one had the desire to risk the marshy area around Kovel'.

The task of the 8th Company of Panthers, which had been transferred by the commander of the SS 5th Panzer Regiment, Muhlenkamp, was the defence of Cherkasy. However, instead of this, Nicolussi-Leck decided to advance further. The company commander viewed the Moshchona axis as unpromising. One may assume that one of the stimuli for the thrust toward Kovel' could have been the information about Gille's radiogram of 25 March, with the idea of the tanks' breakthrough to the fortress, and operations from within to meet the relief group of forces.

On the night of 29/30 March 1944 (at 01.30 on 30 March) there arrived a radiogram from Kovel', which one may describe as 'panicky'. Insofar as the enemy was already occupying the railway junction and was firing over open sights on the area for unloading supplies delivered by air, and that there were no forces for a counterblow, Battle Group Gille was forced to insist that it be allowed to break out on 30 March.[62]

Early on the morning of 30 March Nicolussi-Leck disposed of nine Panthers in line. At 04.00 he began to move out in column formation along the railway embankment. Two tanks were knocked out by mines near 'Cherkasy station' (actually, the railway halt). One of these tanks would later be captured by the Soviet 230th Tank Regiment and would be successfully repaired. Despite the battalion commander's direct order to remain in place, Nicolussi-Leck continued to advance and at 08.15 was already reporting to Gille on his arrival at Kovel' with seven tanks.

The breakthrough to the city by the *Wiking* Division's Panzer Regiment's 8th Company was, undoubtedly, noticed by the units besieging Kovel'. In a report at 16.00 on 30 March by the 125th Rifle Corps' headquarters, it was noted that 'At 12.00 on 30.3 six tanks broke through in the area of the railway and road junction and south of the brick building, where the infantry was cut off from the tanks by fire from the 60th Rifle Division's 1283rd Rifle Regiment. Four tanks passed into the city along the road leading to the south-east.'[63] As regards cutting the infantry off from the tanks, this is most likely wishful thinking. The Panthers arrived in Kovel' carrying infantry. Soviet scouts later found documents on a sergeant major who had been killed on Povurskaya Street on 2 April, showing that he had belonged to the 5th Company of the 131st Infantry Division's 434th Infantry Regiment.

The appearance of armour in the Kovel' garrison was immediately noted in Soviet operational reports. The report of the 260th Rifle Division for 31 March states: 'The enemy, having received reinforcements in the form of 4–6 tanks (Ferdinands), which broke through, has significantly increased his resistance.' In the 260th Rifle Division's evening report for that same day, the actions of the reinforcements were described: 'At 13.00 the enemy counter-attacked the 1030th Rifle Regiment's positions on Broad Street from the direction of Kovel' station, supported by three Ferdinand self-propelled guns.' However, the rout of the Soviet rifle regiment did not follow from this. The 1030th Rifle Regiment's losses for 31 March numbered twenty-two killed and seventy-two wounded. The appearance of the Panthers became more of a psychological factor than a real reinforcement of the garrison.

In the context of the situation around Kovel', it is difficult, on the whole, to describe the decision by Nicolussi-Leck as anything other than irresponsible. The Soviet command's reply to the attack of 29 March was a general offensive against the flanks of the XLII Army Corp's 'guts', which had been pushed toward Kovel'. For this purpose, the 165th Rifle Division, which had just arrived at the 47th Army (the division was quite typical of those transferred to the Second Belorussian Front: an overall strength of 6,980 men as of 25 March, 3,900 rifles, 1,848 Shpagin sub-machine guns, 248 light machine guns, and 81 heavy machine guns), was put into action. It was precisely the arrival of the 165th Rifle Division that enabled it to relieve the 143rd Rifle Division's 635th Rifle Regiment and dispatch it to its parent unit.

Even before the arrival of the 165th Rifle Division in the Cherkasy area, the 328th Rifle Division's 1103rd Rifle Regiment first castled sideways; followed by the 1350th Rifle Regiment from the 234th Rifle Division, which had just arrived at the 47th Army (its main task was covering the 47th Army against Brest). That is, the defence of Cherkasy required no small amount of efforts and a reserve of nine Panthers was quite timely. The Soviet counteroffensive began as early as 30 March. A crisis arose in the Bilichi area, in the 185th Rifle Division's offensive sector. Seven of the *Wiking* Division's assault guns and eight light howitzers were dispatched there immediately after unloading. The situation was relatively stabilized in light of the arrival of 1,000 soldiers on leave and reinforcements from the 131st Infantry Division.

The losses testify to the intensity of the fighting with the XLII Army Corps' relief group. From 20 through 30 March the 143rd Rifle Division lost 364 men killed, for a total, counting the wounded and sick, of 1,727 men, while the 76th Rifle Division lost 470 men killed, for a total of 1,414 men. The 185th Rifle Division suffered the least, losing 102 men killed and 349 overall. On the whole, during 20–30 March the 77th Rifle Corps, which was along the external encirclement front, lost 3,495 men. Documentary data on the XLII Army Corps' losses are missing, but in March 1944 alone the *Wiking* Division alone lost 117 men killed, 48 missing in action and 389 wounded.[64] Considering that these losses were from Richter's quite small battle group only, they may be considered appreciable.

Early in the morning of 1 April the 1350th Rifle Regiment took back Cherkasy. This fact is confirmed by the enemy. There is a radiogram from the XLII Army Corps from 08.00 on 1 April: 'Due to the enemy's powerful attacks from all sides, our forward units have been thrown out of Cherkasy.'[65] Given the presence of the 8th Company's Panthers in Cherkasy, this is hardly possible. The Germans were saved by the continuing arrival of units of the *Wiking* Division to the area of the fighting. At 11.00 on 31 March the SS 5th Panzer Regiment's 7th Company unloaded at Matseyuv station on Panthers. Only an hour later the company was involved in a counter-attack near Perevisa against units of the 185th Rifle Regiment (confirmed by the division's report). Following this, the Panthers were thrown forward to the tip of the spearhead as far as Cherkasy. Following a powerful attack by Stukas[66] against the Soviet defences in the village, the Panthers went into action along with infantry from the 131st Infantry Division. According to the 143rd Rifle Division's report, it was only the sixth attack that brought the Germans success. According to the day's results, six Panthers got bogged down in a swamp, two hit mines, and two tanks were put out of action due to damage from fire from Soviet anti-tank troops, leaving only five Panthers remaining in line in the 7th Company.[67]

The attempt by the 143rd Rifle Division on 2 April to once again take back Cherkasy, which had been occupied by Panthers, was a predictable failure. In the fighting from 30 March through 1 April the 1350th Rifle Regiment lost in killed alone 152 men and another 13 missing in action, while the fighting on 1–2 April cost 87 killed and 289 wounded. Regimental commander Kuleshov perished during an air raid on 1 April. On 3 April the 1350th Rifle Regiment returned to its division.

On the evening of 2 April the headquarters of the VIII Army Corps arrived in Chelm and it was decided to employ it, in place of the XLII Army Corps' headquarters, which had been worn out around Korsun', in conditions of the quite serious struggle that had unfolded around Kovel'. The new corps headquarters also signified a change of command and from 1 April 1944 the VIII Army Corps was commanded by Lieutenant General Johannes Block, holder of the Knight's Cross with Oak Leaves.

Meanwhile, army commander V.S. Polenov decided to concentrate the efforts of the troops entrusted to him toward routing the wedge pushed into the 47th Army's position by the XLII (VIII) Army Corps. According to Combat Order No. 007 of 31 March 1944, two shock fists were to be formed under the command of the 77th and 125th Rifle Corps, the first to the north and the second to the south of the Chelm–Kovel' railway. They were assigned the task of attacking from the north and south along converging axes toward Tupaly and to cut off the 'head' of the German units that had advanced as far as Koshary and Cherkasy. The fresh 234th Rifle Division, which had been reinforced with the 57th and 32nd Tank Regiments, received the additional mission 'to eliminate the enemy who has crossed in the Rudka area and to prevent the crossing of his main forces in this area'.[68] Polenov subordinated the two divisions assaulting Kovel' (the 175th and 260th Rifle Divisions), along with the 18th Assault Engineer Brigade, directly to his headquarters, while retaining the task of eliminating the enemy group of forces in Kovel'. The 123rd Artillery Regiment was included in the army artillery group, with the tasks of suppressing the enemy's artillery in Kovel' and acting against the tip of the wedge moving on the city. The idea was quite logical, but it was not fated to be carried out. Two corps going over to the offensive did not bring rapid success. On 2 April the headquarters of the Second Belorussian Front ordered the 47th Army to go over to the defensive. Among the army's active missions remained the storming of Kovel'. The problem was that the shift to the defensive did not bring about any regroupings in accordance with the new mission. It would have been more logical to move the fresher units into the path of the enemy's likely attack.

Dietrich von Saucken, the commander of the 4th Panzer Division, was a much more dangerous opponent than Mattenklott. The approach of the command of the LVI Army Corps and the 4th Panzer Division to the operation's conduct was significantly different from that of its predecessors. In the headquarters they scrupulously studied not only the topographic maps, but the geological ones as well. The 4th Panzer Division's history states that this was how the route for punching a corridor to Kovel' was chosen: 'A German geological map showed the presence of pyrites north of Moshchena [Moshchona in the maps of the time, A.I.], in the area of Height 192.7, which stretch like a ridge several kilometres from the north-west to the south-east and which will enable us to reach the area north-west of Kovel'. According to this map, practically no other opportunities exist for moving off hard-surfaced roads.'[69]

As a result, the decision was made to attack from Novye Koshary to the north-east and to reach the pyrite ridge, which had been discovered on the map, followed by a thrust along it in the direction of Kovel'. Also, according to German evaluations, the Soviet forces' positions north-east of Novye Koshary were 'not very well fitted out and occupied by small forces'. We should note that the commander of the Panther company, Nicolussi-Leck, had decided to forego the idea of breaking through to Moshchona on the heels of the Soviet forces on 30 March. With the seizure of Moshchona, it was only a short distance to the pyrite ridge.

The LVI Panzer Corps' capabilities as regards armour were significantly less than those of the SS troops. Following the intensive winter campaign, the formations that had been brought in for the offensive could not boast of a large tank park (see table opposite).

At the same time, the Germans remained true to their principles of waging war with heavy artillery. The 4th Panzer Division's 103rd Artillery Regiment was reinforced with the 637th Artillery Battalion's 210mm mortars (minus one battery). I should remind the reader that the 47th Army was trying to storm Kovel' without a single 203mm tube. It was precisely the artillery that became an effective means for breaking through to Kovel'. A.A. Zhitnik, the chief of staff of the 143rd Rifle Division, noted in his report on the results of the fighting: 'The enemy's forces had excellent artillery, demonstrating a high level of centralized control over large artillery groups.'[70]

Table 2.3: The Condition of the LVI Panzer Corps' Armour and Anti-Tank Weapons as of 1 April 1944.[71]

Unit	StuG	Panzer II[72]	Panzer III	Panzer IV (short)
5th Panzer Div.	–	–	–	–
318th Panzer Co.	–	10	3	–
270th Assault Gun Battalion	19	–	–	–
1005th Assault Gun Battalion	5	–	–	–
4th Panzer Div.	–	–	–	1
Total	24	10	3	1

Unit	Panzer IV (long)	PAK (Sfl)	PAK (tow)
5th Panzer Div.	8	6	5
318th Panzer Co.	–	–	–
270th Assault Gun Battalion	–	–	–
1005th Assault Gun Battalion	–	–	–
4th Panzer Div.	30	16	15
Total	38	22	20

Despite the exhaustion of the 131st Infantry Division's capabilities, the VIII Army Corps was also brought in to relieve Kovel'. Aside from a ski regiment, the corps also included the Second Army's assault battalion. As of 3 April, the VIII Army Corps comprised the following:[73]

Thirty-nine Panthers, four Panzer IVs and four assault guns as part of the *Wiking* Division;

Seventeen assault guns in the 270th Assault Gun Battalion (transferred from the LVI Panzer Corps);

Thirteen assault guns in the 190th Assault Gun Battalion.

It was initially planned to open the offensive on 3 April, at 11.00 (Berlin time; on the night of 2/3 April the Germans went over to summer time, moving the hour hand forward). However, as early as the evening of 2 April it was becoming clear that they would not be able to deliver ammunition to their positions in time. This impression was deepened at dawn, when it became clear that the subunits were not able to get to their jumping-off positions in time due to the washed-out roads. The offensive had to be postponed, despite the critical situation in Kovel'. On 2 April Gille radioed that 'The enemy has managed to broaden yesterday's wedge to 2.5km along the front and to break through to the railway junction'. At the same time, it was precisely on 2 April that they managed to land a freight glider in Kovel', containing a military doctor, which sweetened for the garrison the bitter pill of the delay by a day of the offensive by the relief group. The noise of the fighting on 3 April was practically inaudible from Kovel' in the LVI Panzer Corps' forward positions, which also proved the correctness of the decision not to hurry.

As a result, 3 April was lost by the Germans in gathering forces and the general preparation for the offensive. The 4th Panzer Division was supposed to attack in the centre of the LVI Panzer Corps' shock group. Its first objective was Moshchona, with the day's objective the intersection of the road and railway 2km north-west of Kovel'. It was in this place that the Kovel' garrison was holding the so-called 'railway strongpoint'. On 3 April Gille confirmed in a radiogram that it was being held: 'We have already been holding the strongpoint at the intersection of the railways west of Kovel' for 14 days, despite the constant attacks. We have not spotted any construction by the enemy of positions west of it as far as the edge of the woods.'[74] The 60th Rifle Division actually attempted to eliminate this centre of resistance at the end of March, but its efforts were later shifted to other sectors of the fortress.

According to the plan, the VIII Army Corps' 131st Infantry Division was to attack to the right of the 4th Panzer Division, with the task of attacking the grove 1.5km east of Cherkasy. Further on, the division would come up against impassable terrain beyond the railway halt, so essentially the 131st Infantry Division's activities served to tie down the enemy. An attack was also planned along the right flank with the forces of a reinforced *jäger*-ski regiment, the *Germania* Battalion, and the *Westland* Battalion from the *Wiking* Division, with the support of tanks, to the south-east of Koshary. The idea behind this attack, which was directed in the opposite direction of the 4th Panzer Division's offensive, is clear from a glance at the map. In this way, they could free up the road to Kovel', which turned away in this place from the railway to the south.

The 4th Panzer Division's neighbour to the left was the 5th Panzer Division, which had been given the task of advancing from Smidynya to Shaino and then turning to the south-east to its objective of the day – the village of Krasnovolya. The 5th Panzer Division managed to attack toward Krugel' on the morning of 3 April, with the support of the *Wiking* Division's Panther regiment, but was unsuccessful. There is some discrepancy in the German sources, but according to the 185th Rifle Regiment's report, all attacks on Krugel' were beaten back.

In the path of the German relief attack was the same 143rd Rifle Division, which by 4 April numbered 3,937 men (the report was evidently dispatched before the beginning of the attack, as on 1 April the formation numbered 3,996 men). On 3 April the 143rd Rifle Division's 487th Rifle Regiment, which was located along the axis of the Germans' forthcoming attack, numbered only 232 'active bayonets', with eight heavy and twelve light machine guns, ten anti-tank rifles, two 76mm guns and fourteen mortars. The regiment occupied a 3km front. From 29 March through 3 April German aviation regularly bombed the 143rd Rifle Division's positions, making up to more than 100 and more sorties per day, according to the Soviet side's estimate. The enemy's artillery also displayed increased activity.

Furthermore, what was by no means a strong formation ended up at the last moment considerably weakened. In the positions of the 143rd Rifle Division, in the area of the so-called Moshchona Heights (185.7, 192.9 and 189.0 on the map), were the positions of the 1215th Anti-Tank Artillery Regiment. The receipt of reconnaissance information about the concentration of tanks in the zone facing the 185th Rifle Division led to a situation in which the regiment was withdrawn from its positions on the night of 3/4 April and moved to another area. The paradox lay in the fact that the reconnaissance team's information was correct: on 3 April the 5th Panzer Division actually attacked, supported by Panthers, along the neighbouring sector of the front. However, as a result, all three regiments of the 1330th Anti-Tank Artillery Regiment ended up away from the march route of the Germans' 4th Panzer Division toward Kovel'. The 1330th Anti-Tank Artillery Regiment occupied the Butsin–Shaino positions, covering the Brest axis. The 1331st Anti-Tank Artillery Regiment occupied the line Klevetsk–Kalinuvka, south of the Chelm–Kovel' railway. Also, the 1350th Anti-Tank Artillery Regiment's last battalion was returning to its division literally on the eve of the German offensive. It's a paradox, but the shift by the Germans of the date of the offensive by one day led not to a strengthening, but to the weakening, of the defence of the Soviet forces facing the 4th Panzer Division's shock fist. There remained as reinforcements in the 143rd Rifle Division's zone first of all, the 223rd Tank Regiment (five

Shermans and six Valentines) in line as of the evening of 1 April, and secondly, the 60th Rifle Division's anti-tank battalion. The latter had nothing to do in the city, particularly given its division's passive mission, and it was intelligently dispatched to its neighbour along the external encirclement front.

Moreover, the 143rd Rifle Division had an offensive mission for 4 April: at 12.05, following a fire onslaught, a joint attack with the 165th Rifle Division's right flank was to follow on Cherkasy. Against this overall negative background, one must nevertheless emphasize that according to its condition on the evening of 3 April, the 143rd Rifle Division was not experiencing a shortage of ammunition. This, of course, was little consolation.

The operation to punch a corridor to Kovel' began while it was still dark, at 03.15 Berlin time (04.15 Moscow time) on 4 April. Fifteen minutes later a battalion from the 12th Panzer Grenadier Regiment, with five tanks, began the attack. The attack had been thought out to the last detail. By the end of the artillery preparation a group of German infantrymen, which had infiltrated along a quarry, reached the command post of the 143rd Rifle Division's 487th Rifle Regiment, a kilometre from the forward edge, which immediately disorganized the command and control of the defence along this sector. In the 143rd Rifle Division's report on the results of the fighting, it was admitted that on 4 April the infantry 'did not exhibit the kind of resilience it manifested in the fighting on 26 and 29 March'. The exhaustion caused by 20 days of uninterrupted fighting, constant bombing and shelling, and the decline in the strength of the individual units all told on the troops.

Yet another deep attack was the thrust by the 12th Panzer Grenadier Regiment's 5th Company, with the seizure of a strongpoint on the 'pyrite ridge'. Insofar as there was no 'significant fire' at dawn against the attackers, the 5th Company rapidly advanced 1.2km north-east of its jumping-off positions and seized the strongpoint. In this way conditions were created for the German division's unimpeded advance onto the ridge as a whole. The 487th Rifle Regiment, which had been thrown out of its positions, fell back to the line of the heights of the 'pyrite ridge' (although, without getting into the geology of the matter, these were just Heights 185.7 and 192.0 for the Soviet soldiers and commanders). Before long, dive bombers launched a raid along the ridge. They hit the German detachment that had moved forward (in the formation's history, the following is written that 'The attack, during which only shrapnel bombs were employed, looks very impressive, but, fortunately, it passed without almost any losses on our part'), but at the same time prevented the 487th Rifle Regiment from consolidating. Following an attack by Stukas, it fell back further to the north-east under attack from tanks and motorized infantry. The next one to come under attack was the 143rd Rifle Division's 800th Rifle Regiment, which was taken in the flank. There is a remark in the history of the 4th Panzer Division on this score: 'The enemy is waging heavy fire from occupied field positions, which are held by quite large forces, but which face, for the most part, south'. Actually, the 800th Rifle Regiment's positions faced south in the direction of Cherkasy, which they had attempted to recapture during the previous days. Unable to withstand the attack, the regiment fell back to the line of the railway. By evening there remained in one of the 800th Rifle Regiment's battalions twenty-six 'active bayonets', and thirty-one in another.

When the situation cleared up, the commander of the 143rd Rifle Division threw the few Lend-Lease vehicles of the 223rd Tank Regiment into a counter-attack precisely against the Germans' position at the head of the 'pyrite ridge'. The regiment lost two Valentines (one from 'friendly' fire) and two Shermans. The employment by the commander of the 143rd Rifle Division of his reserve 635th Rifle Regiment (the same 200 'active bayonets') did not yield the expected success. Fighting was already going on in the area of the division's command post. The entry of the 143rd Rifle Division's divisional guns into the battle with the tanks immediately revealed tactical shortcomings. They opened fire at long range, revealing themselves and exposing themselves to return fire. The artillery regiment lost four 122mm howitzers and four 76mm guns (ten 76mm guns and four 122mm guns remained in line). Thus all of the 60th Rifle Division's anti-tank battalion's eleven guns had been knocked out.

By midday on 4 April the 4th Panzer Division had seized the offensive's first objective – Moshchona. According to the German version of events, the village was abandoned by Soviet forces and taken without a fight. The 4th Panzer Division's artillery regiment immediately outfitted observation posts on Height 192.7, next to Moshchona. As is noted in the formation's history, 'From there an excellent view opens all the way to Kovel''. That is, the 4th Panzer Division's artillery, including the attacked 210mm mortars, got the opportunity to lay down a road for the attacking tanks and infantry.

Following the first successes, von Saucken demanded Panthers to develop the offensive to link up with the Kovel' garrison, but did not receive them. The SS 5th Panzer Division's 5th and 7th Companies remained tied down by fighting with the 165th Rifle Division, while attempting to free up the road to

Kovel'. The offensive began with an artillery preparation at 06.40 and two tanks from the 230th Tank Regiment, which had been attached to the 165th Rifle Division, were put out of action. The regimental commander later complained that the vehicles had been in one sector for a long time and had been pre-registered by the enemy artillery. The infantry attacks, supported by Panthers, which began after the artillery preparation, began in the early morning and continued the entire day. Nevertheless, the Germans were unable to break the 165th Rifle Division's defence, despite the mass employment of tanks.

One of the defenders' effective manoeuvres was moving their positions by 50m to the depth of the woods, as well as the concealment of the anti-tank artillery in the trees (it was precisely here that the 3rd Anti-Tank Artillery Brigade's 1213th Anti-Tank Artillery Regiment was defending). However, the defensive success did not come cheap for the 165th Rifle Division. On this day the division lost 74 men killed and 288 wounded. There is highly varied data on the Germans' losses along this sector. For example, on 4 April the 131st Infantry Division lost nine men killed, twenty-seven missing in action and eighteen wounded, the *Wiking* Division lost seventeen men killed, two missing in action and 101 wounded, and the *jäger* ski regiment lost twenty-two men killed and sixty-six wounded.[75] That is, they were comparable. On the whole, the fighting for the wooded area near Koshary shows the difference between the relatively fresh 165th Rifle Division (5,157 men on 4 April), which had also been reinforced with an anti-tank artillery regiment, and the very worn-out 143rd Rifle Division.

However, the fate of Kovel' was being decided along the axis of the LVI Panzer Corps' main attack. Following the seizure of Moshchona, the 4th Panzer Division continued the offensive along two axes. The 12th Motorized Regiment attacked the railway embankment to the west of Dubova with tanks, while the 33rd Motorized Regiment was moving to the Kovel' garrison's strongpoint near the loop of the rail junction. A barrier for the latter was flanking fire – Soviet units, not under attack by anyone, remained in the area of the railway halt. This is why Saucken did not submit to the temptation to move to link up with the Kovel' garrison along the shortest route. Also, closer to evening, Saucken managed, through corps headquarters, to detach the *Wiking* Division with its Panthers. There is a sarcastic note on this score in the 4th Panzer Division's history: 'The 4th Panzer Division's soldiers see the formed-up SS tank formations, while they don't receive any kind, even a minimal one, of reinforcement for their tank park.'[76] However, even the arrival of the SS Panthers by 1900 on 4 April did not make it possible to break through to the Kovel' garrison. There was another 1,200m to go to the railway loop, but flanking fire ruled out a final thrust during daylight.

It was in darkness, closer to midnight, when the 4th Panzer Division's forward elements established contact with the garrison. But it is difficult to call this a relief, as with dawn any movement along the short route would be prevented by a flanking barrage. April 5th was to become the decisive day.

One should note that the LVI Panzer Corps' left flank was able to be secured through the offensive actions of the 5th *Jäger* and 5th Panzer Divisions. The Germans managed to drive a wedge into the boundary, where the 234th Rifle Division's understrength 1350th Rifle Regiment, which had just been moved from the Cherkasy area, had taken up defence. The wedge enabled the Germans to turn the 185th Rifle Division's flank and push it to the east. At the same time, significant losses were suffered. If on 4 April the 185th Rifle Division numbered 5,174 men, then the report for 6 April lists 4,463 men. The 5th Panzer Division claimed that as a result of the 4 April fighting 118 prisoners had been taken and that fourteen 76mm and eight 45mm guns had been captured.

An unfavourable factor for the Soviet side was that the commander of the 77th Rifle Corps, N.I. Ivanov, had been put out of action due to a wound, as a result of which Major General V.G. Chernov, who had arrived from the headquarters of the Second Belorussian Front, assumed command on 4 April. A logical decision would have been a counterblow, and this was even planned, but no such order issued from the corps headquarters. At that moment the commander of the 77th Rifle Corps had at his disposal the fresh 32nd Tank Regiment (twenty-one Valentine and Sherman tanks) and the 1204th Self-Propelled Artillery Regiment (SU-76s). Both units were given passive tasks to defend, while the self-propelled artillerymen took up defensive positions at Dubova at night. The 185th Rifle Division's withdrawal evidently played a role.

Frosts on the night of 4/5 April somewhat improved the passability of the roads, which enabled the Germans to prepare for the final attack to link up with the garrison. However, the resumption of the offensive at 04.00 nevertheless remained only a pleasant wish. The 4th Panzer Division went over to the offensive an hour later. The attack only seriously got underway at dawn, after 06.00, when eight Panthers arrived from the SS 5th Panzer Division's 7th Panzer Company. The 4th Panzer Division's artillery did not change its positions due to the washed-out roads and fired at maximum range.

The first target of the 4th Panzer Division's attack on 5 April was the village of Dubova, to the north of Kovel'. Its retention would allow the Soviets not to fear for their flank and rear. Thus the Germans attacked Dubova from the south, temporarily turning their backs on Kovel'. According to a report by the 1204th Self-Propelled Artillery Regiment, its own infantry, numbering sixty men, fell back from the village and the self-propelled guns remained one on one against the German tanks and motorized infantry. According to German data, one Panther was destroyed in the fighting for Dubova, with another heavily damaged. The self-propelled artillerymen claimed to have destroyed seven enemy tanks and disabled two more. The German infantry's infiltration into the village enabled it to fire on the open-topped self-propelled guns from above from the buildings and the SU-76s had soon fired off their ammunition loads. The 1204th Self-Propelled Artillery Regiment abandoned Dubova, leaving behind two burned SU-76s. At around 07.00 Berlin time Dubova was in German hands. There is an estimate of Soviet losses in Dubova in the 4th Panzer Division's history: 'The enemy lost 20 anti-tank guns and anti-aircraft guns, other weaponry, and many men killed.' However, it is not completely clear who the defenders could have been. The 132rd Rifle Division's regiment had not yet arrived and there were no recordings of heavy losses for 5 April in its war diary. The remnants of the 143rd Rifle Division's regiments fell back to the north of Dubova. Perhaps some sort of rear-area elements came under attack.

The question arises: 'What was the 6th Air Army doing?' The answer is 'It was attempting to oppose the breakthrough'. The attempts to attack the German units breaking through to Kovel' immediately cost the 6th Air Army seven Yak-9s that did not return and one Yak-9 that made an emergency landing. According to the pilots' reports, the Germans protected their ground-attack aircraft with Me 109[77] and Fw 190[78] fighters. Despite the fact that it was already April 1944 the Luftwaffe could still achieve local air superiority.

Leaving a screen in Dubova, with its front facing to the north and east, the 4th Panzer Division's 12th Panzer Grenadier Regiment formed a group for the thrust to Kovel'. This included five Panzer IVs with long-barrelled guns and six Panthers. Artillery support for the attack was simultaneously being brought up, as its range from its previous positions was no longer sufficient. At 07.50 the LVI Panzer Corps radioed Kovel', requesting an attack from within the fortress. 'What is the enemy's situation on the northern and western outskirts? If possible, I request you to support the offensive.' The reply was only silence.

Meanwhile, the 6th Company (Panthers) of the *Wiking* Division's panzer regiment, along with the 4th Panzer Division's 33rd Motorized Infantry Regiment, was moving on Kovel'. The Germans' attacking tanks and infantry got into the rear of the 60th Rifle Division's 1283rd Rifle Regiment, which was occupying positions on the outskirts of Kovel'. The regiment was occupying a perimeter defence. The Germans noted that the Red Army soldiers were employing for a defence to the north the positions of the fortress captured earlier and the factory on the outskirts of the city. Gille's reply regarding a meeting attack came during the height of the fighting: 'There is a weak covering force made up of territorial troops, police, railway engineers, and units thrown together along the northern and western front of Kovel'.' That is, Gille refused to employ the Panther company, which had arrived at Kovel' on 30 March, without even bothering to give a reason. Having bypassed the 1283rd Rifle Regiment from two sides, the Germans broke through to the city. At 14.00 Berlin time there followed a radiogram from the LVI Panzer Corps to the headquarters of the Second Army: 'The 4th Panzer Division broke through to Kovel' from Dubova along the road. Contact has been established.'

What happened to the 1283rd Rifle Regiment, which had ended up right in the middle of the corridor made? It numbered 616 men at the time it was surrounded. The encircled elements fell back to an unnamed height to the west of Dubova (south) under German pressure. As early as night the remnants of the regiment undertook a break-out. Throughout 5–6 April small groups of men and officers emerged from the encirclement, for a total of 221 men. Eighteen men came out singly. On the basis of eyewitness accounts, it was established that eighty-nine men were left dead on the battlefield. Another sixty-six men were wounded during the fighting and were evacuated to the medical battalion, where they were discovered in the process of establishing the regiment's actual losses.

As a result, 222 men remained unaccounted for and appeared in the reports as missing in action. As was summarized according to the results of an investigation, 'Part of these were crushed by the enemy's tanks and part remained on the battlefield, wounded and killed'. In official documents they preferred not to employ the obvious word in such circumstances, 'prisoner'. According to a radiogram to the headquarters of the Second Army at 21.00 on 5 April, the Germans captured seventy-three men from the 1283rd Rifle Regiment. According to the results of the fighting on 5 April, the 60th Rifle Division had been torn in two. One regiment remained along the western outskirts of Kovel', while another was surrounded and the third fell back from the northern outskirts of Kovel' to the north-east. The 60th Rifle Division's equipment losses for 4–5 April were four 76mm divisional guns (plus one damaged), four 76mm regimental guns, eleven 45mm guns, six 120mm mortars and thirteen 82mm mortars.

The corridor which had been punched through the 'pyrite ridge' by the 4th Panzer Division on 5 April remained sufficiently narrow on the day that contact was established with the fortress's garrison that it could still be enfiladed by Soviet artillery. Thus the evacuation of the wounded from the fortress on the 4th Panzer Division's armoured personnel carriers, which had begun almost immediately, had to be discontinued.[79] The SS troops' attempt, supported by the Panther company, to establish contact with the 131st Infantry Division along the railway line to Starye Koshary ended in a predictable failure as early as 5 April. This route, according to the terrain conditions, was still good for the breakthrough by Nicolussi-Leck's company into the city, but not for the establishment of a real corridor. The enlargement of the corridor into Kovel' would become the Germans' mission for the following days, and actually until the end of April.

The condition of the LVI Panzer Corps' armour following the pushing through of a corridor to Kovel' is shown in the table. The number of combat-ready vehicles fell by approximately one-third.

Table 2.4: The Condition of the LVI Panzer Corps' Formations' Armour on 6 April 1944.[80]

Formation	StuG	Panzer IV (long)	PAK (Sfl)
4th Panzer Div.	–	19	12
5th Panzer Div.	–	5	7
5th *Jäger* Div.	2	–	–

According to a radiogram to the headquarters of the Second Army, as of the evening of 6 April the SS 5th Panzer Regiment's 2nd Battalion had two command Panthers and twenty-four battle Panthers, and three Panzer IVs (long) operational, six Panthers and one Panzer IV (long) tanks in short-term repair, and twenty-five Panthers in long-term repair.[81] Yet another Panther, according to the same report, was listed as burned. As we can see, the strength of the *Wiking* Division's tank park was greatly reduced in the relief fighting.

In accordance with a later report of 29 April, with a reference to its condition on 10 April, the *Wiking* Division numbered nineteen assault guns (plus three in short-term repair), twenty-one (plus five in short-term repair) Panzer IVs and fifty-eight (plus ten in short-term repair) Panthers.[82] That is, seven Panthers (in the last report the word 'Panthers' is combined with 'Bergepanthers') were written off as a result of the fighting.

The Soviet command's reaction following the relief of Kovel' was interesting. From 24.00 on 5 April the 47th Army, according to an entry in the war diary, was to be subordinated to the First Belorussian Front. In his memoirs, Rokossovskii mentions this in passing as a request from Stalin 'to go see as quickly as possible P.A. Kurochkin, the commander of the Second Belorussian Front, in order to jointly adopt measures for eliminating the enemy breakthrough'.[83] However, the idea of an immediate counterblow was not further developed, possibly not without Rokossovskii's influence. Yet another factor was the weather, which began to worsen on 6 April, and which prevented them from employing air power.

The enemy's breakthrough to link up with the garrison forced the Soviets to call off the assault on the city. The 260th Rifle Division went over to the defensive. The 18th Assault Engineer Brigade was removed from the regiments' combat formations and began hurriedly working to outfit the division's defensive zones. The occupied buildings were prepared for defence and the streets were mined, including with anti-tank mines. Bridges and overpasses were prepared for demolition. Later, already at the end of April, the Germans would carry out Operation Ilsa and push the 125th Rifle Corps back to the line of the Tur'ya River, to the south of the city, inflicting heavy casualties on it (more than 2,000 missing in action). This failure would cost Polenov his job, and before long the entire Second Belorussian Front would be disbanded, with its forces subordinated to Rokossovskii's First Belorussian Front. Half-encircled Kovel' would simply become a city along the front line until July 1944. But that's a different story altogether.

So, what did the struggle for Kovel' cost the 47th Army? The losses of the formations of Polenov's army for the period from 10 March through 10 April 1944 are shown in the table overleaf.

According to the data given, it is clear which formations suffered the most: the 60th, 143rd and 185th Rifle Divisions, which came under the relief attack, and the 260th and 175th Rifle Divisions, which suffered heavy losses in the assault on Kovel'. On the whole, the 47th Army, including its rear establishments and combat support units, lost during the entire period of the struggle for Kovel' 6,434 men killed and 281 missing in action, or a total of 25,086 men.

Table 2.5: Table of the 47th Army's Rank and File Losses From 10 March Through 10 April 1944.[84]

Formation	Killed	Missing in Action	Total
60th Rifle Div.	640	7	2,754
143rd Rifle Div.	688	47	3,096
328th Rifle Div.	330	7	1,140
234th Rifle Div.	390	–	1,514
76th Rifle Div.	659	–	2,186
165th Rifle Div.	608	–	2,427
185th Rifle Div.	1,056	82	3,264
260th Rifle Div.	914	29	4,206
175th Rifle Div.	615	30	2,844
132nd Rifle Div.	124	7	551
3rd Anti–Tank Artillery Bde	124	–	108
18th Assault Engineer Bde	176	12	469

Conclusions

The history of the Kovel' fortress is to a great degree not the history of the storming of the city, but the history of the relief of the garrison. In this sense, Kovel' undoubtedly became for the German command an inspiring example confirming the viability of the fortress concept. Field Marshal Busch,[85] the commander of Army Group Centre, in his 7 April 1944 message to the fortress commandants, directly referred to this event: 'The example of Kovel' showed that there was the encircled garrison's confidence in salvation on the one hand, and the front's desire to relieve the encircled garrison on the other.' Several fortresses were being prepared for the summer campaign in Army Group Centre and Kovel' became for them an example of the development of events.

The gathering and actions of the relief group along the approaches to Kovel' directly influenced the course of the assault on the city. The new formations, which gradually arrived with the 47th Army, were not dispatched to the city walls, but to the external encirclement front. In order to punch a 'corridor', the Germans actually consecutively put into operation two shock groups. These were first Mattenklott's XLII Army Corps, and then Hossbach's LVI Panzer Corps. Moreover, Hossbach's first attempt to break through along the Brest–Kovel' road was unsuccessful. This took place precisely because Polenov's headquarters moved up newly-assigned formations to meet the LVI Panzer Corps. The German command had to shift the axis of its attack in order to achieve its goal.

A quite controversial moment in the history of the fighting for Kovel' is the actions of the *Wiking* Division's SS troops. On the one hand, the SS troops played a significant role in the struggle for Kovel'. On the other hand, the resource of a fresh battalion of Panthers was employed pretty chaotically. The 8th Company's breakthrough to Kovel' became a legend in the history of the SS troops, but the employment of a full-strength company of Panthers for repelling counterblows, and then as part of the relief group of forces subordinated to the 4th Panzer Division, seems to be a more logical employment of this force.

In and of itself, a battalion of Panthers became a more than serious argument in the struggle for Kovel'. One must conclude that opposing the new type of German vehicles was a serious problem for the average Soviet rifle division. In a report by A.A. Zhitnik, the 143rd Rifle Division's chief of staff, it was pointed out that Panther tanks carry out effective fire from a great distance – 1,200–1,500m. Zhitnik wrote: 'At these distances (1,200–1,500m) the enemy's tanks are invulnerable against our divisional weapons.'[86] A positive example was given here by the 165th Rifle Division, which held out against the Panthers' pressure, to be sure, with the support of an anti-tank artillery regiment.

In the Soviet command's actions, given the overall quite energetic conduct of the operation in difficult terrain, we see a turning point in the shift from an offensive to the defensive on 2 April 1944. The decision to forego a regrouping for the purpose of occupying a more suitable position for waging defensive actions (probably in light of the desire to continue active operations) led to catastrophic consequences with the breakthrough of the 143rd Rifle Division's defences and the relief of Kovel'. In this way the undoubted successes in holding the XLII Army Corps and the 5th *Jäger* Division in the preceding days were put in the shade.

From the point of view of the fortress concept, Kovel' showed that even a patchwork garrison was capable of withstanding regular troops, while relying on the old town's stone structures. However, *Faustpatronen* did not play a major role in Kovel'. The struggle was waged with quite traditional means, infantry weapons and light artillery, including anti-tank guns. To be sure, one should make the proviso that an effect was achieved given the besiegers' lack of truly heavy artillery. Overall, the 47th Army disposed mainly of divisional artillery (with an insufficient supply of ammunition at the opening stage) for the storming of the city. 152mm guns were used occasionally, limited by a lack of ammunition, while 203mm howitzers were absent altogether. The 6th Air

Army's aviation, while it inflicted no small amount of unpleasantness on the garrison of the fortress, was unable to fully replace heavy artillery, so vitally necessary in urban fighting.

If one may speak of missed opportunities on the German side, then we see the delayed reaction to the threat to Kovel'. A more favourable line, which already had permanent structures, was that of the Stokhod River. Consolidation along this line with those forces which were ultimately drawn into the fighting around Kovel', appears to be a quite attainable objective. It is possible that for this it would have been expedient to transfer the sector in the Kovel' area to Army Group Centre's Second Army as early as the beginning of March 1944.

In the long term, the Germans' local success around Kovel' became one of the bricks in the foundation of Army Group Centre's disaster in the summer of 1944. The withdrawal of resources from the Third Panzer Army around Vitebsk crossed the boundary between quantity and quality. This concerned both the infantry and artillery, including assault guns and 210mm mortars.

Chapter 3

Poznań: A Fortress in the Right Place

W hen the threat of the Red Army invading the territory of the Third Reich became a reality, the fortress concept was revived. One of these fortresses was Poznań, an important road junction on the way from Warsaw to Berlin. The plan for the defence of the city, which had been prepared as early as 1944, foresaw three different plans for action. The first called for a defence by five divisions along a front 15km from the city, the second by three divisions along a 75km front running 6–8km from the city and the third, the defence of the city itself with the forces available to it.

In accordance with these plans, a non-continuous anti-tank ditch had been dug 8–10km from the outskirts of Poznań, which had its greatest length along the north-eastern and eastern sides. At a distance of 3–5km from the city ran a second and by now continuous anti-tank ditch, 2.5m to 4m deep and 4m to 6m wide, and up to 13m wide along individual sectors. Aside from the anti-tank ditches, a field fortification system had been created: foxholes, trenches, artillery firing positions and machine-gun nests. There were wire obstacles along individual sectors. In view of the speed of the Soviet advance, the only possible scheme of defence became the third one.

Poznań was surrounded by eighteen forts along the third line, numbering from I and Ia to IX and IXa, which had been constructed during the last quarter of the nineteenth century. They had lost their initial significance and were used for purposes very different from that they had been designed for. For example, Poznań's Fort VII was used as a testing ground for gas chambers. By 1945 various depots were located in the majority of the forts. Forts II and IX became shops for an aircraft factory, Fort V sheltered a factory for producing anti-aircraft guns and Fort IVa a barracks. It is interesting to note that the forts' ditches served as shops for the aircraft factory, in which machines were set up, while the ditches were roofed over with glass.

While preparing Poznań for defence as a fortress, the forts were restored to life and even somewhat modernized. Armoured or reinforced concrete cupolas, allowing for all-round fire, were constructed on them. The forts' modernization had not been completed by the start of the assault, but on average they were outfitted with two to four armoured cupolas apiece. The city's residential and industrial buildings were also being prepared for defence by blocking up the lower storeys' windows with bricks.

So, who was supposed to defend Poznań's fortifications? The practice of relying on fortresses had given rise to special fortress units – infantry, artillery and engineers. The 1446th 'Fortress' Infantry Battalion and the 82nd 'Fortress' Machine Gun Battalion were allotted to Poznań. A battery of captured Soviet 76.2mm guns (six guns), two batteries of captured French 75mm guns (six guns apiece) and three batteries of captured Czechoslovak 150mm howitzers were also formed for the city.

We should admit that the numerical and qualitative composition of Poznań's fortress units was not impressive. According to General Mattern, the fortress commandant, the German leadership placed great hopes in the *Volkssturm*.[1] However, of the twenty-four *Volkssturm* battalions planned for Poznań, only one was actually formed.

If the defence of Poznań had relied only on the fortress units and the *Volkssturm*, then it would only have held out for a few days. An infantry school, under the command of General Ernst Gonell, numbering 325 officer-instructors and 1,300 cadets, was based in the city. Gonell formed his staff and students into 12 companies of 27 officers and 135 cadets each. According to the Soviet command's evaluation, this was the most combat-capable part of the garrison. Another 'backbone' of the defence was SS *Obersturmbannführer*[2] W. Lenzer's battle group, which had been formed on the basis of an SS panzergrenadier battalion, including a company of armoured personnel carriers. Three police battalions, the *Landwehr* 312th, 475th and 647th Line and 21st Training Battalions, and a Latvian infantry battalion, which had been formed from a battalion of military translators stationed in Poznań, as well as various small Luftwaffe elements, railway troops, factory security for the Focke-Wulf and DWM works, and others were also in the city.

Besides this, the Poznań garrison disposed of an impressive amount of armour, much more, for example, than the Ternopol' garrison had had in the spring of 1944. First of all, the 500th Reserve (Training) Assault Gun Battalion, consisting of seventeen StuG IIIs, which for a long time had been the 'forge' for the assault artillery's cadres, was stationed in Poznań. Secondly, fifteen StuG IVs,[3] which had been destined for the *Grossdeutschland* Division, had got stuck in Poznań against their will. A train with the self-propelled guns had been headed for Königsberg, but had been subordinated to the commandant of Poznań, due to the urgency of the situation. The self-propelled guns were part of the 500th Assault Gun Battalion. There was also a platoon of tanks in the city, consisting of one Tiger, one Panzer IV and two Panthers. All of the armour was subordinated to Lenzer's battle group, which was the mobile reserve of the fortress.

Soviet troops reached Poznań shortly after the start of the Vistula–Oder operation. During the second half of the day of 22 January 1945, a forward detachment from the 1st Guards Tank Army's 8th Guards Mechanized Corps reached the outskirts of the city. M.Ye. Katukov,[4] the commander of the 1st Guards Tank Army, later wrote: 'Poznań was a typical "tank killer". The Germans would have knocked out all of our vehicles along its narrow streets, which had been well prepared for defence.'[5] However, according to the 8th Guards Mechanized Corps' documents, a 'cavalry thrust' to take the 'tank killer' was nonetheless made. A report by the corps' headquarters states directly: 'A frontal attack on Poznań from the march was unsuccessful, because a strong garrison with a large amount of artillery was in Poznań, as well as tanks and self-propelled guns.'[6] Despite the failure of the first assault, Katukov was unyielding. He ordered his troops to cross the Warta River and to take the city in 'pincers' and capture it through attacks from the north and south. The mechanized corps' motorized riflemen, upon crossing the Warta, attacked the city, but without success. A bridge for tanks was not completed until the evening of 24 January.

It should be noted that at first all of the headquarters of the Red Army's armies and formations attacking Poznań did not regard the city as any different from others that had been taken from the march. Moreover, such victorious attitudes even led to a kind of 'competition'. Major General V.A. Belyavskii, the chief of staff of the 8th Guards Army, openly wrote to the commander of the 29th Guards Rifle Corps: 'Don't be late to take the city of Poznań, or otherwise Kolpakchi's[7] [69th Army] forces, which are approaching the city, might take it.'[8] Poznań actually was formally located within the boundary lines of the 69th Army. I.A. Tolkonyuk, the chief of the 8th Guards Army's operational section, later recalled:

Colonel General V.I. Chuikov,[9] who had been fired up by his chief of staff, Major General V.A. Belyavskii, as well as someone else from his close circle …, decided 'to snatch from right from under Colonel General V.Ya. Kolpachki's nose' such a tempting and tasty, in the sense of glory, chunk as the city and fortress of Poznań. This is how he expressed himself in a conversation with me, referring to the recent experience of Lodz.[10]

All of this renders completely unconvincing the version later put forth in his memoirs by Chuikov about his army's forced turn toward Poznań. One thing we can be sure of is that the Soviet command initially clearly underestimated the ability of the garrison to resist and the strength of the city's fortifications. Moreover, according to Tolkonyuk's testimony, the army's headquarters initially had no information about the nineteenth-century forts, as all the intelligence on Poznań had been prepared for the neighbouring 69th Army.

At first the 8th Guards Army's units moved along the path blazed by Katukov's tank troops. On 24 January 1945 they attacked the eastern sector of the Poznań fortress. First Belorussian Front commander G.K. Zhukov[11] assigned the mission for taking the city as early as the following day. At first the offensive, which had begun on the morning of 25 January, proceeded successfully. The German anti-tank ditch, which had been dug in sandy soil, was scattered in many places by the attackers' artillery fire and did not present any kind of serious obstacle. However, further on the Soviet infantry was met with fire from the forts, which had been scrupulously camouflaged and were practically unobservable, along the fortress's outer ring. The defenders, having waited out the short artillery preparation in the forts' casemates, occupied their positions in just a few minutes and met the attackers with fire. As a result, the first assault on Poznań was unsuccessful and led to appreciable losses, both among the attacking units and among the crews of the guns firing over open sights. Meanwhile, the 1st Guards Tank Army's 8th Guards Mechanized Corps, having cut the road to the west of Poznań, received orders to move further west. One cannot but note that the corps' losses in the attempts to take Poznań by storm were insignificant – it was short only twenty-four tanks and five self-propelled guns during the entire period of the offensive from the Vistula to the Oder. The infantry that remained at Poznań did have armour, although not very much.

Despite the movement of the 1st Guards Tank Army's large mechanized formations from Poznań, the 8th Guards Army command assembled a sizeable force of armour at the walls of the fortress: This included:

259th Independent Tank Regiment (eleven T-34s on 27 January);

34th Guards Heavy Tank Regiment (sixteen ISs[12] on 26 January);

65th Independent Tank Regiment (nine T-34s; there is no report for the time it entered the fighting for Poznań, so these are calculated figures);

371st Guards Self-Propelled Artillery Regiment (four SU-76s on 27 January);

351st Guards Heavy Self-Propelled Artillery Regiment (twelve combat-ready ISU-152s[13] on 24 January, with a minimum of seven self-propelled guns undergoing repair and which were out of action for technical reasons);

516th Independent Flamethrower Tank Regiment (thirteen OT-34s[14] on 28 January);

1200th Self-Propelled Artillery Regiment (six combat-ready SU-76s on 26 January).

This enabled the Soviets, at least during the first days of the assault, to provide a tank shield and sword for all of the formations attacking the fortress. For example, the 1200th Self-Propelled Artillery Regiment moved on Poznań from the east along with the 82nd Guards Rifle Division, but at the beginning of the assault was attached to the 27th Guards Rifle Division, which was attacking from the south toward the western part of the city. The southern shock group got a double reinforcement. The 27th Guards Rifle Division received the 259th Independent Tank Regiment's SU-76s, while the 74th Guards Rifle Division received the 351st Guards Heavy Self-Propelled Artillery Regiment and the 516th Independent Flamethrower Tank Regiment. To replace the regiment of SU-76s, the 82nd Guards Rifle Division received a regiment of IS tanks (34th Guards Independent Heavy Tank Regiment), while the 39th Guards Rifle Division, which was attacking the city from the north, got the 371st Guards Self-Propelled Artillery Regiment's SU-76s.

The 8th Guards Army's formations facing the fortress's garrison were not in very good shape. In 1945 the USSR was already experiencing a shortage of manpower, while the rifle divisions were considerably below their authorized strength (see table). That is, there was little 'reserve strength' in the event of losses.

Table 3.1: Strength of the 8th Guards Army's Rifle Divisions on 25 January 1945.[15]

Formation	Overall Strength	Average Strength of a Rifle Company
27th Gds Rifle Div.	4,780	40
74th Gds Rifle Div.	5,909	74
82nd Gds Rifle Div.	4,545	40
39th Gds Rifle Div.	4,775	45

The failure of the frontal attack forced Chuikov to change the operational plan for taking the city on the run. The 82nd Guards Rifle Division was left along a broad front against the 'East' sector, while the 27th and 74th Guards Rifle Divisions received orders to force the Warta River south of Poznań and reach the southern outskirts of the city. Simultaneously, the 28th Guards Rifle Division was to outflank Poznań from the north. By the end of 26 January the fortress had been encircled along the external perimeter of the line of forts. On 26 January a train was captured along the approaches to the western outskirts of Poznań, loaded with forty-two 105mm howitzers and thirty other guns of varying types and calibres.

The assault on Poznań following the encirclement may be conventionally divided into four stages:

the outflanking and assault of the south-western part of the city;
the assault on the northern and eastern outskirts;
the assault on the city centre;
the assault on the fortress's citadel.

The 8th Guards Army's 28th Guards Rifle Corps' 39th Guards Rifle Division and its entire 29th Guards Rifle Corps were drawn into the fighting for Poznań. By now Chuikov was obviously no longer happy that he had pre-empted his neighbour's units in reaching the fortress. In his memoirs he even moved by a day, to the evening of 27 January, the actual arrival of the 69th Army's 91st Rifle Corps' units at Poznań. However, according to the corps' war diary, its 117th and 370th Rifle Divisions' main forces reached the city as early as 18.00 on 26 January, and the next morning their forward detachments were fighting in the city. Poznań could have become a headache for V.Ya. Kolpakchi, but two of the 91st Rifle Corps' divisions were resubordinated to Chuikov. Zhukov's order placed the responsibility for taking the city on the 8th Guards Army. The 8th Guards and 69th Armies' remaining units continued to pursue the enemy to the west and before long reached the line of the Oder River.

What was the strength of the units surrounded in Poznań? The traditional Soviet estimate of the garrison's strength at 61,000 men is clearly too high. The estimation by a General Staff officer with the headquarters of the First Belorussian Front of 30,000 men, which was made soon after these events, also seems somewhat excessive, although more realistic.[16] The estimate of the

Poznań garrison's overall strength of 25,000 men by the German historian U. Saft was evidently arrived at under the influence of Soviet data.[17] The German documents for the concluding period of the war are full of inaccuracies, but in supplements to Army Group Vistula's war diary for 30 January and 2 February 1945, the strength of 'Fortress Posen's'[18] garrison is put at 12,000 men.[19] Moreover, this includes the 'heads', that is, combat support units and rear area establishments. Colonel Erwin Detbaren, the Poznań garrison chief of staff, gave the same figure during an interrogation in Soviet captivity: 'By the time of the Russians' approach, the city's garrison numbered up to 12,000 men.'[20]

However, this figure does not include units that fell back into the city, but only the garrison itself. It's interesting to note that at the beginning of the assault the 8th Guards Army's war diary offered a close estimate of the strength of the enemy forces surrounded in Poznań as 'more than 10,000 men',[21] which was changed to '12,000 men' in the intelligence report for 1–10 February.[22] At the same time, more than 17,000 men were taken prisoner during the course of the fighting for the city. Even taking into account the instances of overstating the number of prisoners taken in Soviet documents in the first months of 1945, this is a lot. Most likely, this figure takes into account the local residents who were forcibly mobilized during the course of the assault. It is the author's opinion that the estimate of the strength of the units defending Poznań of 15,000–20,000 men is realistic.

Poznań's perimeter defence was divided into four sectors as was traditional (a similar pattern was present at the defence of Ternopol'): 'East' (commanded by General Gonell, 'South' (Major Holfeld, from the staff of the officers' school), and 'West' (commanded by Major Ewert, the former deputy commander of the officer's school), and 'North'.

The flanking manoeuvre that Chuikov came up with following the failure of the frontal attack proceeded quite successfully. Upon forcing the Warta, the 27th and 74th Guards Rifle Divisions deployed to the north and attacked Forts VIIIa, IX and IXa along the outer ring. It's difficult to say whether this manoeuvre contained more in the way of calculation or intuition, but only Luftwaffe units and a *Volkssturm* battalion were defending the south-western forts.

The Soviet forces' accumulated combat experience and professionalism enabled them to deal with the forts with their normal equipment, even without large-calibre guns. Aside from divisional artillery, the two divisions disposed of a total of thirty-one 160mm mortars and sixteen 152mm gun-howitzers.[23]

The artillery fire was concentrated against the forts' upper works, forcing the defenders to retreat to the lower chambers. The embrasures in these internal chambers could not cover the approaches to the fort, which enabled the attackers to infiltrate through the spaces between the forts and to attack them from the rear.

A typical example is the assault on Fort IXa 'Witzleben' by assault detachments from the 74th Guards Rifle Division's 236th Guard Rifle Regiment. Scrupulously prepared artillery fire against the fort's main wall forced its garrison into the internal chambers. The heaviest calibre weapon here was the 160mm mortar. Fire was halted at a signal from the commanders of the two assault groups and the combat engineers attacked the fort, crossing the ditch over an improvised bridge. Upon getting onto the fort's roof, the engineers blew up the armoured cupolas. The engineers began to pour fuel (fuel oil, kerosene and oil) inside through the ventilation shafts. According to some reports, they fired *Faustpatronen* into the ventilation shafts to knock out the partitions. In total, 150kg of fuel was poured in. After that, bottles of flammable liquid with a self-igniting phosphorous mixture were thrown in. The fort burned up from the inside and the ammunition began to explode. The Germans who jumped out into the internal courtyard were met with fire from automatic rifles and grenades. The fort's garrison was wiped out and later about 100 corpses of German officers and men were discovered inside it.

It should be emphasized that the breakthrough of the external line of forts was carried out by the Guards troops of the 29th Guards Rifle Corps alone. The specialized 2nd Assault Engineer-Sapper Brigade did not arrive in Poznań until 28 January, when the fighting for the city was already at its height. By then the rifle units were already advancing towards the centre of the city along the railway line and the streets.

One must say that at that moment the German command was quite pessimistic about the Poznań garrison's chances. For example, in the OKW[24] war diary for 28 January there is an entry that 'The situation in the Poznań area has become exacerbated: 40 per cent of the anti-tank weapons are out of action. According to the available information, the garrison's combat capability is very low, so that its resistance will last only until today.'[25] However, the Poznań garrison managed to hold out for nearly another month. Despite the pessimistic evaluations of the garrison's resilience, it was in fact on 28 January that nine Ju-52s, carrying 17.6 tonnes of ammunition, landed at the Poznań airfield and the 'air bridge' began to operate.

On that same 28 January, Zhukov, the commander of the First Belorussian Front, gave Chuikov a dressing down, sending a directive to the 8th Guards Army headquarters, with the following message: 'Poznań has tied down six divisions and reinforcements. The absence of success can be explained by the poor organization of the assault and the inability to employ the troops at night.'[26] Zhukov also recommended presenting the garrison with a harsh ultimatum and establishing coordination with the air force. Chuikov delivered the ultimatum, but received no reply to it.

One should point out that the fighting for Poznań actually tied down not six but seven Soviet divisions. Aside from the formations taking a direct part in the assault, the 28th Guards Rifle Corps' 88th Guards Rifle Division was positioned not far from the city 'in readiness for actions to destroy the garrison of the city of Poznań, in the event of its break-out to the west'.[27]

However, on the whole, this period of Chuikov's Guards' offensive against Poznań was quite successful. On 28 January the two divisions from the 29th Guards Rifle Corps had been reinforced by the 312th Rifle Division, temporarily transferred from the 69th Army, and reinforced with artillery, including a brigade with eighteen 122mm guns and eighteen 152mm gun-howitzers. This assistance was timely to the highest degree. Despite the fact that on 27 January Fort VIIIa and Lazarus Station had been cleared by the 27th Guards Rifle Division, the enemy reoccupied them. Following a second encirclement and the blockade of the fort, its garrison capitulated, because the officers and men who had occupied the fortifications had absolutely no ammunition left. Following the overcoming of the defence along the external line of forts, the south-western and western parts of Poznań, encompassing an area of 20km², were easily and rapidly cleared of the enemy by Soviet forces.

Two of the divisions, the 27th and 74th Guards Rifle, which had overcome the external belt of forts, were breaking through to the centre of the city. The first was moving to the west of the railway lines, while the second was moving to the east of them. The offensive became more difficult as they moved deeper into the city. For example, the 74th Guards Rifle Division lost 64 men killed and 303 wounded on 26 January and 100 men killed and 820 wounded on 29 January. These are monstrous losses for a single day in 1945.

In all, from 25 to 28 January the 74th Guards Rifle Division lost, according to incomplete data, 253 men killed and 1,321 wounded, while equipment losses amounted to sixteen 45mm guns, five 76mm regimental guns and fourteen (!) 76mm divisional guns. Somewhat lesser losses were suffered by the 27th Guards Rifle Division, which lost 112 men killed and 369 wounded up to 28 January in the fighting for Poznań.

The reinforcement of the assault troops with tanks and engineer troops improved the situation. The 41st Independent Flamethrower Battalion immediately began to torch several dozen buildings per day, laying down a path for the 27th Guards Rifle Division's infantry. However, the lack of coordination with the infantry led to heavy losses for the battalion in the first days of its employment in Poznań: more than forty men killed and wounded. The employment of flamethrower troops was subsequently organized properly.

At this stage, aside from the *Faustpatronen*, the Germans made active use of anti-tank artillery, trying to ambush tanks at short range with fire into their sides as they passed. The garrison also still possessed operational tanks and self-propelled guns.

It's interesting to note that as early as 28 January the flamethrower regiment's tanks had gotten into a tank duel. While moving along the broad Gorna Wilda Street, the 516th Independent Flamethrower Tank Regiment's tanks encountered an enemy tank ambush. While one platoon made a feint attack along a side street, the other two platoons moved around onto the flank of the ambushing group and engaged them at a range of 200m, destroying six 'tanks' (most likely assault guns). The absence of enemy data does not permit us to confirm or deny this episode, but it appears quite likely.

The 351st Guards Heavy Self-Propelled Artillery Regiment's ISU-152 self-propelled guns also operated quite intelligently: they moved along the streets in chequerboard formation, along different sides, while covering each other. On the whole, the self-propelled artillerymen demonstrated a high degree of professionalism, while skilfully manoeuvring their heavy vehicles along the streets. The regiment's reports sounded the refrain: 'No equipment losses.' 152mm shells were a truly weighty argument. Moreover, although the authorized ammunition load was twenty shells per self-propelled gun, the 351st's crews crammed twenty-five to thirty rounds apiece into their vehicles.

Meanwhile, the breakthrough by Soviet forces into the depths of the fortress's defence resulted in the encirclement of the western part of the forts of the outer ring. The first attempt to break out of Poznań was undertaken at this time. On the night of 30/31 January 1945, about 1,200–1,500 men from the garrison of the western forts, Forts VIa, VII and VIII, who were by now completely surrounded, received orders to break out. They attempted to reach the German front far to the west, in small groups. This was a desperate attempt to save themselves. According to Soviet data, some of those blockaded in the western part of the fortress attempted to break through to link up with the garrison's main forces in the 'North' and 'East' sectors.

By 30 January the 74th Guards Rifle Division's infantrymen had reached the northern outskirts of the old city stadium. Before them arose the ancient city walls. They were 1.5–2m high in the city blocks and up to 6m near the bank of the Warta, which was 15–20m wide. The tops of the walls were covered from the corner buildings of the squares and the streets adjacent to them. Gaps in the walls along the intersections of the streets were densely swept by fire from within, including from anti-tank artillery. Here, along the approaches to the walls, one may tote up some of the results of the first days of the assault. From 19 to 30 January 1945 the 74th Guards Rifle Division lost 311 men killed and 1,900 wounded. These losses can be viewed as extremely heavy. The formation lost sixteen 45mm guns, five 76mm regimental guns, fourteen 76mm divisional guns, and two 122mm howitzers. The senior Red Army General Staff representative with the First Belorussian Front, Colonel Solov'yov, later wrote: 'During the first days of fighting the division has suffered more than one-third of the overall losses in the fighting for Poznań.'[28] Solov'yov also reproached the 8th Guards Army command for insufficiently preparing the first attacks on Poznań. The continuation of the offensive would have been impossible without reinforcements. Somewhat later, on 3 February, the 74th Guards Rifle Division received 953 reinforcements.

On the evening of 30 January 1945 a daring operation was undertaken with the participation of the 516th Independent Flamethrower Tank Regiment. One platoon of flamethrower tanks, with a party of assault engineers, moved forward under cover of darkness. The tanks drove at top speed, firing their guns and flamethrowers (this was evidently an unforgettable sight). Dashing across Waly Krolewej Jadwigi Street, one tank broke through into the centre of the city as far as the Catholic church. A second was ambushed on Bram Dembinski Square and was destroyed by an anti-tank gun. Yet another in the same area was knocked out by a tank, identified as a Tiger, which was also lying in ambush. The crews of these two vehicles were almost all either killed or wounded. The tank near the church, now isolated, was forced to withdraw at top speed. By the morning of 31 January nine tanks remained in line in the 516th Independent Flamethrower Tank Regiment. By the evening of 31 January all of the regiment's combat-ready tanks had been refuelled and were ready for battle in a more traditional style, as part of assault groups, with five vehicles with the 236th Guards Rifle Regiment and three with the 240th Guards Rifle Regiment. Despite the raid's failure, it nevertheless told on the resilience of the Germans' defence along this sector and facilitated the breakthrough beyond the walls.

It's a paradox, but it was only after a week of fighting that the formation of assault groups, trained for fighting in city blocks, began in the units assaulting Poznań. For example, two assault groups were formed in the 27th Guards Rifle Division's 76th Guards Rifle Regiment and three assault groups each in the 74th and 83rd Guards Rifle Regiments. The strength of these groups varied from eighteen to forty-one men. Each of the 74th Guards Rifle Division's regiments formed three assault groups, numbering from twenty to eighty men. Each group was supported by one to three 76mm divisional guns, one or two 76mm regimental guns, one or two 122mm howitzers, and one or two tanks or self-propelled guns. The employment of the assault groups immediately reduced losses. For example, on 1 February the 74th Guards Rifle Division lost only twenty men killed and fifty-four wounded.

By 1 February the Soviet units were fighting for the city centre. At this time Himmler became the commander of Army Group Vistula. One of his first acts as army group commander was his appointment of a new commandant for Poznań. General Gonell, the commander of the previously-mentioned officers' school in Poznań, replaced General Mattern. One may evaluate Himmler's capabilities as a military commander in various ways, but his decision as regards the commandant of Poznań definitely altered the fate of the fortress itself and its garrison.

During the first days of the assault on Poznań the Soviet forces assaulted or blockaded the comparatively modern forts, which had appeared during the age of rifled artillery, along the outer ring. The shift of combat operations to the centre of the city led the Soviet forces to older, but still quite strong fortifications. Ancient walls and bastions, which had been built during the early stages of the fortress's construction, covered the old city from the south and west. The Soviet offensive was halted for a time along this line. For the assault on Bastion III ('Grolman') (this should not be confused with the outer ring's Fort VIII of the same name), an assault group consisting of fifty infantrymen and twenty guns of various calibres up to 203mm, was formed from the 74th Rifle Division's 226th Guards Rifle Regiment. One 203mm howitzer (the first such gun deployed in the city, to judge by all accounts), was to punch a hole in the bastion's wall by direct fire at a range of 300m. During the night of 1/2 February, before the assault, the infantry fired on the bastion's embrasures, to cover the gun being brought into position to fire directly at the fort. Powerful 152mm guns were brought up by Studebaker trucks and then manhandled into position. The 203mm gun was moved to its position only once the artillery preparation had begun, already armed,[29] after which it was set up in ten minutes in a previously-prepared pit. The bastion had already been heavily damaged and the upper corner towers had been destroyed. The 203mm gun fired seven rounds against the fort's walls, making two breaches each more than a metre wide. When the fire from the guns was halted by a signal from the regimental commander, flamethrower troops moved forward and let loose several blasts from their weapons into the bastion's embrasures and into the holes in the wall and set fire to the interior. The bastion burned and ammunition exploded inside. The infantry rose to the attack and before long had seized the entire complex of buildings situated around it.

However, the difficulties of the assault did not cease upon overcoming the city walls. The complexity of the offensive in the central part of the city was conditioned by the presence of a large number of multi-storey buildings – more than a third of all military and industrial establishments were located in the centre. The overwhelming majority of buildings in the centre were of old brickwork or stone (granite), with walls up to a metre thick and more. All of the buildings had basements, which were linked together below ground. The centre was also a maze of narrow streets and alleys. Gonell, who had taken personal control of the garrison, was able to restore the integrity of the city's defence following the loss of its south-western part by regrouping forces between sectors.

The fighting for the city blocks immediately revealed the inapplicability of the usual methods of fighting in Poznań. The Germans occupied the corner buildings, from which they were able sweep four sides of the streets with fire. The difficulty of the offensive for the Soviet units in the city quarters was that:

the enemy did not give the infantry the opportunity to attack with machine-gun and automatic rifle fire;

the artillery was also unable to fire from open positions in light of the danger of their crews being hit by enemy fire;

artillery fire from concealed positions was also made difficult due to the buildings shielding each other;

armoured vehicles were hit by *Faustpatrone* rounds.

The general principle of the attack was the sequence of the artillery working over the objective, firing on it from heavy and light machine guns and then breaking into the building through windows, doors and holes in the walls in small groups. The troops sought to cover themselves against flanking fire with smokescreens. Tanks and self-propelled guns operated at high speed, bombarding firing points in the lower floors, while flamethrower tanks set fire to the buildings.

The task of the assault troops was eased only to a certain extent by the seizing of the defensive perimeter. The garrison had employed all their artillery and mortars along the outer ring of the city's defence. Accordingly, when the Soviet troops broke into the centre the defenders' artillery became the attackers' trophies. For the Germans the main means of fighting in the city became infantry weapons and *Faustpatronen*, which the garrison had in abundance. It's sufficient to point out that upon the conclusion of the assault the Red Army captured 19,000 *Faustpatronen*. It was precisely during this period that Soviet documents indicate counter-attacks in approximately company strength, supported by four to six self-propelled guns. Soviet experts also noted the widespread employment of snipers by the enemy.

A large role in the assault was played by FOG[30] flamethrowers, which became standard in assaulting fortresses during the final months of the war. However, their employment required certain precautions. For example, in setting up flamethrowers in a building, particularly an entire battery, from the second floor and up, one had to take into account the sturdiness of the floors. The FOGs had a powerful recoil and could break through a weak floor while firing and set fire to the building they were in. Setting up FOGs in the street required the cover of either darkness or smoke. In Poznań, FOG batteries used a non-standard procedure of first firing unlit fuel which spread throughout the target and then a burst of lit fuel which ignited all the fuel that had seeped into every corner of the building.

One of the means of advance in the city was blowing up obstacles by combat engineers. For example, while assaulting the thirtieth block, the 27th Guards Rifle Division's 83rd Guards Rifle Regiment needed to take a building that covered the entrance into it. All the approaches to the building were enfiladed from the neighbouring buildings. However, a blind wall which led to the objective remained unoccupied. The buildings stood in a row, facing each other with blind walls, without windows or doors. Upon entering a neighbouring unoccupied building through the basement, the combat engineers blew a 1m x 1.5m hole in the blind wall with a 35kg charge. They then threw smoke grenades into the hole and onto the street and made their way to the blind wall of the building under attack under the cover of the smoke. They blew it up with a 40kg charge. An assault group broke into the building through the gap and, as a result of a grenade fight, threw the enemy out of the upper storeys. As a result of this thrust, the enemy's covering fire on the entire street was disrupted, which enabled them to run over to the unoccupied buildings and take the entire block.

While fighting was going on in the south-western and western part of the city, two regiments from the 39th Guards Rifle Division were defending along an 8km front along the line of Forts IVa, V, Va, VI, and VIa in the northern part of Poznań. From 27 January through 1 February it was relatively quiet here, which allowed the garrison to receive supply flights. For example, on 30 January eleven Ju-52s delivered 30.85 tonnes of ammunition, and on 31 January fifteen more delivered equipment and 23.5 tonnes of ammunition.

Upon the successful completion of the attack against the forts along the western side of the fortress, the 312th Rifle Division was pulled out of the fighting and moved for an attack against the 'East' sector, while the 82nd Guards Rifle Division was redeployed during 31 January–1 February to the northern part of the city. G.I. Khetagurov, the commander of the 82nd Guards Rifle Division and an experienced staff officer and the former chief of staff of the 1st Guards Army, was appointed to direct the offensive by the group's two divisions on the citadel from the north.

A peculiarity of the offensive along this axis lay in the breakthrough in the space between the outer ring's forts with their subsequent blockade. The encircled forts fought in isolation for several days. The northern outskirts of the city were made up of loosely built-up blocks with buildings one or two storeys high. At the same time, the occupation of these structures with personnel and weapons forced them to wage the offensive by the consecutive destruction of the buildings or to burn them with flamethrowers. The successes in the fighting in the north of the city enabled Chuikov to free up the 39th Guards Rifle Division and to dispatch it west to the Oder bridgeheads. The number of divisions tied down by the assault on Poznań fell, although it remained inaccessible as a railway junction.

Units of Khetagurov's 82nd Guards Rifle Division slowly took the blocks in the northern part of Poznań. The enemy retained his combat capability and undertook a number of counter-attacks, which most frequently fell upon the

246th Guards Rifle Regiment. The Soviet side viewed these attacks as attempts at a break out. However, these actions by the garrison largely seem to have been attempts to restore the defensive line along Poznań's forts.

The latest obstacle for the assaulting troops became the outer ring's Fort VI 'Titzen', which was quite an imposing structure. The fort was surrounded with a ditch 8–10m deep and 10–12m wide, completely enfiladed from caponiers and counterscarp galleries. The ditch's external wall was topped off with a 3m iron fence. The approach to the fort and around it was blocked by an anti-tank ditch. It was decided before the assault to carry out a careful reconnaissance of the fort with the 82nd Guards Rifle Division's 83rd Independent Guards Reconnaissance Company. The scouts spent three nights, from 3 to 5 February, in feeling out Fort 'Titzen'. On the night of 4/5 February they managed to capture two prisoners belonging to its garrison. According to their testimony, the fort's garrison numbered 180 men.

During the course of another sortie on 6 February, Junior Lieutenant Andreyev, the commander of a reconnaissance platoon, made the decision to make an attempt to assault the fort. After getting across the anti-tank ditch undetected, Andreev and his troops made their way to the gates of the fort. The scouts blew up an armoured door with eight anti-tank grenades and broke into the barracks. The attack proved to be such a surprise that the garrison was unable to put up any resistance. The scouts cut down ten men right there, while the remainder ran away. The successful storming of a fully-fledged fort by a reconnaissance company became perhaps the most daring exploit during the assault on Poznań. They captured a lot of stores in 'Titzen', as it had been used by the Germans as an ammunition depot.

Having seized Fort 'Titzen' and blockaded Fort 'Bonin' (to be more precise, the 'intermediate structure' Va 'Bonin'), units of the 82nd Guards Rifle Division began to advance into the city blocks, which had grown up during the interwar period outside the ring of forts south of Fort 'Bonin'. On the morning of 7 February the 246th Guards Rifle Regiment from Khetagurov's division advanced further to the south and occupied two blocks in the area directly to the north from the heart of the fortress, Fort 'Winiary'. This was a challenge to which the garrison had to reply. Between 15.00 and 16.00 there were a series of German counter-attacks. The most powerful of these was an attack from the south, from Fort 'Winiary', by an infantry battalion with five assault guns and supported by artillery from the fortress. Another two counter-attacks, in approximately company strength, followed from the left flank.

As a result of the German counter-attacks, the 246th Guards Rifle Regiment was pushed out of the newly-occupied blocks and suffered heavy losses: 7 killed, 54 wounded and 103 missing in action. The regimental commander, Colonel V.S. Klepikov, was killed (burned up on a self-propelled gun) during the fighting. This was the most powerful blow by the Poznań garrison, which forced Khetagurov to temporarily go over to the defensive and regroup.

On 5 February the Poznań airfield in the Winiary district, not far from the citadel, was seized, which disrupted the normal work of the 'air bridge'. Up until this moment 110 tonnes of freight had been delivered to the fortress by air and 277 wounded evacuated. From 8 February (there was bad weather on 6–7 February) the Luftwaffe went over to dropping supplies for the fortress's garrison in parachute containers. On that first day seven Ju-52s and six He-111s[31] dropped 16.8 tonnes of ammunition on Poznań.

The turning point in the assault on the fortress was on 9–10 February, when the attackers changed their artillery types. The 184th and 122nd Heavy-Calibre Howitzer Artillery Brigades (203mm B-4 howitzers) and the 34th Independent Heavy Calibre Artillery Battalion (six 280mm Br-5 mortars) arrived at the city. Before this the attackers did not have 280mm guns. The heavy guns arrived after a difficult journey along the ruined railways, with the help of Polish rolling stock. On the other hand, the 189th and 41st Artillery Brigades' 122mm guns and 152mm gun-howitzers were pulled out of the fighting and sent to the Oder bridgeheads, where they were needed for counter-battery fire. Only a single battalion from each brigade remained in Poznań to support the assault groups.

The arrival of the 203mm guns enabled the Soviets to begin the assault on the surrounded forts of the outer ring. Fort Va 'Bonin' was very difficult to take. The fort was surrounded by a ditch 8m wide and 6m deep. Entrance into the fort was possible only from the rear, along ramps. The first attempt to storm it came on 11 February by the forces of an assault group from the 82nd Guards Rifle Division's 244th Guards Rifle Regiment, numbering seventy men and supported by artillery, including two 152mm guns and two 203mm guns. Two T-34 tanks also supported the assault group.

Under the cover of darkness, the 203mm guns were brought up to within 400m of the fort. Following a 10-minute artillery preparation, the assault groups attacked the fort from two sides. However, the enemy, having taken refuge against the artillery fire in the shelters, allowed the attackers right up to the ditch and met them with a hail of fire from the fort's embrasures and from machine-gun nests along its roof. Throughout the day the Soviet infantrymen were unable to get through the fort's gates and into its courtyard.

On the morning of 12 February a powerful artillery preparation was carried out with a large number of guns. Traditionally, the artillery had the task of driving the fort's defenders from the upper works. The mortars initially fired ordinary rounds, followed by smoke rounds, thus shrouding the fort in smoke. The assault group, under the cover of the smokescreen, was to break into the fort's gates behind two tanks and capture the structure covering the entrance into the gates. However, the defenders once again emerged from their shelters and unleashed a hail of fire on the tanks and the 76mm guns that had been moved up to the fort. The assault group, having suffered losses, was forced to take cover. A hail of fire from *Faustpatronen* prevented the Soviets from bringing up guns to fire against the fort's walls.

The third assault on Fort 'Bonin' took place two days later, on 14 February. This time the assault was conducted by two groups: from the rear towards the central entrance, and against the fort's north-western corner. The attackers also divided the heavy guns into two groups. Mortars, divisional artillery, one 152mm gun and one 203mm howitzer fired on the fort's upper works. Under cover from this fire, yet another 152mm gun-howitzer and one 203mm howitzer were brought right up to the fort's ditch (to within 50m). This movement was covered by guns firing over open sights. The 152mm and 203mm guns, upon rapidly deploying, put five rounds into the fort's main entrance. The assault group's attack began after this, with a tank breaking through the gates, followed by infantrymen and combat engineers.

The second assault group, which attacked the fort's north-western corner, operated differently. In order to suppress the fire from the counterscarp gallery, which flanked the northern and western faces of the ditch, a barrel with 220kg of explosives was lowered into the ditch and blown up. The gallery's garrison was put out of action. This enabled the attackers to move into the ditch and capture the gallery. The breakthrough from two directions enabled the attackers to climb up to the fort's main wall. The fort was subsequently burnt out through the ventilation system. The garrison's survivors capitulated and according to Soviet data 70 men and officers surrendered. The destruction of the structures on top of the fort by heavy guns played an important role in the success of the final assault. In all, 151 concrete-piercing shells were fired at Fort 'Bonin'.

The neighbouring Fort V, despite its large size, was taken and burnt out by a small group of combat engineers and the 82nd Guards Rifle Division's reconnaissance company, which on the night of 14/15 February secretly got onto the fort's roof with explosives and flammable materials, poured a flammable mixture into the ventilation system and set fire to it from the inside. The armoured cupolas were blown up by explosive charges. The garrison that ran out into the fort's courtyard was almost completely wiped out by grenades and captured *Faustpatronen*. Fort V burned for a long time as the ammunition there blew up. The garrisons of the remaining forts in the northern part of Poznań capitulated before they were assaulted.

An assault group under the command of Junior Lieutenant I.S. Stupnikov, numbering twenty-two men, was allotted for the assault of Fort V ('Waldersee I'). The group's actions were supported by artillery and the regiment's remaining subunits. Stupnikov's group commenced operations at night, at 24.00 on 14 February. At 01.00 the group destroyed two machine-gun nests and the crew of a 75mm gun immediately by the central gates in a surprise attack. The group, having destroyed the patrols and sentries near the central gates, broke into the fort at 02.30. The invasion of the fort enabled them to begin negotiations for the garrison's surrender. Following negotiations between envoys, the fort capitulated at 07.30 on 15 February. Five hundred and fifty men surrendered, as well as 280 wounded.

There was quite a unique story connected with Fort IVa ('Waldersee II'). On the morning of 16 February battalions from the 82nd Guards Rifle Division's 246th Guards Rifle Regiment isolated the fort and captured several prisoners, some of whom they immediately dispatched to the fort as envoys to conduct surrender negotiations. The fort's commandant, 'with the rank of captain', as noted in the 82nd Guards Rifle Division's war diary, who took part in the negotiations, accepted the conditions proposed by Major General Khetagurov. At midday on 16 February the fort capitulated. More than 500 men surrendered, including 23 officers. However, the story does not end there. There is the following entry in the 82nd Guards Rifle Division's war diary: 'An SS soldier who remained in the fort set fire to the ammunition depot. A powerful explosion took place and the fort caught on fire.' The culprit must have been identified as 'an SS soldier' by the prisoners. However, it seems that this fireworks display was observed from a safe distance. On that day the 82nd Guards Rifle Division lost only eleven men killed and twenty-six wounded, which is not many.

The elimination of the Poznań garrison's northern group of forces was completed on 16 February. Elements of the 82nd Guards Rifle Division were still hunting down individual enemy soldiers and combing through Fort 'Bonin', but, on the whole, the division received a longed-for breather. They counted up the captured equipment, which included more than 500 machine guns of various types, 5,000 rifles, 2,132 trucks, 994 automobiles, 41 armoured personnel carriers and 25 armoured cars. Separately enumerated were 200 recaptured 'Maxim'[32] heavy machine guns and 300 DP machine guns, which were probably captured by the Germans during 1941–2.

The 29th Guards Rifle Corps' losses at this time are illustrated in the following table.

Table 3.2: The 29th Guards Rifle Corps' Losses from 24 January through 16 February 1945.[33]

Unit	Killed	Wounded	Missing in Action	Total
29th Guards Rifle Corps Headquarters	1	4	2	7
27th Gds Rifle Div.	420	2,049	1	2,470
74th Gds Rifle Div.	716	3,102	9	3,827
82nd Gds Rifle Div.	437	1,854	125	2,416
Total	1,574	7,009	137	8,720

It is clear that the 74th Guards Rifle Division suffered the heaviest losses in the fighting for the centre of Poznań.

Following the failure of the first frontal assault against the 'East' sector, combat operations along this axis resumed on 27 January, when the newly-arrived 117th Rifle Division from the 69th Army's 91st Rifle Corps launched an attack in the gap between the forts, successfully blockading Forts Ia and II. However, further on, as was the case with the northern part of the city, the Soviet forces paused until 31 January. The offensive was resumed with the 312th Rifle Division returning to this sector on 1 February. At this moment the 117th Rifle Division numbered 3,999 men and the 312th Rifle Division 4,999.[34]

The elimination of the enemy's resistance in the 'East' sector was entrusted entirely to the 91st Rifle Corps. A distinguishing feature of its operations was the concentrated attacks against individual parts of the enemy's defence for the purpose of breaking through the outer ring, followed by the encirclement and destruction of the centres of resistance. The Soviet units, upon breaking through in the gaps between the forts, encircled and isolated them. There then followed the consecutive destruction of the strongpoints in the buildings of Poznań's suburbs. For example, Fort 'Rauch' (built in 1864), which covered the approaches to the crossing over the Warta River, was simply shot up by a battery of 203mm howitzers. Upon taking up position 450m from the bastion, the battery fired off forty-two shells, as a result of which the front wall was significantly damaged, while ammunition blew up inside and the fort burned. Soviet infantrymen captured it without encountering opposition. The same fate befell the similarly-built Fort 'Prittwitz-Gaffron'. Two batteries of 203mm howitzers were allotted to the fort and they fired eighty shells from a range of 1,000m, forming breaches between 2m and 5m wide in the walls. The round 'Radziwill' bastion, which was located north of Fort 'Rauch' and which was also covered the bridges, was shot up by 203mm howitzers from the western bank of the Warta. Thirty-five concrete-piercing shells made a 4m breach in the bastion's western wall and it burned for a day and was then taken practically without a struggle. Fortifications from the middle of the nineteenth century were practically helpless against artillery from the middle of the twentieth.

What is notable is that the assault on Fort I along the fortress's outer ring did not take place until 14 February. It was already quite deep in the rear of the attacking troops and was being blockaded by a single rifle battalion. However, fire from the fort interfered with the restoration of the railway bridge over the Warta and the fort was taken in an attack by four assault groups following a two-hour bombardment by two batteries of 152mm gun-howitzers and 203mm howitzers.

On 17 February the 91st Rifle Corps' units completely occupied the eastern bank of the Warta River. After this, the 312th Rifle Division was pulled out of the fighting for Poznań and the 117th Rifle Division crossed the Warta and took up positions for the purpose of blockading the fortress's citadel. During February the two divisions lost 3,103 men, including 871 killed.[35]

The most difficult and intensive fighting unfolded along a 4km space in the city centre. The assault methods varied. One of the most common was the caving-in of the facade. The façade of the building under attack was brought down by fire between the windows, burying the firing positions in the basement in rubble. An innovation that was first employed during the fighting for Poznań was the firing of large-calibre M-31[36] rocket-propelled shells from the launchers against the buildings' facades. In this fashion thirty-eight M-31 shells were fired, as a result of which eleven stone buildings were destroyed, including three five-storey ones.

Yet another method was setting fire to the buildings. For example, the enemy was defending a factory complex with a large number of buildings for two days and delaying the advance by the 27th Guards Rifle Division's right flank. The division commander then decided to destroy this centre of resistance by means of setting fire to the buildings one after the other with portable flamethrowers. For this purpose, six small assault groups, consisting of five riflemen and ten combat engineers (including four flamethrower operators), were formed. The factory was divided into six sectors and the assault groups attacked simultaneously. The combat engineers, under the cover of the riflemen and guns, penetrated into the buildings and during the course of several minutes set fire to eight of them. The enemy was forced to abandon the block and partially surrender.

The Poznań garrison's stubborn resistance inevitably affected the Soviet forces' operations along the Oder bridgeheads. In the war diary of the Wehrmacht staff's operational section (KTB OKW) for 16 February 1945 it was noted: 'In general, one may note that as a result of our forces' resistance in Posen[37] and in other fortress-cites, the enemy's advance has noticeably slowed.'[38] In reality, Poznań was a major railway junction from Warsaw to Berlin and its retention interfered with the normal supply of the First Belorussian Front's forces.

By 17 February the Soviet units had practically cleared the city of Poznań of the enemy, having pushed back the remnants of the garrison to the fortress's citadel, the so-called Fort 'Winiary'. The storming of the citadel was entrusted to the 29th Guards Rifle Corps, reinforced by the 2nd Assault Engineer-Sapper Brigade. By decision of the corps commander, the corps' divisions were moved laterally. The 82nd Guards Rifle Division, as the strongest at that moment, was placed along the axis of the main attack, along a 500m front. The 74th Guards Rifle Division was aimed at the citadel's central fort, the so-called 'Kernwerk', along a 350m front, while the 27th Guards Rifle Division was shifted to the northern approaches to the fortress and was given the passive task of preventing the break-out of the citadel's garrison.

Each of the two attacking divisions received four 152mm gun-howitzers and one heavy-calibre artillery brigade. In all, along the 1,000m assault zone there were operating (guns firing over open sights in parentheses):[39]

59 82mm mortars;
29 120mm mortars;
71 (14) 76mm guns;

22 (8) 122mm guns;
8 (5) 152mm gun-howitzers;
41 (22) 203mm howitzers;
6 280mm mortars.

Besides this, thirteen 45mm guns, fifteen 76mm regimental and twenty-nine 76mm divisional guns were operating as part of the assault groups.

A three-hour period of destruction immediately preceded the assault on the citadel. The plan called for the concentration of fire by the entire mass of artillery against targets along the fortress's outer enclosure. In particular, the heavy-calibre battalion's 280mm mortars had the task of destroying Redoubt No. 1 from concealed positions. It should be noted that from 10 February the artillery had begun the destruction of the fortress's fortifications by indirect fire. On 12 February twelve 203mm guns were firing over open sights against the fortress's central entrance from the south. Thus the southern fort ('Kernwerk'), which towered over all the citadel's remaining structures, was already half destroyed by the time the assault began.

At 11.00 on 18 February the artillery rained down fire on the fortress and the approaches to it. The dust and smoke that arose from the explosion of so many shells interfered with observation of the bombardment's results after five minutes. For this reason, they had to take breaks in order to observe their targets, which lengthened the preparation of the attack by an hour. Finally, at 14.50 a salvo from the '*Katyushas*' was fired off and the artillery shifted its fire to the northern and eastern part of the fortress wall.

However, the garrison was defending with the desperation of the doomed. Even the fanatical Gonell had become depressed during the final days of Poznań's defence. On 18 February he radioed the headquarters of the VIII Air Corps: 'Do you want to help us, or is this the German way of war to leave one's comrades to the vicissitudes of fate? Why don't you reply to insistent requests, when we're speaking of the lives of thousands of people?'[40] To be fair, one must say that German transport aviation had carried out 195 sorties, delivering 257 tonnes of supplies, with 147 tonnes dropped by parachute container, to help the fortress of Poznań. On the night of 17/18 February thirteen He-111s dropped 15 tonnes of ammunition to the fortress. Moreover, given the large number of fires, it was not easy to make drops and a part of this total, naturally, fell into the Red Army's hands.

One should note that at the start of the artillery preparation the 82nd and 74th Guards Rifle Divisions and reinforcement units were not yet at the walls of Fort 'Winiary' (the second name of the citadel, named after the builder of the Poznań fortress, the German engineer Johann Leopold Ludwig von Brese-Winiary). A large cemetery, which was occupied by the Germans (according to Soviet data, this was 'Ewart's Group') separated the 82nd Guards Rifle Division's groups from the perimeter of the fort and the 74th Guards Rifle Division from the city blocks still occupied by the Germans. Ewart's Group sat out the artillery preparation in the numerous and quite secure crypts. The assault combat engineers made six passages in the cemetery fence, which enabled the attackers to break into the cemetery. Without waiting to clear the abode of the dead of the enemy's riflemen who had taken up position behind the gravestones and crypts, the infantrymen arrived at the fort's railing. This was a fence typical of the Poznań forts, with spikes inside the ditch. The combat engineers, under the cover of darkness, had already punched through five wide passages with explosive charges and were on the edge of the deep ditch.

Simultaneously, the fortress was being worked over. A battery from the 184th Heavy Calibre Howitzer Artillery Brigade blew a hole in the fortress wall in the area of Redoubt No. 2 by firing over open sights from a distance of 300m, and 152mm and 203mm guns were also firing against the upper part of the ditch's wall, chipping off and damaging it. In this manner positions were created for the placement of assault ladders and for the infantry's approach to the wall. However, the attempt to overcome the ditch on the march, with the help of assault ladders, was unsuccessful. The fort's garrison had long since come to its senses following the artillery preparation and put up fierce resistance, both by enfilading the ditch itself from flanking casemates and by meeting the attacking subunits with frontal fire from the wall. The flamethrower operators who had been moved up to the ditch were unable to suppress the machine guns in the fort's embrasures. The streams of flammable liquid, released from 20–25m, did not have the desired effect.

In order to silence the firing points in the casemates, they decided to resort to a tried and tested method: throwing barrels of explosives into the ditch. Four to six assault engineers, under the cover of infantry fire, rolled the barrel to the corner of the ditch, lit the fuze and tossed it in. The machine guns fell silent from the powerful explosions, which enabled them to overcome the ditch in four places with ladders and to consolidate along the southern slope and the crest of the fortress's ditch. However, within 40–50 minutes the silenced machine guns awoke and opened up a hail of fire. As was later discovered, the exploding barrels did not destroy the casemate, but only put its garrison out of action, which after a while was replaced with a new one. At dawn some of the ladders thrown over the ditch had been damaged by aimed fire. They replaced them under the cover of a smokescreen, but this did not solve the problem of the bullets whistling along the ditch. Flamethrower operator Corporal Iraklii Serbiladze, who reached Redoubt No. 2 and burned out the garrison with a stream of flammable liquid, led to the latest pause for gathering forces in the fortress. However, the infantrymen who had consolidated in the ditch were forced to repel the enemy's counter-attacks.

The 2nd Assault Engineer Brigade's losses for the day of fighting for Fort 'Winiary' were three men killed and seventeen wounded. The 82nd Guards Rifle Division's losses for 18 February were twenty-eight killed and eighty wounded and during the 24-hours from 17.00 on 18 February until 17.00 on 19 February the division lost another seventeen men killed and thirty-one wounded. The commander of the 246th Guards Rifle Regiment, Major Belyaev, died in the fighting, as did Captain Sarychev, a battalion commander in the 244th Guards Rifle Regiment, who had been with the division since Stalingrad. In one day the 74th Guards Rifle Division lost twenty-four men killed and seventy-eight wounded, having captured several buildings on the approaches to the citadel.

The development of the offensive by the 82nd Guards Rifle Division's units within the citadel required the movement of artillery over the ditch. Thus the combat engineers spent the following night, 19/20 February, building a bridge over the ditch on trestles capable of handling 1.5 tonnes. It was initially planned to erect the bridge opposite the breach in the fort's wall that had been made by the heavy-calibre artillery. With the onset of darkness, they began to drag prefabricated bridge parts up to the ditch. However, it proved impossible to build: the Germans constantly fired *Faustpatronen* from the breach and swept the construction area incessantly with rifle and machine-gun fire, forcing the engineers to build the bridge 30m to the east, thus avoiding the *Faustpatrone* rounds flying out of the breach. They suppressed fire from Redoubt No. 1 in the by-now established way: a barrel of explosives. This yielded four or five hours for work. By 07.30 the bridge had been completed, but within 30 minutes it was destroyed by several *Faustpatrone* rounds.

However, the build-up of infantry on the bridgehead inside the fortress continued. Wonders of bravery were manifested in order to suppress the tiresome Redoubt No. 1. For example, flamethrower operator Junior Sergeant Gennadii Kopeikin, who was born in 1926, put up a smokescreen by himself with grenades (!), lowered himself into the ditch by climbing down a rope (!), crawled 15m to the embrasures and set the fort on fire. He was one of the first to get across the ditch and set fire to the fortress's casemate that was hindering the infantry's advance. As a result of the fighting in Poznań, Kopeikin was awarded the Order of the Red Banner.

By 20 February the 74th Rifle Division had reached the approaches to the citadel's ditch in the 'Kernwerk' area. With the assistance of self-propelled guns and 203mm guns that had been brought up to the fortress, by 11.30 two breaches had been made, one in the wall of the southern tower of the central gates and a second in the fortress wall in the south-western part of the 'Kernwerk'. They then suppressed fire from the flanking casemates by dropping explosive-filled barrels into the ditch as usual. Further on, they set up ladders opposite the breaches under the cover of a smokescreen. Individual groups of soldiers from the 236th Guards Rifle Division even managed to cross the ditch and began fighting for the 'Kernwerk's' central tower. As was pointed out in the division's war diary, the enemy 'besides fire from windows and embrasures along the outer walls, holds the long corridors of the prison buildings under constant machine gun fire' (the 'Kernwerk' was used as a prison). The assault groups advanced inside the 'Kernwerk', blowing up the casemate's walls and doors with charges ranging from 0.5kg to 2kg.

The 82nd Guards Rifle Division's losses in two days of fighting for the citadel were 52 killed and 109 wounded. The 2nd Assault Engineer Brigade lost eight men killed, four missing in action and thirty-three wounded. The 74th Rifle Division's losses for the day's fighting for the fortress were 30 men killed and 130 wounded. However, one cannot say that the day did not bring any results. The 82nd Guards Rifle Division's infantry, which crossed over to the fortress, managed to secure the wall in the area of the breach and to create the conditions for a second attempt at building a bridge. They once again suppressed fire from Redoubt No. 1 by blowing up a barrel. By 07.00 on 21 February they finally built the bridge. During the night of 20/21 February and throughout the 21st itself they managed to get fourteen 76mm divisional guns, eight 76mm regimental guns and eight 45mm guns over the bridge near Redoubt No. 2. Meanwhile, the 74th Guards Rifle Division's regiments made up for the time lost along the approaches to the citadel. By 03.00 on 21 February the artillerymen had silenced the enemy's fire from the external walls of the 'Kernwerk' and the 74th Guards Rifle Division's assault groups had crossed the ditch. The 226th Guards Rifle Regiment had consolidated

14. An He-111 bomber abandoned on the airfield at Poznań. In all, according to Soviet data, about 150 aircraft of various types were captured in the Poznań area.

15. A sketch of one of the typical Poznań forts.

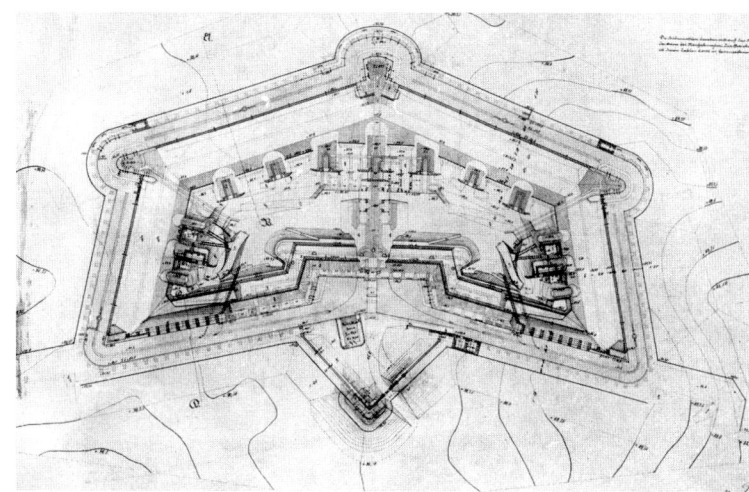

16. General V.I. Chuikov, commander of the 8th Guards Army.

17. A ditch around one of Poznań's forts. Gun limbers have been positioned in the ditch, which was probably used as a storehouse for artillery equipment.

18. Fort Rauch in Poznań. A photograph from the beginning of the twentieth century.

19. Embrasures in one of the casemates of the fortress's citadel.

20. Soviet officers by a redoubt in the fortress's citadel.

21. A building destroyed by heavy artillery on the approaches to the central part of the old city. It had been turned into a centre of resistance by the Germans and suffered heavily during the assault.

22. The ditch of the citadel. The wall running along the centre of the ditch was not an organic structure and most likely speaks to an attempt to employ the ditch as a storehouse or even a factory.

58. Ghost buildings: heavily-damaged buildings, ready to collapse at any time.

59. A column of prisoners from Breslau on the march to a prisoner-of-war camp.

60. A column of prisoners leaves the city. The battle for Breslau is over.

in the 'Kernwerk' to the east, and the 236th Guards Rifle Regiment to the west of the central gates. A battalion from the 236th Guards Rifle Regiment occupied the central gates' tower. At almost the same time as their neighbour, they managed to get fifteen guns (45mm and 76mm) across the bridge over the ditch by 07.00. However, they still needed to overcome the 'Kernwerk's' inner courtyard in order to break into the fortress, for which 76mm and 45mm guns were clearly insufficient to take on the casemates.

The movement of guns into the fortress enabled the Soviets to destroy resistance in the casemates near the wall and advance further. The command of the 82nd Guards Rifle Division's group of guns was entrusted to the commander of the 82nd Guards Rifle Division's 86th Anti-Tank Battalion, Major Pyotr Repin, a veteran of Stalingrad. With the artillery's arrival, the attackers got the opportunity to shoot up Redoubt No. 2's embrasures that faced the courtyard. Repin personally commanded a 76mm gun crew firing on the entrance and the embrasures. Following a few shots, the firing slackened, which enabled them to fire two bursts into the redoubt from a flamethrower. There immediately followed a massive explosion from the ammunition inside the redoubt. It burned for another 36 hours.

Corporal I.G. Serbiladze, the flamethrower operator who has been mentioned earlier, made two successful shots from his flamethrower. He set fire to a building within the citadel from which a white flag soon appeared. Two hundred Germans immediately surrendered. Serbiladze was recommended for the Hero of the Soviet Union for his actions during the assault on the citadel, but was eventually given the Order of Glory Third Class. The reasons for this are not known to the author, although Serbiladze's actions are mentioned in a report by the flamethrower battalion, in the brigade's report and in the artillery troops' report.

The recent days in the fighting for the citadel cost the 82nd Guards Rifle Division thirty-two killed and seventy-nine wounded, while the 2nd Assault Engineer Brigade lost nine killed and fourteen wounded. The 74th Guards Rifle Division lost seventeen killed and forty-eight wounded. The losses suffered forced the Soviets to resort to extreme measures for mobilizing the local population. The morning report by the 236th Guards Rifle Regiment for 22 February indicates the following: '200 mobilized Poles were armed and dispatched to the battalions.'

The development of events inside the fortress showed that it was unlikely that they would be able to finish off the garrison without heavy equipment.

The Germans were firing from the rear side of the central fortification ('Kernwerk') and hindering movement around the fortress. The construction of a bridge or some other structure was needed for moving tanks and heavy-calibre guns into the fortress. A local resident, a Pole who had worked as a plumber in the fortress, supplied valuable information to the Soviet combat engineers. He reported that there was a 3.5m wide archway inside the fortress from an internal corner in Redoubt No. 2. They even included the Polish plumber among the troops of the reconnaissance group, but due to the heavy fire they were nevertheless unable to confirm that the archway opened up a passage into the fort. They decided not to risk it and to attempt to build a bridge in a familiar area, where they had already crossed guns into the fortress.

However, this time the method of throwing in a barrel did not work. The Germans had learned from their experience and had chosen a position in Redoubt No. 1 that enabled them to enfilade the approach to the ditch from which the barrels usually came. They twice attempted to toss barrels and flood the embrasures with a flamethrower, but were unsuccessful. Only after they made a great deal of smoke were they able to throw in one barrel, but they were not able to silence all the embrasures. An attempt to bring flamethrower tanks into the cemetery was similarly unsuccessful. The vehicles carefully moved through the cemetery, which was located on a slope, among the crypts and old trees. However, they were unable to reach the embrasures below the edge of the ditch either with their guns or flamethrowers. One T-34 flamethrower tank was put out of action by a *Faustpatrone*, but did not burn up.

In order to blind Redoubt No. 1's embrasures, they even attempted to block up the ditch with materials at hand: empty crates and barrels, etc. Around 400 local residents were brought in for this work who, as was mentioned in one of the reports, 'coped well with their assigned task'. A mountain of trash blocked the embrasures along the redoubt's lower tier. Nonetheless, attempts to build a bridge during the day cost the combat engineers eighteen wounded.

On the evening of 22 February they found yet another antidote to Redoubt No. 1. Under the cover of a smokescreen they set up two heavy-calibre machine guns in the ditch behind the concrete crosspiece and on its glacis, which fired almost continually on Redoubt No. 1's embrasures. This enabled the combat engineers to reach the bridge unhindered, but what they found did not instil enthusiasm. A significant part of the beams had been broken by the constant bombardment. The bridge's actual capacity did not exceed 10 tonnes and was completely useless for tanks.

All of this caused them to once again remember the archway near Redoubt No. 2, about which the Polish plumber from the fortress had reported. The 2nd Assault Engineer Brigade's vehicles, which had been sent for explosives, immediately returned. They planted five charges with an overall weight of 1.5 tonnes in shafts of various depths on the outer side of the ditch. Following a monstrously powerful explosion, it required only insignificant work to form ramps. This enabled them to move four flamethrower tanks and six 203mm guns into the citadel by 03.00 on 23 February.

Upon advancing from the ditch into the depth of the fortress, the Soviet assault groups made safe the crossing over the bridge to the breach in the wall of Redoubt No. 2. During the night of 20/21 February they moved twenty-two 76mm regimental and divisional guns and eight 45mm guns into the fortress. Guns were moved across the bridge over the ditch into the 'Kernwerk' in the same way along the 74th Guards Rifle Division's sector. This enabled them to shoot up the firing points in the 'Kernwerk's' inner buildings. The fighting continued for two days, 21–22 February, inside the fortress.

Meanwhile, a heavy-capacity bridge was being built over the ditch. They broadened the breach in the wall with the help of 2 tonnes of explosives, and by setting off less powerful charges they formed a ramp for the approach to the ditch. By 02.00 on 23 February the construction of the ramp was completed for the approach by tanks and heavy artillery near Redoubt No. 2. Flamethrower tanks and six 203mm guns were brought into the fortress that night.

However, the 203mm howitzers did not even have to open fire, as the garrison of the citadel capitulated in the morning. Colonel Erwin Detbaren, the former chief of staff of 'Fortress Posen', later described in Soviet captivity the succession of events that led to the decision to capitulate. According to his testimony, radio communications with Army Group Vistula had been lost at about 21.00 on 22 February as the result of the latest artillery bombardment. Before this a radiogram had been sent stating that 'We cannot hold the fortress', to which Himmler's headquarters replied 'Hold'. By midnight they had once again managed to restore the radio link and to enquire from headquarters that 'We have been forced into a narrow space, so should we attempt to break out or surrender?' No reply was received to this message.

Gonell decided to attempt to break out and set the time – at 09.00 on 23 February. Detbaren tried to convince the commandant that it was already too late. The time until 05.00 passed in inaction and ruminations, upon which the commandant finally agreed with his chief of staff. By 06.00 four soldiers who had been in Soviet captivity had been sent with a surrender proposal, which had been delivered to Gonell. At that moment the decision was finally made to capitulate. Gonell drew up a note and sent it to the Soviet command along with the four soldiers and two of his own delegates. Simultaneously, Gonell, according to Detbaren's testimony, declared that he did not intend to surrender. At 08.00–09.00 on 23 February the capitulation of the citadel's garrison began, for which reason the final assault was halted.

However, the struggle for Poznań did not conclude with this. The 27th Guards Rifle Division, which had been covering the citadel from the north, was hurriedly sent off to the Oder as early as the second half of the day on 23 February. As a result, quite a large group from the citadel's garrison managed to escape to the north. In the Steimendorf area, already quite far from the citadel (beyond the enclosure of the forts!), a chemical company from the 82nd Guards Rifle Division began fighting at 09.00 on 23 February with a detachment of Germans, armed with four machine guns, which was approaching from Poznań. The Germans, following a three-hour fight, decided to attempt to break out along another direction, to the north to Glinnow. The 'chemists' cut this escape route as well and through their decisive actions drove the surrounded enemy into a swamp. At this moment yet another group of Germans came out of the woods to the east of Steimendorf (Moraska Hill, which was covered by trees). They had to mobilize twenty-four men from the Polish self-defence forces and arm them with captured weapons in order to repel the break-out. By 18.00 the survivors of the encircled Germans surrendered, with seventy-three men captured while another sixty lay dead on the battlefield. The 'chemists', together with the Polish self-defence forces, lost four men killed and six wounded. Overall, the 82nd Guards Rifle Division's losses for the day were ten men killed and twenty-five wounded.

During the night of 23/24 February there was fighting with individual Germans trying to break out in the Schennerhausen area, immediately beyond the line of the forts. Elements of the 82nd Guards Rifle Division reported seventeen enemy officers and men killed, while their own losses amounted to one man killed and three wounded. But this was not the final gong. At 11.30 on 24 February (more than a day after the official capitulation!) a group of Germans was discovered in the southern part of the woods to the east of Steimendorf, which the chemical company engaged in a fight that lasted to 18.00 and ended with the elimination of the surrounded forces. The 'chemists' took seventy-one prisoners, including thirteen officers. Their own losses were five men killed and seven wounded. It is not impossible that some of the fortress garrison's remnants nevertheless managed to slip away and avoid encounters with the Soviet forces in the rear of the 29th Guards Rifle Corps in the Poznań area.

In all, during the assault on Poznań the 8th Guards Army's forces captured 17,150 enemy officers and men, including one general (Mattern) and one colonel (Detbaren). V.I. Chuikov's headquarters later claimed a larger number of prisoners, but it had declared the garrison's strength to be 40,000 men, in an obvious attempt to justify the time the assault had taken. Ernst Gonell kept his promise not to surrender and shot himself. They discovered his corpse on 23 February in Redoubt No. 4, which was positively identified by captured members of his staff.

Conclusions

From time immemorial, Poznań had been a fortress and sooner or later had to play its role. It was precisely the system of Poznań's fortifications that meant that the city was not taken by the Red Army from the march. On the whole, however, the resilience of its nineteenth-century structures proved not to be very great. Fort 'Winiary's' Redoubt No. 1, which delayed the breakthrough of Soviet infantry into the fortress for a considerable period of time, caused the most unpleasantness.

Poznań became the beneficiary of the *Faustpatronen*, in that way in which they became a factor in Germany in 1945. We are speaking here, first of all, of their mass employment not only as an anti-tank weapon, but as an anti-personnel one as well. In the 27th Guards Rifle Division's report on the fighting in Poznań, it was noted that: 'The effectiveness of the *Faustpatronen* is enormous. Basically, all of the destruction is caused by the force of the explosion. The fragmentation effect is very slight … If a *Faustpatrone* explodes at a distance of 5–7m from a man, then he receives a severe concussion, and often even a fatal one.'[41] The *Faustpatronen* became the garrison's 'pocket artillery', which sharply increased the firepower of the infantry subunits. The Germans would not have been able to put up such stubborn resistance to the assault with infantry weapons alone.

The protracted battle for Poznań can be explained in no small degree by the fact that the attackers received 203mm artillery only on 9 February. After this the fortress did not last more than two weeks. Artillery became the main means of achieving success in the fighting. In all, during the period from 24 January through 23 February 1945, the Red Army's forces assaulting Poznań expended 315,682 shells and rounds of all calibres, including:

2,310 160mm mortar rounds;

4,668 152mm explosive-fragmentation shells;

3,854 203mm shells;

331 280mm shells;

4,107 M-31 rocket-propelled rounds.[42]

This enormous amount of munitions totalled about 5,000 tons in weight, or 400 railway wagons: 3,230 M-31 rocket-propelled rounds were also expended. The numbers for the infantry's expenditure of rounds is also impressive: six million rifle rounds and five million automatic rifle rounds, 130,000 hand grenades of all types, as well as 7,000 captured *Faustpatronen*. The irreplaceable losses of the Red Army's units and formations in the fighting for Poznań amounted to 4,887 men.

The assault on Poznań essentially became a 'dress rehearsal' for the assault on Berlin. Soviet forces gained experience and worked out methods for assaulting residential and industrial buildings. As strange as it sounds, Chuikov's arrogance here played a positive role, as it was his forces who eventually applied the experience of the Poznań 'testing ground' in Berlin.

Chapter 4

Breslau: The Reich's Last Fortress

The city of Breslau, the capital of Silesia, became the largest and last fortress of the Third Reich. Later on, in his memoirs, I.S. Konev,[1] the commander of the First Ukrainian Front, was quite dismissive of the fortress which was under siege by his 6th Army:

> ... the end of the war was not far off and I decided that there was no necessity whatsoever of undertaking an assault on Breslau. Once we were unable to take this fortress-city from the march during the first days, further constant attacks were excessive. We had to keep the enemy in our sights and from time to time remind the Germans with ultimatums that their situation was hopeless and that there was no way out for them.[2]

However, even a superficial study of the Soviet side's combat documents makes us doubt this assertion. Just what took place on the streets of Breslau at the end of winter and spring of 1945?

It is an irony of fate that Breslau became one of the cities from the streets of which the Second World War began. At the end of August 1939 an endless flow of Wehrmacht vehicles and columns of infantry moved through the city towards the Polish border. It was from Silesia that Army Group South launched the main attack in September 1939. Breslau had 630,000 inhabitants in 1939, but the subsequent evacuation to Breslau of factories located in areas subjected to Allied bombing and the influx of refugees increased the size of the city's population to nearly a million.

Breslau was declared a fortress as early as the summer of 1944. However, its transformation into an actual fortress made only moderate progress. On 25 September 1944 Major General Johannes Krause, an artillery officer who had spent a large part of the war in Greece and had only limited combat experience, was appointed chief of the Breslau garrison. The garrison initially included two battalions, made up mainly of elderly reservists. Krause, being a rational man and capable of making elementary calculations, immediately evaluated the plan for evacuating Breslau's inhabitants at the rate of 100 trains a day as utopian. Krause proposed to *Gauleiter*[3] Hanke[4] the evacuation of 200,000 of the city's residents, including the elderly, the sick, children and young mothers, before catastrophe struck, but this was categorically refused. Hanke replied that 'The *Führer* will order me shot if I propose this right now, at a time of great peace!' It's difficult, of course, to describe as 'a time of great peace' when the Red Army seized bridgeheads over the Vistula, only 300km as the crow flies from Breslau.

However, the Red Army was actually already at the threshold of the Third Reich and the latest convulsive decision by the Nazi top brass became the formation of the *Volkssturm*. Breslau, as a fairly large city, could, at least on paper, put up thirty-eight *Volkssturm* battalions, with a total strength of about 15,000 men.

As was mentioned earlier, fortress artillery batteries of several field guns or howitzers were formed for the fortresses in eastern Germany in the autumn of 1944. Being a large city, Breslau nevertheless ended up being done out of its fortress guns. By an OKH[5] directive of 29 November 1944 eight captured Schneider 1912 model 75mm field guns from the Yugoslav army (known in the Wehrmacht as FK 249(j)) and three Italian 37 model 75mm guns (known in the Wehrmacht as FK 249 (i)) were to be transferred to Breslau, but in fact the city got no howitzers, not even captured ones. Moreover, in the autumn of 1944 the inhabitants of Breslau were mobilized not for strengthening the city, but for the construction of the 'Barthold' position along the border of Poland and Germany.

The preparation of Breslau for defence was sharply accelerated with the start of the Soviet offensive from the Vistula bridgeheads. On 26 January 1945, by order of the OKH, the 609th Special Designation Division (Division z.b.V. 609) was to be formed in Breslau from units of the Breslau garrison. The division combined part of the city's *Volkssturm* in three regiments of two battalions apiece. However, the formation formally included an artillery regiment and even a tank company. Major General Siegfried Ruff, who had earlier commanded artillery units and who had been the commandant of Riga in 1944, led the division.

On 31 January 1945 General Krause was relieved of his duties due to illness (pneumonia) and Colonel Hans von Ahlfen, who reported taking up command at 10.20 on 3 February 1945, was appointed in his place. He had earlier commanded the Seventeenth Army's engineer units. Only a few days remained before the encirclement of the city and the beginning of street fighting.

The fortress's condition made a depressing impression on von Ahlfen as a military engineer. He later recalled:

I could not shake the sensation that here the order issued by the high command in August 1944, as in many other places, had not been taken seriously. How otherwise could one explain omissions, the chief of which I will list below:

- the absence of a main headquarters, which could have busied itself with transforming Breslau into a fortress immediately from August 1944;
- the insufficient level of the fortress troops' organization;
- the insufficient armament and poor supply of munitions;
- the omission of the opportunity to supply the city by air in the event of a siege.

Actually, in Breslau there was only the Gandau airfield in the western part of the city, practically on the outskirts. Its loss in the event of an assault on the city was only a question of time. The construction of a landing strip in the city seemed more expedient. One had to be built in any event, but already under fire. However, the coordination to raze buildings and to transform one of the streets into a landing strip seemed a difficult task for those in the city. It's human nature to hope that things will work out.

The seizure by the First Ukrainian Front of bridgeheads on the left bank of the Oder during the Vistula–Oder operation became the prerequisite for the encirclement of Breslau. The city of Breslau fell into the area of responsibility of Lieutenant General V.A. Gluzdovskii's[6] 6th Army. At that moment it was hard to call Gluzdovskii a commander held in high regard. In Vladimir Alekseyevich's background was the negative experience of the winter positional fighting of 1943–4 on the Western Front, where he commanded the 31st Army and from which he had been relieved in May 1944. However, Gluzdovskii's return to the western direction took place fairly smoothly, although the 6th Army only received a supporting role in the overall offensive.

According to Operational Directive No. 0051/op of 31 January 1945, Konev's headquarters ordered the 6th Army to launch an attack against the rear of the enemy group of forces defending Breslau and 'by the close of the fourth day of the operation to take Breslau'. The Breslau axis was not a priority one – according to the same directive, the First Ukrainian Front's forces were directed to reach the Elbe and take Berlin. The capture of Breslau essentially pursued the same goals as did the capture of Poznań: to free up a major road junction for the unhindered supply of the *front*'s forces.

One must say that the preparation for a new offensive immediately following the January thrust from the Vistula to the Oder was not an easy task. The First Ukrainian Front's lines of communications had become extended and railway transport was still unavailable. This forced the Soviet forces to transport ammunition and fuel from their unloading points on the right bank of the Vistula to the bridgeheads by road transport. Even after taking motor vehicles from formations and units occupying defensive positions at the bridgehead, the 6th Army only managed to scrape together 170 motor vehicles to transport 350 tonnes of ammunition and 180 tonnes of fuel. The supply problems forced them to postpone the date for the beginning of the offensive from 6 to 8 February 1945. By the morning of 8 February from two to five units of fire for the artillery and mortars and one-and-one-half to two units of fire for infantry weapons had been accumulated in the units and at army depots. As of the evening of 7 February, Lieutenant General of Tank Troops I.P. Korchagin's 7th Guards Mechanized Corps numbered in line 186 T-34s, 21 ISU-122s,[7] 21 SU-85s, and 21 SU-76s;[8] that is, it was almost at authorized strength. Only six T-34s were undergoing repairs. The 6th Army had no other tank formations during this period.

The offensive developed quite successfully. At 08.35 on 8 February the artillery preparation began and lasted 55 minutes. Units of the 7th Guards Mechanized Corps crossed over to the bridgehead under the artillery preparation. At 12.00 the 24th Guards Motorized Brigade and the 57th Guards Tank Brigade, which were moving in the 7th Guards Mechanized Corps' first echelon, bypassed the infantry and raced into the depth of the German defence.

Despite the overall favourable development of events for the Red Army, it's hard to call the 7th Guards Mechanized Corps' breakthrough to the south of Breslau an entertaining stroll. The corps' two forward brigades encountered stubborn resistance from the enemy along the line of the railway running from Breslau to the south-west. On 10 and 11 February 1945 the 57th Guards Tank Brigade fought for the station and village of Koberwitz, and the 25th Guards Mechanized Brigade for Domslau station and, as was mentioned in the corps' war diary, 'suffering heavy losses in tanks and personnel from the enemy's tank and artillery fire, as well as from tank destroyers armed with *Faustpatronen*, who have holed up in the buildings' basements'.[9] The brigades were also subjected to enemy air strikes. The 57th Guards Tank Brigade and the 25th Guards Mechanized Brigade, upon uniting their efforts, broke through between Domslau and Koberwitz, but ended up being isolated. During these days (10–11 February), the 7th Guards Mechanized Corps' 24th and 26th Guards Mechanized Brigades, which had been in defensive positions facing south, were subjected to attacks by German tanks along the front Gross-Baudis–Kostenblut. The task of the counterblow was evidently to punch a corridor through to Breslau and prevent the closing of the 'cauldron'. Before long the failure of the offensives of 10–11 February made the launching of counterblows along this sector pointless. On the morning of 12 February the 309th Rifle Division's regiments, which had been brought up following the completion of the fighting for Liegnitz, relieved the 7th Guards Mechanized Corps' 24th and 26th Guards Mechanized Brigades. Bringing up the rifle units strengthened the defence along the external front of the developing encirclement.

At the moment when the encirclement of Breslau had practically closed shut, a tragic event took place that echoed throughout the entire Red Army. On 11 February one of the most outstanding Soviet bomber pilots, Major General of Aviation Ivan Semyonovich Polbin, was shot down by anti-aircraft fire over the capital of Silesia. His Pe-2 crashed on the outskirts of Breslau.

From 18.20 on 12 February, and during the following night and on 13 February a new counteroffensive was launched by the Germans, this time involving changing the axis of the attack to the east, to the Kostenblut–Kant front. The repeated attacks along this sector may be explained quite simply – this was the narrowest part of the ring around Breslau. The external and internal encirclement fronts around the city were only 30km apart. Soviet intelligence included among the attackers units of the 8th Panzer Division, the 19th Panzer Division, and *Volkssturm* and anti-aircraft units, which corresponds to German data. Upon achieving a local success with the capture of Gross-Peterwitz, the relief group was before long forced back to its jumping-off positions by a skilful flank attack. Further on, the situation for the Germans continued to worsen and the 273rd Rifle Division was arriving at the battlefield from the west and north. The division threw the enemy back further to the south and took up defensive positions along the line of the Striegauer Wasser River, thus securing a tenable external encirclement front. As early as 14.00 on 13 February the 309th Rifle Division was freed up and was removed from positions along which it had repelled the counterblow and was approaching Breslau from the south-west.

The closing of the 'cauldron' took place on the morning of 13 February, when the 6th Army's 7th Guards Mechanized Corps linked up with the 5th Guards Army's forward detachments in the area of Rotsurben, a road junction directly to the south of Breslau. As early as about 08.00 a scouting party dispatched by the 25th Guards Tank Brigade encountered a self-propelled artillery regiment from the 5th Guards Army near Rotsurben. At around 10.00 the 12th Guards Tank Regiment met the 252nd Tank Regiment from the 5th Guards Army's 31st Tank Corps. The fortress's communications with the outside world had been cut.

However, the formation of a ring around the fortress was not yet complete at this time. The most powerful formation in the Breslau area was the 269th Infantry Division, which was falling back to the north-eastern outskirts of the city. On 3 February the 269th Infantry Division had been replaced by the Moor Independent Fortress Regiment, named for its commander Lieutenant Colonel Walther Moor. With the appearance of the threat to outflank Breslau, the 269th Infantry Division began to rapidly fall back to the south. On the night of 13/14 February units of the 269th Infantry Division and elements of other formations that had ended up in the Breslau area reached the internal encirclement ring. Simultaneously, there followed an attack from outside the 'cauldron' by the forces of the 19th Panzer Division. The two groups of German forces linked up in the area of the village of Tinz. Two brigades from the 7th Guards Mechanized Corps were involved in a difficult night battle for eight hours and the situation was not stabilized until 11.00 on 14 February. As the German historian Rolf Hinze maintains, not only the military, but tens if not hundreds of thousands of refugees from the city managed to break out in the direction of Zobten, from where they were evacuated by railway.[10] Such an outcome cannot, of course, be excluded.

From this time on the fortress could only rely on its own forces. All the calculations that the garrison would be reinforced by formations retreating in the Breslau area collapsed. The completion of the formation of the internal encirclement ring around Breslau took place during 14–16 February, when the 6th Army's rifle formations consolidated the success of the mobile units by arriving at the near approaches to the city. As early as the night of 14/15 February the 7th Guards Mechanized Corps was pulled out of the fighting in light of the sharply exacerbated situation in the Striegau area, where the Germans were launching counterblows. On the evening of 14 February there remained in line in General I.P. Korchagin's mechanized corps 108 T-34s, 9 ISU-122s, 17 SU-85s, and 13 SU-76s. That is, the losses in the fighting to encircle Breslau may be rated as fairly heavy.

In connection with the forthcoming removal of the 5th Guards Army to another sector of the front, the 294th Rifle Division, which was approaching Breslau from the east, was transferred from A.S. Zhadov's[11] army to the 6th Army. The 77th Fortified Area (UR), which was defending along the northern bank of the Oder River, was also transferred to Gluzdovskii's army from the 52nd Army. Somewhat later, from 18 February, the relief of the 5th Guards Army's units to the south-east of Breslau by elements of the 273rd Rifle Division and the 6th Army's reserve regiment took place. All of the future participants in the siege and assault on the fortress had been gathered together.

Who, in the end, fell into the trap of the fortress? The Moor Regiment, which had relieved the 269th Infantry Division, consisted of four infantry battalions, four mortar battalions and a company of radio-controlled 'Goliath'[12] tanks. I should remind the reader that during this period the regiments of the Wehrmacht's regular infantry divisions had an authorized strength of two battalions. Officially, the Moor Regiment was called Regiment 'B' and was formed from the 49th Reserve Training Battalion and the 83rd Infantry Training Battalion. The Moor Regiment occupied a 15km front from Stein (along the highway to Breslau from the north-east) and then along the bank of the Weide River as far as Polanowice. If a Regiment 'B' existed, then it is logical to suppose the existence of a Regiment 'A'. Indeed there was – the Ganf Independent Fortress Regiment, which had been assembled from various subunits and which was officially named Regiment 'A'. It consisted of 'only' three battalions.

In all, there were five regiments with a letter designation in Breslau. Regiment 'C', which was also listed as the Sauer Independent Fortress Regiment (named after its commander, Lieutenant Colonel Sauer), occupied a 13km front along the bank of the Weide River as far as its confluence with the Oder. It was made up of five battalions, which had also been formed from training subunits. That is, this 'regiment' was also different from the usual Wehrmacht two-battalion regiments of this period. To the west of Breslau was the next in alphabetical order, Regiment 'D', which was more often called the Besselein Independent Fortress Regiment, in honour of its commander SS *Obersturmbannführer* Georg Besselein. It had also been formed from SS training elements and included five infantry battalions, two battalions of 120mm mortars and an anti-aircraft battery. Two *Volkssturm* battalions were additionally subordinated to Besselein's regiment.

The Wehl Regiment, which had been formed from Luftwaffe ground personnel, was the next in line. It included four infantry battalions and several independent companies. It occupied an 8km front from Hermannsdorf to Klettendorf, to the south-west of Breslau. Finally, the remaining 19km sector along the city's defensive perimeter was occupied by three regiments of the previously-mentioned 609th Special Designation Division. The 609th Division's regiments, according to the already established tradition in Breslau, were also named after their commanders: the Kersten, Reinkorber and Schultz Infantry Regiments and the Siebert Artillery Regiment.

The fortress also received the Breslau Fortress Artillery Regiment, consisting of six fortress batteries (formed in the autumn of 1944) and two artillery training battalions, one light and one heavy, from Bunzlau. Later on, elements of the 859th Heavy Battalion and the 269th and 17th Infantry Divisions' artillery regiments were blockaded in the fortress. The Breslau Anti-Tank Battalion, consisting of a tank regiment (one Panzer IV, two Panzer IIIs, six StuG IVs from the 311th Assault Gun Brigade,[13] six Panzer IIs from the FAMO factory, and four *Wespe*[14] self-propelled guns with 105mm howitzers).

On 15 February von Ahlfen announced the following: 'Residents of Breslau! Our fortress has been completely surrounded. This should not come as a surprise for you, because a fortress must constantly live with the thought that it will have to fight encircled ...'[15] The commandant went on to describe the inevitable difficulties which the residents of the encircled fortress would encounter and recommended hiding in the basements and warned of the possible blowing up of the bridges over the Oder.

As if to confirm the commandant's words, heavy shells rained down on Breslau. On 16 February the 315th Independent Heavy Artillery Battalion, armed with 280mm Br-5 heavy mortars, fired on the city post office, where, according to intelligence information, there was an ammunition depot, and on the electrical plant from a distance of more than 10km. One gun, positioned to the north of Breslau, fired off nineteen concrete-piercing rounds. A large explosion was observed in the area of the post office. On 18 February the 280mm guns' targets became the oil storage facility with its cement cisterns buried in the ground, on the north-eastern outskirts of Breslau. According to the 315th Independent Heavy Artillery Battalion's report, 'two centres of flame rose up, which were accompanied by five explosions of enormous force'. The water tower became yet another target, with the Soviets firing six rounds at it and hitting their target.

On the same day that von Ahlfen announced the forthcoming travails, the Red Army made an attempt to seize the fortress from the march. In the middle of the day on 14 February Major General F.V. Zakharov, the commander of the 22nd Rifle Corps, issued an order which did not allow for misinterpretation. 'The corps … is to seize the south-western outskirts of Breslau and by the close of the day is to reach the line of the group of lakes in the central part of the city.'[16] However, attacks against the suburbs of Breslau undertaken in the following days were unsuccessful. The 309th Rifle Division overcame the Lobruck–Opperau line with difficulty, while the 218th Rifle Division stormed Kritern. There could be no thought of any thrust directly into the city centre.

A significant success for the Red Army in the initial period of the battle for Breslau was the seizure of the railway embankment in the south-western part of the city. It was not fated to become a serious obstacle for the attackers as was the case around star-crossed Pogost'ye in 1941–2. The 218th Rifle Division's regiments began the fight for the embankment on 18 February and overcame it as early as the following day. Later, von Ahlfen explained the defence's lack of success along the line of the embankment in the following manner: 'In January we decided to forego blowing up the railway lines, which ran along four lines, for a variety of reasons. If fortification work had begun near there in time, then it would have been possible to prepare this massive transportation structure for defence.'[17]

One of the key moments in the German descriptions of the initial period of the fighting for Breslau was the 20 February counter-attack in the southern park (now beyond the railway embankment) by the 55th *Volkssturm* Battalion, which had been formed from Hitler Youth[18] teenagers. According to the German version, this attack was a tactical success and brought about the withdrawal of the Soviet forces from the park. Is there any confirmation of this in the Soviet documents? There is. In the war diary of the 218th Rifle Division's 667th Rifle Regiment there is the following notation on this account: 'At 14.00 the enemy, numbering up to two infantry companies in strength and supported by seven self-propelled guns, got into the rear of the first battalion, after four enemy attacks had been beaten off, which was forced to fall back to the railway under the pressure of superior enemy forces and there consolidate.'[19] The participation of armour (assault guns?) in the attack somewhat changes the description of what took place. In all events, the conclusion had been reached about the utility of employing elements of the Hitler Youth in frequent counter-attacks in view of the inability of the teenagers to withstand a prolonged positional struggle.

Having failed to seize the city from the march, the 6th Army command paused to prepare a planned assault. According to the plan prepared by the 6th Army staff by 18 February (confirmed by Konev on 19 February 1945), it was planned to launch the main attack against the city from the south, from the 2.5km front Oltaschin–Sudpark. The shock group would consist of the 273rd and 218th Rifle Divisions and two regiments from the 309th Rifle Division. Artillery, to the tune of 572 guns, was massed along the attack zone. A supporting attack was to be launched along both banks of the Oder for the purpose of eliminating the 'appendix' of the fortress's defensive perimeter which jutted out along the river to the north-west. One may call the plan's pace for the assault 'lightning like', and the shock group was to reach the city centre and advance as far as Stadtgraben as early as the first day. Yet another day was allotted for the assault of the central island, containing the university, post office and telegraph office. V.A. Gluzdovskii's staff found a basis for its optimism in its evaluation of the enemy. According to data presented by the chief of the 6th Army's intelligence section, Colonel Gorchinskii, the strength of the city's garrison was 18,060 men who disposed of 141 guns and 45 tanks and self-propelled guns.[20] The 315th Independent Heavy Artillery Battalion's 280mm mortars were to be transferred south from the northern sector, to the 22nd Rifle Corps' zone, to support the assault. It was planned to be ready to begin the assault by 20 February 1945.

The Soviet divisions at the walls of the capital of Silesia may be described as satisfactorily equipped by the standards of 1945 (see table). The better-equipped divisions were assigned to the shock group.

Table 4.1: The Strength and Availability of Infantry Weapons in the 6th Army's Formations as of 20 February 1945.

Formation	Men	Rifles	Degtyaryov and Shpagin Sub-machine Guns	Machine Guns	
				Light	Heavy
218th Rifle Div.	5,036	2,962	1,542	209	69
309th Rifle Div.	5,084	2,352	1,887	117	48
181st Rifle Div.	4,319	2,198	1,322	159	52
359th Rifle Div.	4,319	2,743	1,482	154	61
273rd Rifle Div.	5,439	2,931	1,687	196	66
294th Rifle Div.	4,358	2,542	1,060	95	34
77th Fortified Area	2,230	1,479	333	98	92

One cannot but note that according to the Table of Organization No. 04/550, which was in force at that time (with changes as of July 1943), a non-Guards rifle division was supposed to have 9,380 rank and file, 6,274 rifles and carbines, 1,048 sub-machine guns, 494 light and 111 heavy machine guns. According to the data presented here, it is quite clear that the 6th Army's divisions, while disposing of approximately half of their authorized strength of officers and men, had sub-machine guns above authorized strength alongside a shortage of heavy and light machine guns. At the same time, this corresponded to the overall concept of the development of the Red Army's infantry. For example, according to the new Table of Organization No. 05/40 of December 1944 (which only a limited number of formations had gone over to in 1945[21]), 11,706 men were to have 3,594 sub-machine guns while retaining the former number of light and heavy machine guns. That is, the presence of 50 per cent of the authorized amount of automatic weapons corresponded approximately to half of the division's strength, while relying on sub-machine guns, a practice which was codified in the table of organization after the war. Moreover, the rifle companies were especially heavy with sub-machine guns. In the 359th Rifle Division the amount of automatic weapons was raised to 50 per cent, not counting machine guns, by removing them from non-combat subunits. In the 273rd Rifle Division's three assault battalions there were 872 men armed with 439 rifles, 424 Shpagin sub-machine guns, 65 Degtyaryov sub-machine guns and 24 heavy machine guns. That is, approximately 50 per cent of the troops were armed with sub-machine guns.

At this time the 6th Army was poorly supplied with armour. Following the departure of the 7th Guards Mechanized Corps, the understrength 349th Guards Heavy Self-Propelled Artillery Regiment would be subordinated to Gluzdovskii's army. On the evening of 19 February 1945 it counted eight combat-ready ISU-152s and six in repair.[22]

Three assault battalions (one for each regiment) were created in each division for attacking in urban conditions. In all, including the 22nd Rifle Corps commander's reserve, the shock group numbered ten assault battalions. An assault battalion was supposed to have the following strength:

a rifle battalion;
two 152mm guns;
two ISU-152s or two B-4 203mm 1931 model guns;
a battery of 76mm guns;
a combat engineer demolition group;

a combat mine/obstacle removal group;

a group of portable flamethrower operators (ROKS);

a group of anti-tank riflemen;

a sniper group;

a sub-machine gun group;

a group with captured *Faustpatronen*.

This composition made it quite possible for an assault battalion to destroy the enemy's firing positions, remove obstacles and minefields and combat the enemy's tanks and self-propelled guns.

We should offer more concerning the combat engineer demolition and mine-clearing groups. The 6th Army's engineer subunits were divided into groups for the storming of Breslau for:

demolition, consisting of three or four combat engineers with 200kg of explosives, and three or four men with ROKS flamethrowers (for making holes in the walls of buildings and fences and clearing passages through barricades);

heavy sapping, consisting of combat engineers with 400kg of explosives, and three or four men with ROKS flamethrowers (in the division commander's reserve for blowing up major structures);

mine clearing, consisting of a section or platoon with mine detectors, probing rods and grapnels, with a supply of explosives (for widening passageways, clearing streets and checking anti-mining activities).

The demolition groups were part of the assault groups, but might be given an independent task.

The Red Army already had considerable experience of urban warfare and Gluzdovskii's staff prepared specially printed instructions (dated 17 February 1945; that is, strictly before the beginning of the assault) for the formations designated for the assault. The instructions recommended creating assault groups for city fighting of the following composition:

a rifle company (60–70 men);

two 203mm guns or SU-152s;

a battery of 76mm guns;

a group with *Faustpatronen*;

a group of combat engineers/demolition men.

As was noted in the 6th Army's instructions, 'The assault groups, through blockading and destroying key targets in urban buildings and structures, secure the advance by the rifle units' combat formations within the city'.[23] Other groups were created for supporting the assault groups: mine clearing and artillery support (by a battery or battalion).

The elaboration as to a company's strength in the guidebook was not superfluous. By 20 February 1945 only a few of the 6th Army's rifle division's companies contained 60–70 men. The average company strength in Gluzdovskii's army was 40–50 men. The 273rd Rifle Division was the strongest in this regard, with its companies averaging 59 men.

The chief weapons for accompanying the infantry in street fighting were the 45mm anti-tank gun and 76mm divisional and regimental guns. Combat experience showed that the 76mm armour-piercing round could penetrate any wall in a common urban building, while also striking the enemy's riflemen firing from it. In general, the divisional artillery of Soviet rifle divisions was employed entirely for firing over open sights, without exception. The 122mm M-30 howitzer, due to its great weight, of course was not very suitable for rolling behind an assault group. However, they were also employed for firing over open sights. These howitzers' shells completely penetrated brick buildings at a distance of 300–400m. The complete destruction of a two or three-storey building was achieved by fifteen to twenty shells.

The 152mm ML-20 gun-howitzer and 203mm B-4 howitzer were employed in street fighting in a traditional manner for the Red Army of 1945. The 152mm and 203mm guns required six to fifteen shells to destroy a three or four-storey building. However, as was noted in materials for the study of the 6th Army's war experience, bringing these guns up for firing over open sights 'involved great difficulties in conditions of street fighting'.[24] Therefore they only employed these guns for destroying particularly solid structures that were resistant to lighter guns and engineer weapons.

On the night of 21/22 February the 6th Army's forces regrouped and occupied their jumping-off positions for the assault on the city. It should be noted that at that moment the 273rd Rifle Division had not yet concentrated completely along the approaches to Breslau and one of its regiments had begun its march from the Streigau area only on 22 February. The 22nd Rifle Corps' combat formations were organized quite traditionally into two echelons, with two rifle regiments in the first line and one in the second (in the case of the 273rd Rifle Division, it was absent). However, a regrouping was also taking place in the enemy camp. Literally a few hours before the start of the Soviet offensive, the Wehl Regiment, made up of Luftwaffe personnel, to the south of Breslau was relieved by the more combat-capable Moor Regiment. Von Ahlfen later admitted: 'The transfer of the Moor Regiment took place at the most critical moment.'

The first assault on Breslau began at 08.00 on 22 February with an artillery preparation lasting two hours and 40 minutes. The start of the assault was heralded by a true hurricane of fire from heavy guns. On 22–23 February the 315th Independent Heavy Artillery Battalion fired off 113 280mm rounds (eight heavy, twenty-four concrete-piercing and eighty-one French grenades[25]) against the Germans' strongpoints in the southern part of the city, at the close range, for guns of such calibre, of 4.5–5km.

The broad Kurassierstrasse became a serious test for the assaulting units in the southern part of Breslau. Fire from machine guns, automatic rifles and *Faustpatronen* prevented the Soviets from crossing it. It was decided to set off two powerful explosive charges in the south-eastern part of Block 569 on the other side of the Kurassierstrasse. At night, under the cover of darkness, combat engineers planted the charges and at 08.00 on 24 February two powerful explosions followed, The block was also set on fire in eight places. Taking advantage of the element of surprise, the infantry and combat engineers threw themselves into the assault. The attackers carried out more demolitions during the attack. As a result, the enemy fled and the 955th Infantry Regiment captured four blocks (582, 581, 578, and 569) north of Kurassierstrasse. Losses for the entire 309th Rifle Division were seventeen men killed and seventy-four wounded.

During this period fire became the attacker's main ally, in the literal sense. Flamethrower operators with special covering groups, consisting of one soldier with a light machine gun and one or two automatic riflemen (apart from the infantry elements operating in this sector), worked from the front against the buildings. The machine gun would suppress the enemy's firing points or even silence them. The automatic riflemen fired on the buildings' windows and basements. The flamethrower operators would move up to the designated target under cover of this and would set the building on fire with a ROKS round. Thus the defenders of the building being attacked either perished or hurriedly fell back.

Aside from the flamethrowers, as early as the end of February the Red Army employed special groups for setting fire to buildings in the enemy's rear in the fight for Breslau. The groups consisted of four or five combat engineers and predominantly operated at night. During the day the groups at the front would discover lanes and passages into the rear and the enemy's firing points. With the onset of darkness, the group, taking with it two bottles of flammable liquid and three grenades per man, would infiltrate behind the enemy and set fire to buildings, forcing the Germans to abandon their positions. However, this method was quite risky, so technical means were later used to set fire to buildings. These were improvised ampoule launchers, which the Soviet combat engineers learned to easily make from the casings of 76mm shells. Such an ampoule launcher (more exactly, a bottle launcher) was developed by Major Novodvorskii's 59th Combat Engineer Brigade and acquired the name 'Novodvorskii's ampoule launcher'. The capsule plug would be unscrewed from a 76mm shell casing and in place of it a steel rod would be driven in and fastened with a steel cylinder (trunnions). The cylinder was fastened with clamps to a supporting plate made from 2mm of iron. Simultaneously, bipods made from steel pipes were fastened to the shell casing with clamps. Such a strong construction enabled them to aim the bottle launcher quite accurately. The bottle with flammable liquid was launched a distance of up to 700–800m by a charge of black powder, which was ignited by a Bickford fuse. They sought to employ these weapons *en masse* for the purpose of causing huge fires in the enemy's immediate rear, which would be impossible to extinguish. Sixty or seventy ampoule launchers, which could launch up to 1,000 bottles during the artillery preparation, would operate in a division's offensive zone.

The effectiveness of setting fire to buildings was so great that in the 309th Rifle Division they even employed captured *Faustpatronen* for launching bottles of flammable liquid into buildings. The detonator would be removed from the *Faustpatrone*'s grenade and a bottle of flammable liquid would be inserted into the cone of the hollow charge of the unit. A shot into a building's window from such a '*faust*' would not cause an explosion, but would start a fire. The weapon's range was 150–200m. The author of this invention is listed in the documents as Master Sergeant Maslennikov, from the 309th Rifle Division's chemical defence company.

There was still one more effective means of fighting, which was the blowing up of positions interfering with the infantry's advance. Heavy demolition groups operated with very powerful explosive charges. For example, during February 1945 Soviet units reached the approaches to Hindenburg Square. A massive barricade, with built-in platforms for artillery and machine guns, blocked one of the streets in the area of Hindenburg Square. The entire street could be enfiladed from the barricade, which prevented the attackers from engaging it with artillery over open sights. Lieutenant Genin's heavy demolition group received orders to blow it up. Following a thorough study of the terrain, Genin decided to approach the barricade through the basements and to then get out through a window into the dead space at the foot of the barricade and to plant his charges. The assignment was accomplished at night, secretly and without losses.

Despite the presence of armour in Breslau, it was employed extremely carefully by the Germans at the beginning of the assault. They threw tanks and self-propelled guns into the fighting in 'exceptional cases' along the most dangerous axes. February also saw the debut of the 'Goliath' tankettes in Breslau. They did not make much of an impression on the Soviet units. As was noted in the army's report on the results of the February fighting, the Germans attempted to employ the tankettes against tanks and self-propelled guns, but they 'did not reach their targets and would run into buildings and telegraph poles and blow themselves up'. Two 'Goliaths' were captured by the Red Army. Nonetheless, there was one example of the successful employment of remote controlled tankettes. At 15.00 on 25 February, in the area of the cemetery on the Lerchenberg Hill (so-called Block 707), the Germans launched the 'Goliaths', two of which were destroyed by artillery fire, while the third tankette reached its target building and destroyed it with an explosion. About forty Red Army soldiers died as a result. By the way, Breslau did not mark the debut of the 'Goliaths' in urban fighting. Before this the tankettes were quite actively employed by the Germans in street fighting during the course of suppressing the Warsaw Uprising.[26] However, this was with only very limited success.

In a number of cases, the fact of burning out buildings did not in and of itself guarantee success. In Block 567 (Habitzstrasse), to the west of Hindenburg Square, the Germans were defending in the basements of almost completely burned-out buildings. During the course of the fighting on 25–26 February the infantry of 309th Rifle Division's assault groups was able to occupy one of the basements under cover of darkness. After this, the work of the combat engineers began. One basement wall after another was blown up by explosive charges weighing from 1kg to 5kg. A charge fastened at the height of half a metre would blow a hole 1.3m high in an 80cm wall, while simultaneously hitting the enemy in the neighbouring basement with the shockwave and ruins. As the buildings were seized, a group of combat engineers moved parallel through the ruin above, blowing up the covering over the heads of the enemy occupying the basements. In all, the combat engineers blew up twenty-two walls in Block 567. Moving from basement to basement by blowing up the walls was also employed by the combat engineers attached to the 309th Rifle Division's 955th Rifle Regiment in the fighting for Block 599 (on the north side of Hindenburg Square). It was necessary to blow up eighteen basement walls here.

Gauleiter Hanke's connections with the powers that be facilitated the arrival in Breslau of additional reinforcements at a critical moment during the first assault. On the night of 24/25 February about twenty heavily-laden Ju-52s arrived from Jüterbog with paratroopers from the 26th Airborne Regiment's 1st Battalion. In fact it is a stretch to call them 'paratroopers', because the regiment was formed from unsuccessful pilots from the Luftwaffe's ground personnel. Moreover, among the 'paratroopers' who had just arrived were quite a few of natives of Silesia and the Sudetenland, and they preferred to fight for the capital of Silesia rather than in Pomerania. Von Ahlfen almost immediately committed the battalion into the fighting, but this was probably under duress, as the 'airborne troops' were clearly lacking in infantry training. These were far from those airborne troops who had landed on Crete[27] and defended Monte Cassino.[28] Later, on the night of 6/7 March, a battalion from a special designation airborne regiment arrived in Breslau.

It's doubtful that the arriving airborne forces had any influence on this, but as the Soviets advanced further toward the city centre the garrison's resistance increased. In a daytime report by the 22nd Rifle Corps, it was noted that 'During 27.2.45 the enemy's resistance in the centre and along the left flank of the corps has sharply increased'.[29] In the 273rd Rifle Division's daytime report for 26 February, alongside the entry on the enemy's increasing resistance, it was noted that 'The fighting in some blocks has become hand to hand, involving the use of knives, bayonets and bricks'. On this day the 273rd Rifle Division lost 65 men killed and 205 wounded, a figure clearly higher than average for the 22nd Rifle Corps as a whole. On this day the comparatively strong 273rd Rifle Division collided with an industrial quarter on the outskirts of Breslau. They reported: 'The map indicates that this sector contains no buildings, when it is actually a complete factory-industrial area.' Moreover, this area did not even have a number on the city map and was classified as an 'unnamed quarter'. Its capture was reported, but in reality they captured only the approaches to this 'mini-Stalingrad'. There's one more detail characterizing this period's fighting: in the 28 February fighting for a building in Block 704, elements of the 273rd Rifle Division's 969th Rifle Regiment fired 400 *Faustpatronen* at the embrasures, windows, attics and basements. At the same time, the division's advance was halted, while the fighting in Blocks 704 and 705 continued for several days. One of the signs of the enemy's increasing resistance was the reduction in the number of prisoners taken. From 24 to 27 February the 22nd Rifle Corps took 169, 209, 168 and 213 prisoners respectively, but on 28 February this figure fell to 64 men, and during the days that followed the number of men captured in a single day did not exceed a few dozen.

The increase in resistance came about due to changing defensive tactics. Earlier the Germans would take up defensive positions on all the floors of the buildings, which led to fatal consequences in the event it was set on fire. It was sufficient to set fire to one storey and the garrison would abandon the entire building (those running away from the fire would bring everyone along with them). Having realized the vulnerability of such a method, the Germans began occupying only the basements, leaving only snipers, observers and soldiers with automatic rifles in the other storeys. In the event the building was set on fire, the core of the garrison remained secure for a long time. Now the main problem for the assault groups was breaking through to the objective through multiple layers of fire, which were laid down by the enemy in front of the forward edge. Various methods were used for this: creating smoke and moving into the attack as soon as possible after the last salvos of the artillery preparation, and even air strikes on the attackers' part (forcing the defenders to take cover).

As the 6th Army's units moved deeper into the labyrinth of Breslau's streets, the estimate by Soviet intelligence of the garrison's strength also grew. As was noted above, on 20 February the strength of the defenders was estimated at 18,060 men. After a week of fighting, by 27 February the estimates had increased more than half again – to 30,960 men.[30] At the same time, the Germans were in no hurry to surrender. In all, during the period from 20 to 28 February 1945, the 6th Army reported the capture of only 730 prisoners, 929 rifles and 74 machine guns.[31]

At the beginning of March the 6th Army's forces were preparing for a new assault on the city. According to Order No. 0022/op from Gluzdovskii's headquarters on 2 March, the main attack toward the centre of the city would be made by the 22nd Rifle Corps (273rd, 218th and 309th Rifle Divisions), while the 74th Rifle Corps was to support its neighbour by securing the flank of the main forces' shock group. The 22nd Rifle Corps' shock group consisted of the 218th and 309th Rifle Divisions, deployed in two echelons (four regiments in the first line). They were to advance along the axis of *Strasse der SA* (Storm Troopers' Street) from Hindenburg Square to the university. The 218th Rifle Division was to be reinforced by an armoured ram of four ISU-152s, three ISU-122s and three T-34s, while the 309th Rifle Division was to be reinforced with four ISU-152s, two ISU-122s and four T-34s. The 273rd Rifle Division was to be pulled out of the industrial 'unnamed quarter' (it was to be turned over to a fortified area's machine-gun battalion) and positioned along a narrowed front on the flank of the shock group.

The troops were ordered to break into the centre of the city as early as the offensive's first day, while also overcoming a water barrier, the so-called 'City Moat'. It was probably expected that after the Germans' first defensive line was overcome that the garrison's resistance would collapse. This estimate of the enemy did not correspond to reality.

At the same time, on 2 March 1945 Konev appealed to Moscow, to Stalin personally, in an 'especially important' coded telegram:

Due to the fact that the city of Breslau is fortified (an old fortress), has large buildings and that the garrison numbers no less than 50,000 men, in order to capture the city as quickly as possible, I request your permission to continuously bomb day and night the city of Breslau, using Golovanov's[32] Long-Range Aviation and heavy bombs.

Breslau was more like a new industrial fortress, with its old fortifications of only third-rate importance. The idea of bombing Breslau with the forces of Long-Range Aviation during the day looked more than doubtful in light of the closeness of the Germans' fighter aviation to the outer encirclement ring. However, the leader did not remain deaf to the appeals by the commander of the First Ukrainian Front. Long-Range Aviation actually did later bomb Breslau, although not every day. It had more than enough targets during the spring of 1945: Danzig, Swinemunde and others.

During the night of 2/3 March the troops in Breslau regrouped and were committed into the fighting as individual assault detachments. At 10.30 on 3 March the artillery began an hour-long bombardment along the 22nd Rifle Corps' front. The 315th Independent Heavy Artillery Battalion also took part in the artillery preparation with its 280mm mortars. Its targets were the strongpoints in the corner buildings in six blocks in the 22nd Rifle Corps' attack zone. Having expended twenty-four concrete-piercing shells, the 315th Independent Heavy Artillery Battalion scored twelve hits. The attack began at 11.30. The FOG flamethrowers demonstrated their usual high effectiveness in street fighting. For example, on 2 March the 218th Rifle Division's 667th Rifle Regiment was given the assignment of taking Block 635. The regiment was reinforced with two ISU-152s, three ISU-122s, one T-34, and twelve portable flamethrowers and artillery. However, the trump card was to be the FOGs. A company of the 25th Flamethrower Battalion set up seventy FOGs, which were aimed at the buildings in the block under attack. On the day of the attack, within seven minutes after the start of the artillery preparation, all the FOGs were ignited and a sea of flame enveloped the entire southern part of the block. Nineteen buildings began to burn immediately. The stunned Germans fell back in panic, the 667th Rifle Regiment's infantrymen advanced behind the wall of fire and by the end of the day had completely occupied Block 635.

Block 604, in which a large enemy garrison was hiding, was covered from the front by a thick and high (3m) wall, which hindered firing on it with artillery over open sights. In turn, the street which this wall came out on was raked with machine-gun fire. On 5 March Lieutenant Klimov's heavy demolition group received orders to collapse the wall. They suppressed a machine-gun nest which was enfilading the street with captured *Faustpatronen*. When the machine gun fell silent, the combat engineers quickly crossed the street and planted five 30kg charges, tying them together with a demolition fuse. Not waiting for the machine-gun nest to 'wake up', the demolition troops fell back into a shelter and detonated the charges. The wall collapsed, enabling the artillerymen to fire on the building behind it.

However, despite the tactical successes, there was as yet not even a hint of a swift breakthrough into the centre of Breslau. The 22nd Rifle Corps' offensive came to a standstill. In the war diary of the 218th Rifle Division's 667th Rifle Regiment it was noted that as they advanced into the depths of the city, 'the enemy is putting up stronger and stronger resistance'. The tenacity of Breslau's defence was noted by many participants in the fighting. Senior Lieutenant Vladimir Filippovich Belik, a company commander in the 22nd Flamethrower Battalion, wrote the following in his diary for 5 March 1945: 'Only a few days in Breslau seems like an eternity. Just in these few days I lost 20 men out of 70, and almost all of them were killed. The cursed Germans fight like those doomed – soldiers, civilians, men, and women. They fight for each building, storey and room.'[33]

Meanwhile, in the fortress the conflict between *Gauleiter* Hanke and General von Ahlfen was growing. One of the reasons for the friction was the need to establish a new airfield within the city. Even before the encirclement ring closed, von Ahlfen saw the possibility of building one to replace Gandau. He considered the so-called Frisian Meadow and the adjoining stadium the most suitable site. Western literature on the subject delicately fails to mention that this sporting venue was called the Hermann Göring[34] Stadium in 1945. Given the *Reichsmarshall*'s build, this was a very subtle dig. Actually, on a map of the highly built-up area of Breslau, this area appears appealing. But this is only at first glance. The Frisian Meadow is located practically on the outskirts of the city, although separated from the territory controlled by the Soviet forces by a river. An airfield here risked coming under fire not only from artillery, but from mortars as well. Yet another shortcoming of the grass landing strip was the prospect of employing it with the onset of spring when the ground would be wet.

Apropos of this, Fritz Morzik, in his study of the Luftwaffe's air bridges, is quite sceptical of the possibilities of using the Frisian Meadow. He writes that 'as a result of natural barriers blocking the approach for landings and take-offs, it [the Frisian Meadow] could be used only in emergencies and by the most experienced pilots'.[35]

An alternative to the stadium in honour of 'Fat Hermann' was the long and straight *Kaiserstrasse*, which was closer to the city centre. This would make it possible to build a landing strip about 1,300m long. However, in order to transform the street into an airfield it would be necessary to remove the streetlights and the trolley car cables. Moreover, it would also be necessary to raze a Lutheran church to ensure safe landings. It is sometimes maintained that it was necessary to raze several churches, but there was only one on the *Kaiserstrasse*, according to a 1941 map of Breslau. The choice of a street in the northern part of the city for an airfield, which was protected by the I-Werk concrete fort, but not on the outskirts, seems quite rational. The *Kaiserstrasse* also began near a bridge over the Oder, which provided a landmark for approaching aircraft, although the design of the bridge itself excluded its use as an extension of the landing strip. Hanke received permission from Berlin to build an airfield within the city from Hitler personally. Von Ahlfen was to supply the *Gauleiter* with explosives and specialists.

On the evening of 5 March 1945 the new commandant of the fortress, Lieutenant General Hermann Niehoff, arrived in Breslau by plane. From the formal point of view, he was a much more impressive figure than von Ahlfen. First of all, Niehoff had experience of the Eastern Front dating back to June 1941, as well as the quite lengthy and intensive experience of commanding an infantry division in Ukraine during the winter of 1943/1944, including 'the Hube Pocket'. I should remind the reader that von Ahlfen became a general only before his appointment as commandant of Breslau, and before this he was only an engineer colonel. Secondly, Niehoff received the Knight's Cross in the summer of 1944 and at the time of his appointment to Breslau, on 5 March, he received the Swords to it. Being of the same generation as von Ahlfen (both were born in 1897) and also having started out as a colonel in 1939, Niehoff was clearly advancing along the career ladder more successfully.

Not being constrained in his evaluation of his comrades while in Soviet captivity, General Niehoff raised the veil of secrecy over his appointment:

> In the Seventeenth Army, to which I was subordinated, they pointed out to me as the reason for changing the fortress command the unsuitability of my predecessor, Major General von Ahlfen. The latter was an engineer officer who had recently received the rank of major general, and who lacked sufficient military knowledge. Besides this, he was reproached for his insufficient ability to control himself and his tendency to excessive drinking.[36]

The tendency to drown one's sorrows with schnapps adds some colour to this simple comparison of service records. In light of what Niehoff said, the image of von Ahlfen as an honest old veteran harried by a despotic Nazi fades somewhat. The conflict with *Gauleiter* Hanke over the airfield was evidently of secondary importance. The army group command, in a moment of relative stability, found and appointed a more suitable commander to lead the large garrison, and that's all.

Upon his arrival, Niehoff immediately noted the serious shortcomings in the city's defence. First of all, the Moor Regiment and the 609th Infantry Division's regiments, which were defending along the southern defensive sector, had not been relieved or replaced with fresh or better units. They only received reinforcements from reserve units. Secondly, the defence was being waged in contravention of standard Wehrmacht procedure. While in Soviet captivity, Niehoff painted the following picture: 'No shock reserves had been allotted for counter-attacks, and when the enemy penetrated our lines the

German command limited itself to simply withdrawing, which was a quite short-sighted measure, pregnant with fatal consequences in the near future.'[37] Counter-attacks and counterblows were the backbone of German defensive tactics during the Second World War. Oversights in the organization of the defence meant there was a danger of Breslau's defenders being split up into three parts by the continuing Soviet offensive from the south into the city centre.

Beginning on 5 March the Germans began to carry out energetic measures for reconstructing Breslau's defence. First of all, the Moor Regiment, which had been worn out in the fighting, was relieved from the southern defensive sector and replaced by the fresh SS Besselein Regiment. The Moor Regiment was transferred to the quieter, for the moment, western sector of the fortress's front. Secondly, reserves were created in the immediate vicinity of the front line, through the ruthless denuding of the first line. During his interrogation in Soviet captivity, Niehoff explained his decision as follows: 'During the enemy's offensive, the outcome of the fighting did not depend whether or not the front line was completely manned. The more people on the front line the more there were killed by the enemy's powerful fire.'

At night these reserves were employed for strengthening the first line and preventing enemy infiltration through it. During the day, they would undertake a counter-attack in the event of an offensive. Fortress reserves were also created in Breslau from two well-trained battalions which the commandant could quickly transfer to the threatened sector in two motorized columns. Simultaneously, these two battalions, not being tied down on the front line, had the opportunity to undergo intensive training and enjoy proper rest. The reserve battalions were reinforced, including by pulling worn-out but experienced subunits from the front line.

A second line was being built immediately behind the first one, to prevent the rapid exploitation of any breakthrough. The *Volkssturm* was mobilized to work on this line, and in certain cases engineer units. The elderly *Volkssturm* troops were not suitable for the harsh conditions of defending the first line, but were able to hold up the Soviet breakthrough elements until the reserves arrived. The *Volkssturm* troops worked on the second line at night and during the day rested at their positions, being ready to give battle in critical situations. Here, along the second line, was the main part of the infantry's heavy weaponry, which also kept the *Volkssturm* from running away under the first attack.

In general, ideas about manoeuvre defence, which at first seem strange in urban circumstances, permeated all Niehoff's measures. Pulling back into the reserve from the first line, away from attack by Soviet artillery, affected not only people, but heavy weapons as well:

> I only attached part of both infantry weapons and artillery to the infantry. In this case I operated according to the principle that 'The reserves decide the outcome of the fighting'. I had the main mass of heavy infantry weapons (which was also supported by motor vehicles for rapid movement) at my disposal and could transfer it, depending upon need, to the sector of the Russians' main attack.[38]

75mm 1eIG18 light infantry guns and mortars provided support for the defending infantry. In urban conditions their undoubted advantage was that they were capable of plunging fire over buildings with the shot barely being heard. Light machine guns were mostly employed and at first heavy machine guns were used without a mount. Thus it was easy to shift one's position. Heavy machine guns retained their importance only in open areas.

Anti-tank defence was supported by the forces of the units occupying the defence and relied on anti-tank guns, mines and *Faustpatronen*. Besides this, the commandant's reserve contained a mobile group consisting of the following:

1) 'Armoured Group Retter';
2) two platoons of *Faustpatrone* troops;
3) several batteries of various types of guns, including anti-aircraft.

'Armoured Group Retter' at that moment disposed of several self-propelled guns of various types. Among the latter Niehoff especially noted during his interrogation 'two StuG IV-type modern tank destroyers with long barrels'. The comparison of this statement with other eyewitness accounts forces us to draw the conclusion that we are not speaking here of the StuG IV, but about the *Panzerjäger* IV,[39] with a 75mm gun with a barrel length similar to that on a Panther tank.

A group of *Faustpatrone* troops consisted of young men on bicycles, each of whom carried two *Faustpatronen* each. There were similar groups, for example, around Berlin. During his interrogation, Niehoff spoke in ecstatic terms about this decision: 'I regretted that the overall shortage of men did not allow me to form an even larger number of such special units. I recommend them as an excellent combat weapon in a similar situation.'[40]

According to Niehoff's orders, the main mass of the fortress's artillery remaining in line (three–four battalions) was concentrated in the city centre for the purpose of guaranteeing all-round fire of the defence's entire perimeter. Lieutenant Colonel Urbatis, the fortress's artillery chief, commanded this centralized group. This distribution enabled the defenders to concentrate barrage fire in front of any defensive sector in the event of a Soviet attack, thus mitigating the factor of surprise. On the other hand, the location in the city centre limited the fortress artillery's opportunities and practically excluded its employment against Soviet artillery. In Soviet documents, attention was paid to the fact that the Breslau garrison devoted practically no attention to counterbattery fire. Only in rare instances were the Germans' artillery batteries moved up to previously-prepared positions closer to the front line for firing on important targets. A restraining factor was also the shortage of ammunition and of communications equipment, most of all radio.

The German 150mm heavy infantry guns (the 15cm sIG33) were an ideal weapon for employing in the city for direct infantry support. Their ability to carry out plunging fire over buildings, their high degree of accuracy and the 150mm shell's great penetrating power made them very effective. However, there were only a few of them in Breslau and little ammunition for them. As of 24 March, the Breslau fortress had fifteen sIG33 guns, with a unit of fire of only 300 rounds, and thirty-three leIG18s with a unit of fire of 1,500 rounds (2,500 rounds, according to other data).[41]

Gauleiter Hanke took advantage of his connections with the Third Reich's leadership to secure precisely these artillery systems for the Breslau garrison. Heavy infantry guns would not fit into the Ju-52 transports so was decided to deliver them in transport gliders. Despite the overall collapse of control in the Third Reich, the *Führer*'s personal intervention caused the necessary levers of power to turn. The transport gliders, with eight sIG33s, ammunition and a battalion of artillerymen, nevertheless took off. However, only one glider made it to the fortress with one gun and its crew, while the remainder were shot down. This saved no small number of men in Gluzdovskii's army.

Here we cannot but emphasize the poor thinking behind the fortress idea by the German command as a whole, although there had been a great deal of time for this since the appearance of Directive No. 11 in March 1944. The selection of the most suitable artillery systems for urban warfare and the priority supply of the fortress garrisons with them were not carried out. Supplies for precisely this type of gun had not been accumulated.

In summing up the evaluation of the qualitative composition and role of the artillery in the struggle for the Breslau fortress, it is expedient to present data on the availability of ammunition for the various artillery systems in the city (unfortunately, there are no figures for the earlier dates).

Table 4.2: The Availability of Artillery Ammunition in Breslau on 24 March 1945.

Artillery Type	*Availability of Ammunition as of 24 March 1945*[42]
7.5cm 1eIG18	19.9 tonnes (2,500 rounds)
KWK42 SprGr (Panther gun, high-explosive fragmentation shell)	1.4 tonnes (2,500 rounds)
15cm sIG33	13.5 tonnes (300 rounds)
KWK42 PzGr (Panther gun, BB shell)	12.2 tonnes (635 rounds)
10.5cm 1eFH18 (105mm field howitzer)	71.3 tonnes (1,720 rounds)
1KH 290 (r) (Soviet 1927 model 76.2 regimental gun)	28.7 tonnes (2,520 rounds)
15cm sFH18 (150mm field gun)	20.3 tonnes (370 rounds)
K.H. 390 (r) (Soviet 1931 model A-19 122mm gun)	18.7 tonnes (350 rounds)
21cm Mrs (210mm howitzer)	1.5 tonnes (10 rounds)
F.H. 349 (j), (probably a mistaken entry; actually 249 (j)	0.8 tonnes (67 rounds)
sFH 396 (r) (Soviet 1938 model M-30 122mm howitzer)	0.3 tonnes (9 rounds)
2cm Flak (20mm anti-aircraft cannon)	178 tonnes (356,000 rounds)
7.5cm Pak SprGr. (PAK-40 high-explosive fragmentation shell)	6.0 tonnes (485 rounds)
3.7cm Flak (37mm anti-aircraft cannon)	5.2 tonnes (2,540 rounds)
7.5cm Pak PzGr (PAK-40 armour-piercing shell)	0.9 tonnes (58 rounds)
8.8cm Flak (88mm anti-aircraft gun)	265 tonnes (14,324 rounds)
7.5cm KWK 40 SprGr (75mm gun Panzer IV and StuG (high-explosive fragmentation shells	2.2 tonnes (178 rounds)
FK16 nA (1934 model 75mm field gun)	0.35 tonnes (29 rounds)
7.5cm KWK 40 PzGr (75mm gun for Panzer IV and StuG, armour-piercing shells	2.9 tonnes (189 rounds)

It is clear that the garrison only had an abundance of rounds for all types of anti-aircraft guns. At the same time, the 88mm anti-aircraft gun's capabilities in urban warfare were very limited. They sought to hide them in basements and use them against tanks, but with limited success. 20mm automatic anti-aircraft guns were more widely employed. Moreover, the clumsy quadruple *'Vierling'*[43] platforms were taken apart with single 20mm guns placed on improvised mounts.

Simultaneously, worthy of attention is the fact that by 24 March only an insignificant number of rounds for the 75mm anti-tank guns and for the 75mm long-barrelled gun for assault guns and Panzer IV tanks (they were not interchangeable) remained in Breslau. One may say that there were no shells for 210mm howitzers, which were the Wehrmacht's mainstay throughout the entire war. There was also a limited number of shells for the sFH18 150mm field howitzer, another mainstay of the German artillery. One should also note that what was said above about the 75mm 1eIG18 is inapplicable to the Soviet 1927 model 76.2mm field regimental gun, although they formally belonged to the same class. The Soviet gun was not designed for plunging fire and could not fire over buildings.

Against the background of the measures undertaken by the fortress's new commandant, the assault on Breslau by Soviet forces continued. On 9 March the target of the 315th Independent Heavy Artillery Battalion's 280mm guns once again became the corner buildings in the blocks in the 22nd Rifle Corps' offensive zone, in the basements of which the enemy's firing positions were located. Thirty-six concrete-piercing rounds were expended, with seventeen hits observed. Moreover, fire against Block 622 was corrected with the aid of an observation balloon (as noted in the 315th Independent Heavy Artillery Battalion's war diary, this 'was the first time in the battalion's experience'). Taking into account the proximity of Army Group Centre's airbases, the launching of an observation balloon over Breslau was an undertaking not without danger and fighters could have appeared over the city at any moment. The fire correction yielded positive results, as the explosions of the 280mm shells could be seen clearly from the observation balloon.

Individual positions interfering with the advance were destroyed by heavy demolition groups. For example, on 11–12 March a church in Block 593 (on the *Hohenzollernstrasse*, running north toward Hindenburg Square) became an obstacle for the forward advance of the 309th Rifle Division. Strongpoints in the nearby buildings covered the approaches to the church. A heavy demolition group, under the command of Lieutenant Klimov, received orders to blow it up. The decision was made to operate at night and during the day to carefully reconnoitre the terrain and to study the object of the attack. Having crept up to the buildings near the church under cover of darkness, the combat engineers set them on fire simultaneously in several places. The garrisons began to fall back, returning fire. Taking advantage of the enemy's confusion, the demolition troops crept up to the church and 540kg of explosives were planted, after which the combat engineers returned to their jumping-off position. A large part of the church was destroyed by the explosion and the garrison wiped out. The infantry attacked and on 13 March occupied the entire block.

Technical weapons were also employed. On 11 March, in Block 575, the attacking elements of the 359th Rifle Division encountered stubborn enemy resistance in the power station. A 'Galitskii-type' cart was employed to blow up the building with a 100kg explosive charge. They pushed the cart as far as the wall of the power station with six poles and blew it up. Without allowing the enemy to recover, the assault group immediately broke into the hole.

However, against the backdrop of these successes, the measures for improving the defence's organization taken by the new commandant began to have an effect. If in the first days it was sufficient for a Soviet assault group to break into a building for the garrison to abandon it, now at the end of February and beginning of March the Germans would continue to resist, even after the capture of the greater part of the building by Soviet infantry. Defensive activity also increased. In a report on the 6th Army' combat experience of 15 March 1945, the following was noted: 'It has been noted lately that the enemy has begun to frequently carry out counter-attacks, which sharply reduces the pace of advance of our combat formations.'[44] The counter-attacks were conducted by groups ranging from fifty men to a company or battalion in strength. The Germans' more active employment of *Faustpatronen* was simultaneously noted.

Aside from the overall increased organization and stubbornness of the defence, it also began to become modernized and perfected. General Niehoff immediately noted the problem of the fires that undermined the fortress's defence. Later, during interrogation, he wrote: '... the greatest losses and damage were the consequence not so much of the explosions [of bombs and shells, A.I.], as the fires that resulted from them.'[45] A countermeasure was the ruthless clearing of the buildings of all flammable objects, under the slogan of 'Set it on fire, so as not to burn up yourself'. Moreover, this concerned not only the buildings adjacent to the front line, but in the centre of Breslau as a whole. The civilian population was conscripted into the work to clear the buildings of furniture and other flammable materials.

Passive measures were also adopted against fires. The cleared rooms were sprinkled with sand and a bucket of sand was left in them. Hand-held fire extinguishers and 'Minimax' industrial container mounts were used most often. These means were employed not only for putting out a fire that had just started. A. Vasil'chenko cites this fact: 'General Niehoff decided to consult with one of the professors at Breslau Technical University. The professor, in turn, recommended that the general employ for extinguishing fires the one chemical substance that was kept in abundance in large containers in the northern part of the city.'[46] We are most likely speaking here of tetrachloride methane. The Hitler Youth began to pack up this substance in beer bottles and deliver them to the front line for pouring on fires. These measures significantly reduced the danger of fires for the Breslau garrison.

As a result, under the new commandant, in the second half of March the nature of the struggle for Breslau changed radically. The garrison's surviving soldiers and officers had acquired experience of street fighting and, under the leadership of the experienced General Niehoff, began to adapt themselves to and attempt to counter the Red Army's tactics. For example, the Germans began to configure for defence the blocks' structures which were enclosed by the buildings facing the street against artillery firing over open sights and '*Andryushas*' (M-30[47] rocket-propelled artillery). The fire system began to be based not on machine guns emplaced in the corners of buildings, but on machine guns moved back 40–50m into the block. This enabled them to rake both the street and the buildings occupied by the attackers with fire. Fire from flanking machine guns was duplicated by frontal fire from within the block.

If one could formalize the German defence plan, then it appeared as follows. The buildings located directly along the front line were set on fire so that only the walls remained. The next row of buildings was outfitted as the actual forward edge of the defence. For this the basement was prepared as a strongpoint and fortified. The entrance into the basement was from the courtyard in the rear. Further on, all the furniture of the rooms, apartments and offices in these buildings were set on fire. After this, the walls of the buildings were carefully blown up so that their ruins covered the basement, but not so that its roof collapsed. A basement covered with debris from above became more resilient to bombardment from guns and mortars. According to the Soviet side's observations, such firing positions were reinforced by covering them with bricks and placing railway sleepers and beams on them. At the same time, false embrasures were built, while the real ones were carefully camouflaged. Overall, more attention began to be paid to camouflage:

uniforms, helmets and camouflage nets adapted to the colour of the terrain were more actively employed by the Germans.

The next series of buildings behind the consciously destroyed ones, on the contrary, remained intact, with observation posts and firing points established in them. Yet another method of defending entire buildings became the placing of the embrasures of the firing points in the rooms' internal walls. This narrowed the sector of fire, but also reduced the defenders' vulnerability to artillery fire. We should add that firing points in depth made it harder to spot the muzzle flash.

The advantages of such a defensive organization are obvious. First of all, the burnt-out buildings shielded the actual forward line from observation, including while it was being constructed. Secondly, the seizure of these blackened skeletons did not bestow any advantage on the attacker: they were raked with fire from deeper in the block and easily collapsed under fire, or were even deliberately blown up by mines left in them. Aircraft bombs, 300–400kg explosive charges, or a pair of containers with either hydrogen, acetylene or oxygen were employed as mines. The detonation of the containers was carried out by a special intermediate charge. They hid the mines under the mountains of charcoal and trash typical of basements. The effect of the explosion was impressive: a six-storey building folded up in seconds.

Of course, there were few volunteers ready to risk sitting next to such a mine under fire. Explosives or an acetylene container could increase the effect of a hit by a Soviet shell several times. Such a method was suitable only for deliberately abandoned positions. However, it was also necessary to hold the false forward edge, if only with weak forces. Correspondingly, containers of explosives were only planted in some tactically suitable buildings. Following the abandonment of the false forward edge, the 'ghost' buildings without mines were bombarded by artillery and *Faustpatronen*, as the Germans sought to collapse them on the attacking groups. Overcoming a series of 'ghost' buildings forced them to battle the enemy's previously unobserved fire system, which combined squat pillboxes in destroyed buildings and entire buildings towering over them. Later during interrogation, Niehoff, the commandant of Breslau, rated this new plan highly: 'This arrangement greatly justified itself. The soldiers felt invulnerable in positions outfitted in the described manner.' One should note that Niehoff was not the sole inventor of the tactics of the garrison's actions. For example, in the 22nd Rifle Corps' report for 28 February, it was noted that 'part of the buildings are being mined and have been prepared for demolition' by the enemy 'with the aid of powerful mines'.[48] That is, the idea of blowing up buildings with mines appeared at least a week before the new commandant's arrival, but Niehoff may be credited with establishing the overall organization of the defence and combining the methods employed into an integrated system.

Niehoff's innovations involving the return to the practice of defending through counter-attacks was noted by the Soviet command. In the evaluation of the enemy contained in the 6th Army's war diary for March 1945, it was noted that in the event of seizing a 'bridgehead' in a block, the Germans 'tried to prevent the group from spreading through the building and tried to throw it back with an unexpected counter-attack'. This forced the Soviets to reinforce the assault group with a consolidation group with light machine guns.

Simultaneously, the shortcomings in the tactics employed by the 6th Army's forces began to manifest themselves in the fighting. The employment of 300mm '*Andryushas*' along the entire length of the block led to the partial destruction of the building that the assault group was trying to break into. This deprived the attackers of a foothold in it and facilitated the destruction of the buildings under attack by *Faustpatrone* rounds. The employment of '*Andryushas*' also hindered infantry weapons fire in support of the attack. The riflemen would end up too close to the explosions of the '*Andryushas*' and, as they delicately wrote in one of the reports, 'there were incidents of losses among the rank and file'. At the same time, the '*Andryushas*' were not all-destroying annihilators: when the rocket-powered shells hit the buildings' first and second storeys, the garrison in the basement nevertheless retained its combat capability and was in shape to fire.

SN-42 steel breastplates somewhat disappointed the Soviet troops during the street fighting for Breslau. As was noted in the 309th Rifle Division's report, they could be penetrated, often fatally for the wearer, by rifles, machine guns and 'automatic rifles of a new design' (*Sturmgewehren*), even from a range of 250–300m. In the 273rd Rifle Division's 971st and 967th Rifle Regiments, they conducted an experiment upon receiving the breastplates: they hung up the armour and fired at it with a TT[49] from a distance of 15m. The breastplate was penetrated. The soldiers began to treat the weighty 'armour' with scorn, although it nonetheless provided protection against fragments and pistol rounds (the 9mm German rounds were less powerful than the 7.62mm TT rounds), and they recommended wearing it in urban conditions for defence against brick and concrete fragments. The creators of the SN-42 never claimed that it provided protection against rifle rounds.

Continuing the theme of protective measures, one may note that the extra mesh armour fitted on Soviet tanks and self-propelled guns, despite all the doubt as to its effectiveness (experiments on the testing range did not confirm any benefit from the shields), did not work badly as a psychological tool. In a report on the employment of armour in Breslau, it was noted: '*Faustpatrone* troops fight our tanks from basement or semi-basement rooms. Typically, the *Faustpatrone* troops fire on our self-propelled guns with mesh side armour from the second or third floor, aiming at the self-propelled gun's upper armour.'[50] That is, the *Faustpatrone* troops were not aware of the real effectiveness of their weapons and, seeing in their sights the shields on the armoured vehicles, believed that the shot would be ineffective and sought another angle. In the chaos of the Third Reich, if they did carry out tests on the effectiveness of the *Faustpatronen* against such armour (the author is not aware of any such tests), then the results of these tests were not transmitted to the weapon's ultimate users.

The new defensive methods were inculcated gradually, but manifested themselves as early as the middle of March. Lieutenant V.F. Belik, who was mentioned earlier, wrote in his diary on 11 March 1945 that 'uninterrupted fighting is going on and we have advanced only two buildings in three days, while many people have died. We seized the first storey and the enemy sits in the basement; we seize the basement and he's sitting above us and throwing hand grenades at us. On 8 March the enemy blew up a building, the first storey of which our troops had captured. There were a lot of casualties, including six of my men wounded.'[51]

During nearly a month of street fighting the 6th Army's forces suffered significant losses among the rank and file. The strength of the divisions' rifle companies varied from twenty to forty men. This forced Gluzdovskii to halt the assault. The 6th Army went over to the defensive on 20 March. The rifle battalions were pulled back into the rear in turns, in order to refit and prepare for a new attack. The pause was also used to reconnoitre the enemy's defensive positions.

Table 4.3: The Strength of the 6th Army's Rank and File on 20 March 1945.

Division	Rifle Division Strength	Rifle Regiment Strength	Average Strength of a Rifle Company
218th Rifle	3,339	526–586	31
273rd Rifle	3,569	576–696	20
309th Rifle	4,161	719–729	33
181st Rifle	3,347	522–769	33
359th Rifle	3,915	800–806	32
294th Rifle	3,298	465–645	37

The Attack from the North

The slow advance through the city blocks in the southern part of Breslau forced the Soviet command to search for alternatives. The attempt to break into the centre of Breslau from the north along the railway line was one of them.

The 294th Rifle Division and two companies from the 77th Fortified Area's 421st Machine Gun Battalion, as well as a battalion from the army reserve regiment, were drawn into the offensive. The fresh 87th Guards Heavy Tank Regiment, consisting of fifteen IS-2s[52] (which had been part of the *front* reserve) was to serve as the tank ram for the new offensive. The two companies from the fortified area's machine gun battalion were supposed to support three SU-76 self-propelled guns from the 294th Rifle Division's 350th Independent Self-Propelled Artillery Battalion. To judge from this, the Soviet command counted on overthrowing the defence by a powerful tank attack with the heavy IS-2s.

The offensive began at 09.40–10.00 on 9 March. According to the war diary of the 294th Rifle Division's 857th Rifle Regiment, the tanks being delayed on the southern outskirts of Petersdorf at the start of the attack had a negative effect on the course of the fighting. As a result, the infantry, met with fire, hit the dirt and the element of surprise was lost. The IS tanks subsequently advanced, but along the enemy's forward line near Oswitz station they encountered a broad anti-tank ditch across the road. At the same time, the March rains and the overall swampy terrain to the north of Breslau restricted the tanks to the roads. As a result, the 294th Rifle Division did not advance on the offensive's first day. The 77th Fortified Area's 421st Machine Gun Battalion was only able to advance 300m, losing ten men killed and fourteen wounded.

On the following day an attempt was made to resume the offensive along the railway. However, according to the new plan, it was decided to direct the IS tanks around and through the village of Weide, along the bank of the river of the same name, to get into the rear of the Germans at Oswitz station. The 294th Rifle Division's infantry managed to get to within 60–100m of the enemy's positions, but any further advance was halted by anti-personnel minefields, heavy fire from infantry weapons, mortars and *Faustpatronen* (which had come to replace artillery for the Germans even in field conditions). The tanks of the 87th Guards Heavy Tank Regiment, due to the soggy soil, were forced to move along the road and once again came up against the anti-tank ditch across it.

Attempts to move the tanks off the road led to the heavy vehicles getting stuck in the bogs and mud. The roads, in turn, were blocked by obstacles and anti-tank ditches, through which, as was noted in the report by the 6th Army's administration for armoured and mechanized troops, 'the combat engineers were unable to clear passages for the tanks'.[53] As of the evening of 14 March, six IS-2s were still in line and another four under repair in the 87th Guards Heavy Tank Regiment. The shock capabilities of the IS regiment had been seriously undermined as the result of the attempt to break through from the north.

Here I will allow myself to digress somewhat from the main course of the story. A feature of the war was the reconnaissance missions similar to E. Kazakevich's[54] *The Star*, although on a smaller scale. Moreover, the scouts could not count on the population's support on German territory. In the 77th Fortified Area's war diary there is the following entry: 'The four-man scouting party sent out by a rifle battalion from the 173rd Army Replacement Rifle Regiment on 13.03.45 in the direction of Weidebrueck did not return to its unit.' What became of these men only a few weeks before victory? How did they die? This will most likely remain a mystery.

At the same time, one should note that in 1945 deserters became a valuable source of information for the intelligence services. One cannot say, of course, that they arrived in a continuous stream, but on the night of 14/15 March three Germans crossed the lines and gave themselves up in the 421st Machine Gun Battalion's sector.

The Struggle Continues

On 20 March the assault on Breslau was halted, although the Soviet command had in no way given up on the idea of crushing the garrison's resistance. A comparatively large party of 1,460 reinforcements arrived. Gluzdovskii ordered that they be put into the ranks according to the tasks for the assault on the city. In order to create combat-capable assault units, alongside the reinforcements, which included battle-hardened soldiers with experience of fighting in Breslau, each regiment in the divisions pulled a rifle battalion apiece out of the fighting. The remaining battalion occupied the front and operated in small groups with local missions.

As before, the main attack was to be launched from the south toward the city centre by the forces of the 22nd Rifle Corps, reinforced with the 25th Heavy Calibre Howitzer Brigade, the 40th and 315th Independent Heavy Calibre Artillery Battalions, two brigades of RS M-31s, and the 349th Self-Propelled Artillery Regiment, with ISU-152s. The 309th and 218th Rifle

Divisions were supposed to move shoulder to shoulder along the direction of the main attack along *Strasse der SA* and break through to Breslau's main train station, which was only a few blocks away. The 273rd Rifle Division was to launch a supporting attack on the gas factory near the city's freight depot. The 74th Rifle Corps was also given the supporting task of cutting the south-western corner of the front in Breslau. The start of the new assault on the fortress was initially set for the morning of 24 March, but the late arrival of trains with ammunition forced them to postpone it to the 25th. The engineer troops were assigned to prepare '1,000 bottles of flammable liquid for distance launching', 40 'tankette-torpedoes' and ten 'mine-torpedoes'. In March 1945 Soviet combat engineers from the 62nd Combat Engineer Brigade discovered 'Goliaths' ('tankette-torpedoes') in the captured German artillery depots in Liegnitz. It was these that they decided to employ in the latest stage of the fighting for Breslau. The combat engineers of the 62nd Combat Engineer Brigade studied the new equipment for several days, taking note of the ease of guiding the tankette. The 'mine-torpedoes' mentioned in the same breath as the 'Goliaths' were M-13 rocket-powered shells with a wooden body filled with explosives placed over them.

The artillery preparation for the new assault began at 09.00 on 25 March and continued for three hours. The 'Goliaths' were not put into action on the offensive's first day. They limited themselves to traditional weapons. The 315th Independent Heavy Calibre Artillery Battalion's 280mm Br-5s methodically fired on the corner buildings in Blocks 602, 614 and 619, in the 309th Rifle Division's attack sector. Seventeen concrete-piercing shells were fired at each block and direct hits were scored. This secured the breakthrough of the 309th Rifle Division's infantry into these three blocks, but they were unable to advance further. For example, the 309th Rifle Division's 955th Rifle Regiment was assaulting Block 591. Following the shifting of the artillery fire to the rear, the 'chemists' showered the street with smoke grenades. The enemy opened fire on the smokescreen. Yet another smokescreen was created along another flank within 5–7 minutes. The Germans shifted their fire to the new source of smoke. Within another couple of minutes the firing died down. At that moment the flamethrower operators attacked the firing points that had revealed themselves. The new smokescreen covered the attack and the assault groups broke into a large building without losses and began a grenade battle within it. The neighbouring 218th Rifle Division, despite the support of the 40th Independent Heavy Calibre Battalion, also only managed to achieve a breakthrough into the blocks along the front line. The following day failed to bring decisive success. The fighting was going on within the blocks and the advance was measured in tens of metres. It was now necessary to employ smokescreens not only for breaking through, but for covering the evacuation of the wounded. On 26 March the assault group of the 218th Rifle Division's 372nd Rifle Regiment ended up being blockaded from three sides in an occupied building in Block 630 and was subjected to several counter-attacks. The enemy's fire made it impossible to bring up ammunition and to evacuate the wounded, but the 'chemists' kept the smokescreens up for six hours, which enabled them to bring up food and ammunition and to carry out twenty-eight wounded men. Five hundred smoke grenades and a hundred smoke charges were expended.

The hour of the captured 'tankette-torpedoes' came two days after the beginning of the new assault. On 27 March the combat engineers launched five 'Goliaths' in the 309th and 218th Rifle Divisions' sectors. Two tankettes hit a building in Block 592 and two a building next to Block 695. The attack on the following day was much less successful, when the 'Goliaths' had lost the element of surprise. The combat engineers launched six tankettes in the 218th and 309th Rifle Divisions' attack zones, of which only one reached its target, blowing up the corner building in Block 630. The remainder were knocked out by heavy enemy fire, including from *Faustpatronen*. Moreover, there were casualties among the Soviet combat engineers, because the tanks were knocked out and exploded not far from their jumping-off positions. According to the results of employing 'tankette-torpedoes', it was concluded that there was a need to mask the sound of their engines with something.

The new German tactics were employed with unpleasant regularity. In the 22nd Rifle Corps' daytime report for 28 March, it was noted that 'A group of soldiers from the 957th Rifle Regiment, which was operating in the southern corner of Block 592, suffered losses as the result of the enemy blowing up the building and fell back to the northern part of Block 593 [with the church that had been demolished earlier, A.I.]'.

In March 1945 the assaulting troops continued to improve their incendiary devices. Aside from the previously-mentioned Novodvorskii bottle thrower made from a 76mm shell casing, other innovations included a bottle launcher made from an anti-tank rifle and a rifle mortar for firing thermite globes. The former was made from a 76mm shell casing fitted around the anti-tank rifle's muzzle brake and the bottle was propelled by a blank 14.5mm round with a reduced powder charge. The range was up to 250–300m. The inventor was the chief of the 359th Rifle Division's chemical service, Captain Kuz'min. The rifle grenade launcher for thermite globes and bottles was invented by the chemical chief of the 309th Rifle Division's 955th Rifle Regiment, Captain Fomin. The range was about 150m. In order to evaluate the scale of employment of incendiary devices in Breslau during this period it is expedient to cite data on ammunition expenditure. During March 1945 940 bottles of flammable liquid were expended, 9,235 'Molotov cocktails' and 1,656 thermite globes. The bottles of flammable liquid were used less, although they were rated more highly by the troops than the other types.

Shifting the Direction of Attack

The forty-day assault on Breslau from the south continued and gradually led to the concentration of a significant part of the garrison in the city's southern part and to increased resistance and the creation of a deeply-echeloned defence in the urban area. This forced Gluzdovskii to shift the direction of the main attack for the new assault. It was planned to launch an attack not from the south, but from the west. The Lowe River facing the western part of the city was the buttress of the garrison's defence and Breslau's suburbs, which had been transferred into strongpoints and centres of resistance. However, this defensive system was clearly weaker and was defended by fewer men than was the central part of the city.

The army commander decided to launch the main attack with the 74th Rifle Corps' three divisions from the Schmidtfeld area to the east. In general, the mission of the 6th Army's forces was 'To cut off the western group of enemy forces through a vigorous offensive to the east and to destroy it in detail'.[55] It was decided to launch a supporting attack on the 22nd Rifle Corps' left flank to the north, along the railway in the direction of the factories listed as Sites 52 and 63 (one of them was the 'Hydrometre' mechanical factory). As opposed to the previous plans which supposed a breakthrough to the centre of the city, the plan for the new offensive laid out the mission of 'destroying the enemy's northern group in the Klein Gandau, Pilsnitz and Kosel areas, and the southern group in the area of site 43, Klein Mochbern'. According to the order, the limit of the advance would the railway going from north to south from the bridge over the Oder as far as the industrial area south-east of the city. That is, according to the plan by the 6th Army headquarters, it was planned to seize a large slice of the fortress's garrison and in this way to undermine its defensive capabilities. Although this was not openly stated, an offensive from the west would also deprive the garrison of the Gandau airfield, through which, despite the bombardment, Breslau continued to be supplied by air.

In order to create his shock 'fist', Gluzdovskii transferred the sector to the north of Breslau to the 77th Fortified Area. In this way, an enormous sector was occupied by only 1,679 men, although they did dispose of 92 heavy machine guns and 48 76mm guns. On the other hand, a breakthrough to the north clearly did not promise those encircled any kind of advantage, as it would only bring them into the rear of the First Ukrainian Front, and not to their own forces. The 294th Rifle Division, which had been freed up in the northern sector, was transferred to the 74th Rifle Corps along with the worn-out 87th Guards Heavy Tank Regiment with its IS-2s. One must say that this formation did not impress with its numbers, having only 3,353 men as of 1 April. Yet another division (359th Rifle Division – 4,023 men) was removed from the group of forces assaulting Breslau from the south. On 29 March it turned over its sector to its neighbours and on the night of 29/30 March it marched to Operau, taking up its jumping-off positions for the offensive. Also, on 27 March the 112th Rifle Division (4,593 men on 1 April) became part of the 6th Army and was transferred to the 74th Rifle Corps' shock group. As a result, the 'ram' aimed at the western part of Breslau contained the 112th, 294th and 359th Rifle Divisions. The 74th Rifle Corps was reinforced with eleven artillery units, including both battalions of 280mm mortars and both tank regiments (the 87th and 222nd). They transferred the 87th Guards Heavy Tank Regiment's IS tanks to the fresh 112th Rifle Division. Besides this, in order to revive the assault on the city, the 194th Howitzer Brigade, with its ML-20 152mm guns, was returned to Breslau from the town of Neisse and on 31 March took up positions along the western outskirts of the city. One cannot but note that aside from its organic artillery, the 74th Rifle Corps disposed of a considerable park of captured artillery: sixteen 105mm guns, twelve 75mm guns and three 75mm self-propelled guns (probably captured *Sturmgeschützen*, with all three in the 294th Rifle Division). The 74th Rifle Corps' 181st Rifle Division had the passive mission of acting as the link between the two corps' shock groups.

However, a serious problem for the offensive from the west was the poor concealment of the operation. Niehoff, the fortress commandant, later noted during interrogation that '… the Russians very poorly masked their concentration of forces for the offensive: at night one could note the mass movement of vehicle columns, moving with switched-on lights, to the place of the future main attack, and one could hear commands being issued in a loud voice'. He also drew attention to the fact that a strengthened artillery preparation was carried out at the location of the future offensive, while the artillery was silent along the other sectors of the front. All of this meant the loss of the element of surprise.

The regrouping was completed on 30 March and by the morning of 31 March Soviet forces had occupied their jumping-off positions for the offensive. At 08.30 registering fire began, and at 09.30 the artillery began its two-hour working-over of the forward edge and the tactical depth of the enemy's defence with an onslaught of fire. Some documents give the length of the artillery preparation as three hours. Aside from the artillery preparation to destabilize the enemy's defence, captured 'Goliaths' were also employed on 31 March. Fourteen tankettes were launched in the morning in several groups of two or three vehicles each. Only three reached their target, two in the Schmidtfeld area and one on the approaches to Pilsnitz. Yet another one had been blown up in the enemy's trench. The remainder were knocked out by the Germans. The artillery preparation was supplemented by aerial bombardment. Groups of five to eighteen Pe-2s from the 6th Guards Bomber Corps carried out 221 sorties in three hours and dropped 204 tonnes of bombs, including 15 FAB-500 and 498 FAB-250 aerial bombs. Despite the intensive anti-aircraft fire, they suffered no losses.

Artillery firing over open sights destroyed the fortified buildings and structures along the western outskirts of the neighbourhoods under assault. Elements of the 112th and 359th Rifle Divisions began fighting in the streets of Maria-Hofchen, Klein Mochbern and Schmidtfeld. There was fighting for every building. All of the passages in the kitchen gardens, gardens and streets had been mined. It was noted in the 112th Rifle Division's war diary that '*Faustpatronen* were heavily employed in this battle as powerful weapons in close-quarters fighting'. The garrison also called upon aircraft to bomb the attacking 'units'. There was no rapid breakthrough on the first day.

Losses suffered by the 74th Rifle Corps' formations on the first day of the offensive are shown in the table. Although not disastrous, they were nevertheless appreciable.

Table 4.4: Losses Among the 74th Rifle Corps' Formations on 31 March 1945.[56]

Formation	Killed	Wounded
181st Rifle Div.	30	105
112th Rifle Div.	19	34
359th Rifle Div.	59	132
294th Rifle Div.	73	178

During March 1945 the 6th Army's forces expended more than five million 7.62x54mm rifle and machine gun rounds, four million 7.62x25mmTT rounds for sub-machine guns and pistols, 128,000 hand grenades and nearly 6,000 anti-tank grenades (the 'Voroshilov kilogram'). The expenditure of mortar rounds and shells was as follows (see table).

Table 4.5: The Expenditure of Artillery Munitions by the 6th Army's Forces in March 1945.

Type of Munitions	Amount Expended
82mm mortars	143,678
120mm mortars	25,547
160mm mortars	1,725
45mm shells	55,694
76mm shells (1927 model regimental gun)	7,140
76mm shells (1943 model regimental gun)	7,649
76mm shells (divisional gun)	34,290
122mm howitzers (1910/30 and 1938 models)	6,228
152mm gun-howitzers (1937 model)	5,824
203mm howitzers	2,220

In March the entire First Ukrainian Front expended 10,760 203mm rounds and 73,300 152mm rounds for its 1937 model gun-howitzers. That is, one cannot say that the 6th Army consumed the bulk of the *front*'s heavy artillery ammunition. The share of 76mm divisional shell expenditure was quite meagre: during March the First Ukrainian Front expended 691,000 shells of this type, with the 6th Army accounting for less than 5 per cent.

Despite the insignificant number of tanks in the army, the expenditure of 85mm tank shells was 1,496 rounds and the number of 122mm 1931 model rounds was 1,017. The expenditure of captured ammunition was also quite impressive. Gluzdovskii's forces expended 8,500 75mm, 26,000 (!) 105mm and 3,000 150mm shells. Captured 105mm howitzers made up a considerable share of the 6th Army's artillery 'orchestra'. The expenditure of a few thousand 7.92mm and 9mm pistol rounds pales against this background. The 6th Army's expended 944 captured *Faustpatronen* during March (and this is only the amount listed by artillery supply).

The 6th Army's losses from 1 March through 1 April 1945 were 2,727 men killed, 37 missing in action and 8,758 wounded, which, taking into account sick and non-combat losses, equals 12,886 men.[57] Details of the losses by the army's formations are shown in the table below.

Table 4.6: Losses by the 6th Army's Formations from 1 March through 1 April 1945.

Formation	Killed	Missing in Action	Wounded	Total
218th Rifle Div.	533	4	1,839	2,449
273rd Rifle Div.	429	8	1,623	2,124
309th Rifle Div.	373	1	1,634	2,122
112th Rifle Div.	206	–	374	731
181st Rifle Div.	329	6	1,260	1,691
294th Rifle Div.	292	–	822	1,156
359th Rifle Div.	280	–	928	1,262
77th Fortified Area	83	–	367	491

The 22nd Rifle Corps' divisions, which were attacking in the southern part of Breslau, suffered heavy losses, as might be expected. Moreover, the 273rd Rifle Division, which was operating along a broad front along an auxiliary axis, suffered losses equivalent to those of the shock divisions. The decision to shift the axis of the main attack to the western part of the city was adopted only at the very end of March.

During March 1945 the 6th Army's tank forces lost five IS-2s, six T-34s, three SU-122s, and one ISU-152 burnt out, seven IS-2s and two ISU-152s knocked out, and four T-34s and two SU-122s that blew up on mines.[58] The data cited here clearly show that a significant part of the March losses in Gluzdovskii's entire army were due to the unsuccessful attempt by the 87th Guard Heavy Tank Regiment to attack in the northern part of Breslau.

In 1945 Easter in Germany fell on Sunday, 1 April. Thus the Soviet offensive, which began on Holy Saturday, 31 March, became known among the Germans as the 'Easter Offensive'. The resumption of the offensive on the first day of April did not yield significant successes for the 74th Rifle Corps' shock group. Only by 2 April did the 112th and 359th Rifle Divisions conclude fighting for the city blocks (reduced to ruins) and reach the line of the railway embankment to the west of the industrial area and south of Gandau airfield.

For this reason, one should say a few words regarding the legend of the Red Army's missed opportunities in the fighting for Breslau. General Niehoff, after being freed from Soviet captivity, later recalled:

We were very surprised when the Russians, after their first major success, did not continued to attack along the right flank, while advancing further, but turned to the north-east in the direction of the engineer barracks. Meanwhile, night fell. Major Tilgner's group, which had not suffered any losses during the night, was placed in trucks and delivered to the regiment. Of course, we had to leave the heavy guns in place. When the second day of Easter dawned a new defensive line had been created in the west. Later, after my capture, I had a conversation with a staff officer from General Gluzdovskii's army headquarters. In reply to our question as to why the Russians, following the successful breakthrough of our defence during the second half of Eastern Sunday, did not turn to the right, the officer was quiet for a little bit. He then looked at the map and stated: 'We had other plans'. Evidently, the Russians were simply unable to take advantage of this unique chance.[59]

In essence, what Niehoff was saying was this: as a result of the Soviet forces' actions, the Moor Regiment, which was defending the Gandau area, ended up cut off from the rest of the garrison. The regiment's elements were forced to fall back to the north, over the Oder, from where they were transferred on trucks to form a new defensive line in the west of Breslau. A gap yawned while the transfer was taking place. A direct comparison with Soviet documents does not confirm this thesis. It was on Easter Sunday and the next two or three days that the 74th Rifle Corps was engaged in stubborn fighting on the outskirts of Breslau. The movement to the east, which had been succeeded by a movement to the north, cannot be seen in the operational reports. The 74th Rifle Corps' evening report for 1 April maintains that the corps, 'having encountered the enemy's fire resistance, was not successful'. The 112th Rifle Division's war diary directly indicates the nature of the fighting following the arrival at the railway embankment: 'Combat activities by the division's units were limited to a firefight with the enemy along the former line until 6.4.45.'

Memoirists rarely manifest scrupulous accuracy and here Niehoff is no exception. A comparison of the facts forces us to put forward another candidate for the missed opportunity (if there really was such a thing). The turning point in the Soviets' 'Easter Offensive' was noted around 3–4 April, when the commander of the 359th Rifle Division, Colonel P.P. Kosolapov, made the decision to change the axis of the attack to the left flank and to attack Height 118.4 and Klein Gandau with two regiments. The regiments were reinforced with six tanks, upon which they placed a group of automatic riflemen. The shift in axis brought success. Following an hour-long artillery preparation, at 15.00 on 3 April the division went over to the attack and by 19.00 broke into Klein Gandau.

In the 359th Rifle Division's report on operations in Breslau, there is the following phrase: 'The division commander decided not to attack further against the blocks in the western part of Breslau and, under the cover of powerful artillery fire and a smokescreen, to slip through to the airfield and assault the blocks from the north, which the enemy in no way expected.'[60] The same thing was written in the division's morning report for 4 April: 'The division commander DECIDED: Upon carrying out a regrouping, to launch the main attack by the 1198th and 1196th Rifle Regiments in the direction of the road junction north of Block 69, and by a turning movement from the north to capture Blocks 69, 87, 88 and 89.'[61] The formation's war diary openly states that at the same time one regiment placed its front facing east as a cover against the trough-shaped railway bridge over the tangled paths in the industrial area as far as Klein Gandau. At 14.30 on 4 April, following a brief half-hour artillery preparation, two of the 359th Rifle Division's regiments went over to the attack. The riflemen, supported by tanks and self-propelled guns, took only a half an hour to overcome the airfield, but were later met with fire from the cemetery north of the airfield. Further on, there was fighting until evening for the area to the site listed in the reports as 'The Building of the Blind', and Block 69 on the outskirts of Breslau. An attempt to bypass the city blocks from the north did not bring the expected success. According to German data, the headquarters of the Moor Regiment, which had activated a reserve platoon for defence, was located in the boarding school for the blind.

Before us we have a picture which unambiguously resembles the description of a 'turn to the north'. It's difficult to evaluate an attack to the north as a deliberate mistake. We only have Niehoff's expert opinion. According to Soviet data, the blocks adjacent to the airfield from the east were by no means abandoned by the defenders. Up to 08.00 on 5 April elements of the 359th Rifle Division were assaulting Blocks 88 and 89 along the outskirts of Breslau (the mission of the turning movement was their seizure). If there had been a breach here in the defence, then the assault on the blocks would not have been necessary. There was also fighting for Block 90, directly to the east of the airfield, on 5 April. The linchpin of the defence here was two four-storey buildings with sturdy basements and thick walls. The capture of Block 90 by a reinforced company of automatic riflemen from the 1194th Rifle Regiment required considerable effort and was completed only by the morning of 6 April. Attacks on the next block, 103, on the way to the centre of Breslau, encountered 'Heavy fire from machine guns and heavy-calibre machine guns [evidently 20mm anti-aircraft cannon, A.I.]'. The offensive was also beginning to burn out in light of the shortage of ammunition, because in the 359th Rifle Division's report for 6 April it was pointed out that 'The division is experiencing a severe shortage of regimental and divisional shells' (by 'divisional' we must understand both 76mm guns and 122mm howitzers, for which there remained less than one-tenth of a unit of fire). It is not impossible, of course, that the continuation of the offensive by the 359th Rifle Division on 4 April from Klein Gandau to the east along the railway lines could have brought success.

The second candidate for the turn to the north is the 294th Rifle Division. The 359th Rifle Division's breakthrough opened the road to the Gandau airfield for this division. It captured 47 non-operational aircraft that had been scattered over the field, as well as 125 abandoned vehicles and other equipment. In moving forward, the 294th Rifle Division's 857th Rifle Regiment turned the flank of the northern group of the fortress's defence. The groups of Germans falling back in front of the regiment retreated to the northern bank of the Oder (from where they were taken to form a new defensive line). A battalion from the 857th Rifle Division forced the Oder on the heels of the retreating groups from the Moor Regiment and destroyed a platoon-sized screen left on the island in the river here, then crossed the river into the flank and rear of the positions which they had unsuccessfully assaulted along with the regiment of IS tanks three weeks ago. Overall, 5 April was an uncommonly successful day: forty-seven prisoners taken and five 105mm guns, one 37mm gun, six 75mm and 88mm guns, mortars, shells, and 147 motor vehicles (out-of-order). To judge from everything, these were the very same 'heavy guns' which, in Niehoff's words, 'they left in place'. The advance by the 294th Rifle Division's regiment across the Oder may also be interpreted as a 'turn to the north'. It's possible that Niehoff had in mind the possibility of the Russians continuing the offensive along the western bank of the Oder in the direction of the city centre.

In reality, they tried to shake the defence in the northern part of Breslau with the aid of the 294th Rifle Division. On the following day two battalions crossed the Oder and on 7 April ammunition was brought up. However, a joint attack by two battalions from the 294th Rifle Division and the 77th Fortified Area against the flank of the German position was not successful. The battalions that attacked in the hope of surprise, because of the lack of artillery preparation, ended up being spotted by the enemy, were illuminated by rockets and hit the dirt. As there was no prospect of developing the attack, the bridgehead was evacuated. Before long, the entire 294th Rifle Division handed over its positions to its neighbours and was pulled out of the 6th Army and received orders for an attack along the Dresden axis. Ahead of it lay a German counterblow and the final encirclement in the war of Soviet troops around Bautzen. In such a case, one wants to say that 'It would have been better to have remained in Breslau'.

In order to develop the success that had been achieved by the 359th Rifle Division's breakthrough and the seizure of the Gandau airfield, the Soviet command actually took quite realistic measures. Having bogged down along the line of the railway embankment, Colonel Zhukov's 112th Rifle Division was pulled out of the fighting, turned over its zone to the neighbouring 181st Rifle Division at 02.00 on 6 April, and as early as that same morning took up positions on the approaches to the house of the blind along with reinforcement weapons (the IS tanks of the 87th Guards Heavy Tank Regiment and some 160mm mortars). They reinforced the shock group along this axis with the ISU-152s of the 374th Heavy Self-Propelled Gun Regiment, which had arrived as part of the 6th Army. However, although the 74th Rifle Corps' units had advanced, it was at only a slow pace. In the 112th Rifle Division's war diary, the formation's actions in the area of the house of the blind were characterized as 'an extended and stubborn firefight with a slow forward advance'. On 8 April the regiment of IS tanks was withdrawn from the 112th Rifle Division and left Breslau.

One cannot but note that the officers and men of the Breslau garrison were in no hurry hurry to surrender, despite the doubtful prospects for the defence of the fortress. For example, during the period of fighting from 10 to 28 March, the 6th Army's forces captured only 444 men. Of course, the 6th Army's intelligence officers inquired as to the reasons for such behaviour when they questioned prisoners. Sergeant Karl Heiner, from the 4th Company of the Sauer Regiment's 2nd Battalion, during interrogation explained the situation as following follows: 'There would have been a lot of deserters to the Red Army, but being afraid of Russian captivity and the supposedly difficult conditions of life (evacuation to Siberia, heavy and prolonged work and poor food) restrained many soldiers.'[62] He explained his surrender as being due to the desire to avoid an almost inevitable death: 'I was personally led in going over to the Russians by the fact that I could see no prospects for remaining alive in Breslau. In captivity I will at least have some hope of remaining alive.'[63] Sergeant Theodore Gregert, from the 12th Company of the Moor Regiment's 3rd Battalion, was more blunt, stating 'If it were the Americans here instead of the Russians, then everybody would have surrendered long ago'.[64] Only the threat of almost inevitable death forced them to cross the lines.

To be fair, there was some basis for these fears. The bitterness of the Soviet-German conflict, which had arisen from having beheld the Wehrmacht's and the *Einsatzgruppen*[65] crimes in occupied territory left its impression on the armed struggle in the final months. For example, in an order from 6th Army headquarters of 10 April, the rank and file were warned that shooting prisoners was forbidden.[66] A more realistic method for the soldiers to escape from the hell of Breslau was self-inflicted wounds, which offered the chance of being evacuated by plane. However, self-inflicted wounds were severely punished. Prisoners under interrogation stated, for example, that on 1 April 1945 an order was read out loud to the Wehl Regiment announcing that five soldiers had been executed for self-inflicted wounds. Moreover, with the loss of the Gandau airfield the possibility of being evacuated evaporated.

The strip that had been built along the *Kaiserstrasse* was never used by transport aircraft. The constantly burning city was almost always covered by smoke, which made a landing on the *Kaiserstrasse* unlikely. However, one cannot say that its construction was completely useless. The strip was employed for gliders (which also landed on the Frisian Meadow).

If the 'Easter Offensive' in the west had some tangible success, the 309th Rifle Division's attacks in the city did not achieve much. Even the most basic actions required great efforts. For example, one of the problems of street fighting was the creation of a network of communications trenches for safe movement in the captured blocks. This was particularly relevant in case it was necessary to cross a wide street. The 309th Rifle Division's breakthrough across *Grebschener Strasse*, which ran along nearly the entire centre of the city, required the construction of communications trenches. The street was controlled for the most part by the Germans and was kept under heavy fire.

Every attack across it resembled a game of 'Russian roulette'. To play this game while being loaded down with rifles, grenades and mortar rounds was no picnic for anyone. The street was covered with asphalt and cement on a concrete base. As a result, on the night of 3/4 April the digging of a communications trench across *Grebschener Strasse* was carried out with the aid of explosives. Thirty combat engineers took part in this work and expended 360kg (!) of explosives. A communications trench 35m long and 1.5–1.6m deep was made, which enabled people to cross the street reasonably safely. This unique method of blasting a trench determined its shape, which was 2m across at the top and 0.8m at the bottom.

The 273rd Rifle Division, which had been employed in the south-eastern part of the city at the end of March and the beginning of April, went over to the defensive, while engaged in training reinforcements and preparing for the fighting in the city. As the headquarters of the 273rd Rifle Division reported on 11 April, four understrength rifle companies apiece remained in the division's regiments. For example, the 971st Rifle Regiment's 4th Company had a strength of ten men, the 5th Company thirteen men, the 7th Company twenty-two men, and the 8th Company twenty-three, while the 967th Rifle Regiment's 4th Company had twenty men, the 5th Company twenty-two men, the 7th Company thirty-three men, and the 8th Company thirty-five.

The 273rd Rifle Division's foes were the subunits of the Germans' 609th Infantry Division. The defence's strongpoints along this sector were the *Heiliggeistkirche* (Church of the Holy Spirit) and a school to the north of the *Steinstrasse* (running parallel to the front line). The compact modern concrete school building had been heavily damaged, but was being held by a battalion from the Reinkorber Regiment. Fighting went on inside the building, when a Soviet assault group was in one classroom and the Germans in the next. An effective means of defence in the area of the school were the 88mm *Puppchen*[67] ('Dolls') anti-tank grenade launchers. Colonel Reinkorber later recalled: 'An undoubted virtue of the "dolls" was that this weapon could be fired from the upper storeys without the risk of being noticed by an enemy observer. The sound of firing would be muffled in the schoolrooms and the flash was almost invisible from the street.'[68] The Soviet documents also contain material on the employment of the *Puppchen* in Breslau as a manoeuvrable crew-transported weapon weighing 120kg[69] (which was, for example, not much compared to a 45mm gun). The following was written regarding the effect of a round: 'A grenade hitting a brick wall 1.5–2m thick pierces it and starts a fire.'

Here it makes sense to say a few words about the 'underground' war in Breslau. Soviet specialists studied the underground layout of the captured part of the city and in accordance with these data made their assumptions about the outline of the underground communications in the blocks in Breslau remaining in enemy hands. Simultaneously, prisoners were questioned and maps of the underground structures were sought in all captured buildings. By the middle of April the Soviets had quite a full picture of the underground structure of the fortress under assault. However, the underground network did not play a significant role in the struggle for the city. As was noted in the report by the chief of staff of the 6th Army's engineer troops, Guards Lieutenant Colonel Aristov, 'The underground structure of Breslau played almost no role in the assault on Breslau, if one does not count several exits for the reconnaissance parties into the enemy rear for the purpose of divining his forces' manoeuvres'.[70] This can be explained by the fact that the Germans kept the underground communications under constant observation and sealed off the entrances with barricades and blocked the viewing shafts.

The limited success of the 'Easter Offensive' had put Gluzdovskii in a difficult position. They had begun taking resources from him, which were so desperately needed for the assault on Breslau, in order to use them for the far higher-priority mission of attacking Berlin. The 6th Army did not have time to turn the situation around during the operational pause preceding the Berlin operation. During the night of 10/11 April units of the 294th Rifle Division were relieved by the 112th Rifle Division and the 77th Fortified Area and left for the 52nd Army. The day before being relieved, the 294th Rifle Division made a final sprint and occupied the Dampfer Company's river harbour, thus moving the front line forward toward the railway embankment, which had been marked as the 74th Rifle Corps' target in the 31 March offensive plan.

On that same 10 April the 25th Heavy Calibre Howitzer Brigade (203mm guns) was removed from the 6th Army. The next to go was the 194th Heavy Howitzer Brigade, which had been supporting the troops on the streets of Breslau until 9 April. It also left for Berlin. Also on the 10th the 37th Flamethrower Battalion left the army. However, one should not say that Konev had given up on Breslau. Aside from the usual supplies, a penal unit was supplied, as were additional ammunition (primarily artillery shells) and rocket artillery units.

Given the great wealth of choices, the alternatives for continuing the offensive along the former axes were not promising. The terrain in the north and east did not promise success, while the 22nd Rifle Corps had gotten firmly bogged down in the labyrinth of streets and burned-out blocks. As a result, the new plan called for resuming the attacks toward the centre of Breslau from the west. Following a brief period of contemplation, V.A. Gluzdovskii made the decision to regroup his forces and to resume the assault. On 12 April orders were issued to pull the 218th Rifle Division out of the 22nd Rifle Corps in the southern part of Breslau and transfer it to the 74th Rifle Corps' zone. The 77th Fortified Area's 334th Machine Gun Battalion was relieved by a battalion from a reserve regiment and pulled back to the Pilsnitz area to cover the 74th Rifle Corps' flank along the bank of the Oder, thus reinforcing the 112th Rifle Division.

According to the plan of the commander of the 74th Rifle Corps, Major General A.V. Vorozheikin (Combat Order No. 0027 of 14 April 1945), the main attack would be launched by the 359th and 218th Rifle Divisions, reinforced by heavy-calibre artillery, as well as six and eight ISU-152s respectively. It was planned to break through toward the bend in the Oder and to force a crossing of it. The 181st Rifle Division was to launch a supporting attack along the railway lines to the Freiburg Station. Another six ISU-152s from the 349th Guards Heavy Self-Propelled Artillery Regiment remained in the 74th Rifle Corps commander's reserve in readiness to develop the success of either the 218th or 359th Rifle Divisions. However, the plan was cancelled at literally the last minute and a new operation was planned.

The basic idea of the 6th Army's new operation in the western part of Breslau was the employment of that fact that in the rear of the German subunits defending the line of the railway embankment the Oder bends and ends up being behind their backs. The railway embankment along this sector was of truly impressive size: up to 6m high and 40m wide. Tanks and self-propelled guns could not overcome it without engineer preparation. The situation was further exacerbated by the fact that that empty railway carriages stood quite thickly along the railway lines all the way to the bridge over the Oder. That is, in and of itself the idea required impeccable realization.

According to the renewed plan (Combat Order No. 0028 of 16 April 1945), the main attack was to be launched by the forces of Colonel D.T. Zhukov's 112th Rifle Division, with the entire 374th Guards Heavy Self-Propelled Artillery Regiment attached to it. The 112th Rifle Division's front was to be narrowed as much as possible through regrouping. The 4th Battery from the ISU-152 regiment, with a squad of fifty men, was to be allotted for the decisive thrust. It was planned that upon the infantry's capture of the railway embankment, the battery would rapidly bypass the infantry formations, reach the bridge over the Oder (so-called Target No. 25) and seize and hold it until the infantry's arrival. The 1st and 3rd Batteries of heavy self-propelled guns were assigned to directly accompany the 524th Rifle Regiment's infantry and the second the 385th Rifle Regiment's infantry. It was planned to break through across the Oder and to seize the block and power plant along its eastern bank. The element of risk included the 112th Rifle Division's advanced jumping-off positions, which made it vulnerable to a counterblow. Of course, the newly-committed 218th Rifle Division promised to cut off the salient along the 112th Rifle Division's flank, but obviously not to cover its neighbour's flank with its attack during the course of the offensive.

The 74th Rifle Corps' remaining formations were to essentially support this thrust to the bridge. Three self-propelled guns from the 222nd Tank Regiment were to be attached to the 181st Rifle Division, six ISUs from the 349th Guards Heavy Self-Propelled Artillery Regiment to the 359th Rifle Division, and eight ISUs from the 349th Guards Heavy Self-Propelled Artillery Regiment to the 218th Rifle Division. One must admit that despite allowing for the possibility of a breakthrough by the self-propelled guns with infantry into the depth of the defence, the new plan made more sense than the one outlined in Combat Order No. 0027. The old order left the bridge over the Oder (the very same Target No. 25) at the disposal of the garrison's group that was being outflanked and required the forcing of the Oder along with seizing a bridgehead on an island. That is, further advance once again required the forcing of a water obstacle within the confines of the city.

On the evening of 16 April Gluzdovskii reported to Konev that the 1,500 reinforcements from front resources and another 500 men found within the army in rear units had been incorporated into the shock group. The delivery of the ammunition assigned to the army was completed on 16 April. For example, on 15 and 16 April the 359th Rifle Division received 600 reinforcements. On the whole, the reinforcements received by the 74th Rifle Corps in April were organized into rifle companies with a strength of fifty to sixty men and armed on a scale of 40 per cent automatic rifles, 10 per cent light machine guns and 50 per cent carbines.[71] One hundred and twenty-five rounds were allotted for the carbines and 300 for an automatic rifle, and 800 rounds for a light machine gun, with each soldier also receiving four RGD-42 grenades and one anti-tank grenade. Each rifle section was also supplied with four captured *Faustpatronen*.

They trained the reinforcements seriously, which included 28 hours of tactical training, eight hours of fire training, eight hours of engineer training, and only two hours of political instruction.

The 6th Army's forces prepared for a new assault. Reconnaissance was carried out involving the capture of prisoners. Ramps were prepared on the railway embankment for the passing of the self-propelled guns. Also in the embankment, under the rail bed, passages were cut for the infantry. In the rear, assault groups trained in the ways and methods of operating on an ISU-152. Along the line of contact with the enemy the assault groups continued to seize individual buildings and positions. The losses testify to the intensity of the fighting during this period of 'quiet': from 14 to 17 April the 359th Rifle Division lost 73 men killed and 295 wounded. The artillery took up positions for firing over open sights. On the night of 16/17 April the 218th Rifle Division was put into the first line, thus getting a day to master its positions. A reconnaissance in force was carried out at 04.00–04.30 on 18 April. Aside from prisoners, a deserter from the German side was noted on the night before the offensive.

The artillery preparation, which was already quite traditional for Breslau, lasted for three hours until 10.00 on 18 April (with the equally traditional approximately hour-long registration fire). However, with the beginning of the operation nothing went as planned. The assault party, which had been placed on the combat vehicles, while under fire, 'jumped off their vehicles and scattered, while at the same time suffering losses'. The heavy self-propelled guns moved forward toward the bridge without infantry support. The 112th Rifle Division's infantry subunits, as a whole, encountered the enemy's heavy fire and hit the dirt, and then when the fire increased even fell back to the embankment's western slopes. In their turn, the Germans undertook a counter-attack about midday, supported by two armoured vehicles, identified as Panthers. Most likely these were '*Jagdpanzer* IVs',[72] which were identified as Panthers by the sound of their firing, as their gun was the same. During the course of the fighting German self-propelled guns and *Faustpatrone* troops managed to set fire to three ISU-152s.

This episode is covered in the memoirs of the commander of an assault gun, Lieutenant Hartmann, who on that day was fighting in a *Panzerjäger* IV: 'I halted on the road near the Popelwitz station. I began to examine the territory of the garden through the periscope. There I spotted giants with 152mm guns. I hit the first of them without any problem and it was immediately engulfed in flame. The long barrel enabled me to fire at a pretty great distance.'[73] The Popelwitz station was located right on the railway embankment.

During the second half of the day there took place an unpleasant but expected event: the 112th Rifle Division was subjected to a counterblow in the flank from Block 112 (Ironically, the number of the division and the block coincided) and was forced to fall back to its jumping-off position. As a result, by 16.30 the 374th Guards Heavy Self-Propelled Gun Regiment, which had penetrated into the enemy lines, ended up cut off in the area to the west of the shooting range. They were later attacked by tanks and assault guns and were also subjected to a bombardment by *Faustpatronen* from all sides. While tightening the ring, the Germans gradually destroyed the ISU-152s that had broken through. In all, in a day of fighting the self-propelled gun regiment lost eighteen ISUs, of which fourteen burned up in encirclement. The 112th Rifle Division itself lost on 18 April, that bloody day for the self-propelled artillery troops, 32 men killed and 136 wounded.

Events developed less dramatically in the offensive sector of the 74th Rifle Corps' other formations. Along the 359th Rifle Division's offensive sector the first line of the German defence collapsed, swept away by a hurricane of fire, although the lengthy artillery preparation gave the Germans time to gather their reserves. With the first peals of the cannonade, which heralded a major Soviet offensive, the reserves, which had occupied defensive positions along the line of the railway embankment in Block 107, began to move up to the axis of the attack. It was precisely in the 359th Rifle Division's attack zone that the railway lines split into two branches with high embankments. The infantrymen overcame the first embankment, but were met with fire from the next one. The artillery for firing over open sights had been delayed in front of the already captured embankment and fell behind the assault groups that had forged ahead. The Germans had already barricaded and mined the passages through the embankment. New passages had to be blasted with explosives for the artillery to pass through. As a result, the newly-arrived reserves held off the further advance by the Soviet infantry. The vigorous thrust forward did not materialize.

The 181st Rifle Division achieved much more impressive results on 18 April along the auxiliary axis. The success was not accidental, but was the natural product of military guile. The 181st Rifle Division stood on the approaches to the industrial area in the south-east of Breslau. Ahead towered the factory shops, the battle for which threatened to turn into a bloodbath. In the morning, accompanied by a three-hour artillery preparation, plumes of smoke rose above the Soviet positions. In all, four centres of smoke release, with 150 charges apiece, were organized along a 400m front. The 181st Rifle Division's 'chemists' ignited 21–22 charges simultaneously. The wind, which was blowing that morning exactly in the right direction, carried the smoke to the factory structures. The enemy unleashed heavy fire against the area of the smoke discharge, while expecting an attack precisely from this direction. However, the attack came along the neighbouring sector, where the 181st Rifle Division's 288th and 243rd Rifle Regiments attacked at 10.00. This attack proved to be completely unexpected. The two regiments managed to break through the maze of railway lines north of the factories into Blocks 107 and 108 in the area of the munitions factory. In this way, the factories ended up being turned from the flank. At the same time, losses were moderate: during 18 April the 181st Rifle Division lost 32 men killed and 136 wounded. On the morning of 19 April the 181st Rifle Division reached the *Nikolaitor* (the Nikolai Gates) railway platform. The Germans' attempts to counter-attack and throw back the 181st Rifle Division's regiments that had penetrated were not successful. The turning of their flank forced the Germans to abandon the major Linke-Hoffman factory (listed on the Red Army's maps as Site No. 43). The positions seized by the 181st Rifle Division became the jumping-off point for the 6th Army's next offensive.

The losses of the shock group of the 6th Army's 74th Rifle Corps on the first day of the new assault (see the table) may be rated as appreciable, but still not exceeding the numbers of the reinforcements received.

Table 4.7: Losses by the 74th Rifle Corps' Formations in the Offensive of 18 April 1945.[74]

Formation	Killed	Wounded
181st Rifle Div.	32	136
359th Rifle Div.	46	151
218th Rifle Div.[75]	22	96
112th Rifle Div.	32	136

At the same time, one must note the record 'harvest' of prisoners on the first day of the new assault. On 18 April the 74th Rifle Corps' forces captured 245 enemy soldiers and officers belonging to the Moor Regiment, the 26th Airborne Regiment, the *Volkssturm*, and other subunits.

The 22nd Rifle Corps also took part in the 18 April offensive in the southern part of Breslau. The Soviet command was aware of the possibilities presented by attacks from different axes simultaneously, thus scattering the reserves of the fortress's defence. The commander of the 22nd Rifle Corps, Major General Zakharov, decided to break through to the centre of Breslau from the south-east along the railway lines with the forces of the 273rd Rifle Division. The offensive's goal was the so-called 'Site 20', the main freight station and the railway shops. A breakthrough to them would mean getting into the rear of the Germans in the blocks to the south of the centre, which up until now had been attacked without any particular success. From the freight station it was a stone's throw, once again along the railway lines, to the city's main station. Two of the 273rd Rifle Division's regiments, reinforced by six ISU-152s and a company of flamethrower operators, made up the shock group. Four assault detachments, each with a strength of fifty to seventy men, were created in each of the 273rd Rifle Division's regiments. Two assault detachments of seventy men apiece, reinforced with four ISU-152s and 76mm, 105mm (captured) and 122mm guns, were to operate in the 967th Rifle Regiment in the first line. In the 967th Rifle Regiment a single assault detachment, reinforced with two ISU-152s and 76mm, 105mm and 122mm guns, was to operate in the first line. Moreover, according to tradition, a single day was allotted for the breakthrough to the freight station. The 22nd Rifle Corps was to launch yet another attack with the forces of three of the 309th Rifle Division's battalions, but this time in the interests of the army's main shock group.

The regrouping of the 273rd Rifle Division's units began on the night of 17/18 April. At 03.00 the assault detachments occupied their jumping-off positions and attacked at 10.00. None of the assault detachments was successful. As early as evening the 971st Rifle Regiment, as a consolation prize, managed to occupy the Knoper Muhle mill on the outskirts of Breslau. However, at about 03.00 on 19 April a powerful artillery bombardment was launched against the mill, as a result of which, as was noted in the report by the division's headquarters, 'the regiment's subunits, having suffered significant losses, abandoned it'. Two ISU-152s of those supporting the 273rd Rifle Division's offensive were burned in the northern part of the Wolfe metallurgical factory (listed as Site No. 50 on Soviet maps).

In all, from 10.00 on 18 April to 19.00 on 19 April, the 273rd Rifle Division lost 36 men killed, 348 wounded and 12 missing in action. The 971st Rifle Regiment suffered the heaviest losses – 10 men killed, 6 missing and 230 wounded. Evidently these were the consequences of the nighttime artillery bombardment. The attempt to break through along the railway lines to the centre of Breslau was a failure. The attack by the 309th Rifle Division in the interests of the main shock group was also a failure. It ran into the 'Niehoff Line', with landmines in the buildings of the first line. As was noted in the daytime report, 'Up to a platoon of infantry from the 309th Rifle Division died in a mined building'.

The failure of the offensive and the heavy losses of equipment forced the Soviets to abandon the attempt to break through the railway embankment. Although the infantry had already managed to advance beyond the embankment, the element of surprise had been lost. Without a rapid breakthrough to the bridge, pushing the Germans out of the area of the shooting range would be pointless, as the defenders could fall back behind the Oder and blow up the bridge after them. This is actually what happened, and 'Site No. 25' was indeed ultimately blown up by the Germans.

At the end of April Gluzdovskii's headquarters once again began to regroup the army's forces along the fortress's perimeter. On the night of 20/21 April the 112th Rifle Division was relieved by a company from the 77th Fortified Area's machine-gun battalion and marched to the area of Hindenburg Square in the southern part of the city and by 08.00 had relieved units of the 309th Rifle Division in positions in the city blocks. The 309th Rifle Division, in its turn, was transferred to the western part of Breslau and subordinated to the 74th Rifle Corps. In this lateral movement one can discern the desire to take advantage of the experience of the 309th Rifle Division, which had become quite skilled in urban fighting in the western part of the city.

Besides this, from 20 April Gluzdovskii had at his disposal yet another rifle division – the 135th Rifle Division from the 59th Army. However, the new division was transferred by march and it was only on 22 April that it arrived at the approaches to Breslau. The 6th Army's headquarters ordered that the time before the arrival of the fresh (more likely 'fresh') formation should 'be maximally employed for training the rank and file in street fighting in the conditions of a major city'.[76]

Combat Order No. 0025/op of 22 April 1945 from the 6th Army's headquarters read as follows: 'The army is resuming the assault on Breslau and, while launching the main attack from the west, is to cut up the enemy's central and southern group of forces and consecutively destroy them and capture the city.' According to the plan for the new offensive, the 22nd Rifle

Corps was ordered to break into the outskirts of Breslau, with the forces of the 181st Rifle Division and the fresh 135th Rifle Division, along the railway lines north of the 'Hydrometre' factory in the industrial quarter to the south-west of the city and to then break through directly to the city centre and to force the Oder. Actually, it was the 181st Rifle Division that had mostly captured the industrial quarter during the preceding days. Moreover, the corps' auxiliary task was the encirclement of the enemy. Upon coming out into the area of the Freiburg station and the Guta factory, part of the forces was to attack the German units in the southern part of Breslau in the rear and link up with the 112th Rifle Division. Accordingly, they stationed the 112th Rifle Division in the salient, where Soviet units had advanced furthest in the direction of the city centre during the attack from the south (the so-called Block 659 on the corner of Habnitz and Hohenzollern Streets). According to an order by the commander of the 22nd Rifle Corps, Zakharov, the left-flank 135th Rifle Division was to break through to the centre of Breslau, while the right-flank 181st Rifle Division was to undertake an encirclement operation along with the 112th Rifle Division. The 374th Guards Heavy Self-Propelled Artillery Regiment and three tanks from the 222nd Tank Regiment were attached to the 181st Rifle Division, while the 135th Rifle Division received seven tanks from the 222nd Tank Regiment. A new wrinkle in the latest assault was to be the denser combat formations of the attacking units. It was noted in the 22nd Rifle Corps' order that 'The division's combat formations should be organized in three echelons'. Earlier, the usual order of two regiments in the first line and one in the second was employed in the 6th Army.

According to the new plan, the 74th Rifle Corps (309th, 359th and 218th Rifle Divisions) was to launch a second attack shoulder-to-shoulder with its neighbour. Its task was to break through to the centre of Breslau in a dense formation from due west along the city blocks. The 74th Rifle Corps' order stressed: 'The divisions are to have a combat formation of three echelons, regiment behind regiment.' The 218th Rifle Division retained the old formation of two regiments in the first line along the auxiliary axis. The 349th Guards Heavy Self-Propelled Artillery Regiment remained the 74th Rifle Corps' armoured ram. The 359th Rifle Division received five self-propelled guns, the 309th Rifle Division two, and the 218th Rifle Division two. The corps also received the mission, upon arriving at the Oder, to turn to the north and to destroy the enemy group of forces in the area of the firing range (where the ISU-152s burned on 18 April were). The aviation preparation of the offensive was entrusted to the 1st Bomber Air Corps. I should remind the reader that the fighting for Berlin was going on at this time. Nonetheless, the front command did not abandon hopes for the fall of fortress Breslau.

On the night of 22/23 April the first echelons of the 135th and 309th Rifle Division were moved up. The following morning, at 09.30, following a 2.5-hour artillery preparation, the 6th Army's shock group, consisting of five rifle divisions, resumed the assault on Breslau. They also cleared the road for the 22nd Rifle Corps with fire from heavy-calibre guns. On 24 April the 315th Heavy-Calibre Artillery Battalion fired off eighty-eight concrete-piercing 280mm shells and achieved forty direct hits. The battalion's targets were also located in Blocks 299 and 159, that is, at the exit from the defile between the industrial buildings and the urban quarters.

The artillery preparation was carried out according to a complex plan, with 15–20-minute breaks for deceiving the enemy. The Germans usually moved deep into the basements and the attack following the false cease-fires was a complete surprise. This enabled the Soviets to immediately capture two to three blocks in a 'rush attack'. Many garrisons ended up being locked up in the basements and were destroyed or they surrendered. According to the results of the first day, 111 prisoners were taken from the Moor, Sauer and Besselein Regiments.

On 24 April the 359th Rifle Division's lead 1198th Rifle Regiment in the 74th Rifle Corps' shock group made a fighting advance through Blocks 140 and 141. The second-echelon 1196th Rifle Regiment was committed into the fighting to develop the success. However, the neighbouring 135th Rifle Division, lacking experience of urban warfare, advanced more slowly and thus the 359th Rifle Division's flank was exposed to bombardment from its neighbour's zone. This interfered with the actions of artillery firing over open sights and the 1196th Rifle Regiment did not achieve any success. The 135th Rifle Division's second-echelon regiments were not even committed into the fighting. Also, the Germans, true to their active tactics, launched counter-attacks. The 1198th Rifle Regiment's assault group, which had broken into Block 152, was pushed back by an enemy counter-attack.

Having knocked the 359th Rifle Division's assault group out of Block 152, the Germans set fire to the buildings along its western edge. Thus the resumption of the offensive on 25 April enjoyed only partial success: if the infantry could still make it through the smoke and heat along the basement or semi-basement structures in the flaming buildings with difficulty, it then proved impossible to drag the artillery through the burning block. It was not possible to continue the assault without artillery firing over open sights. As a result, the Soviets were only able to capture Block 152 by the evening of 26 April. Events developed in the 135th Rifle Division's zone in a similar fashion. The Germans met the attack against Block 160, which bordered on Block 152, by setting fire to the buildings and also by flanking fire from the south.

On the night of 26/27 April, when the assault groups of the 359th Rifle Division's 1196th Rifle Regiment broke into the buildings in the western part of the neighbouring Block 153, the Germans once again employed their former tactics and set fire to the entire western part of it and fell back into the eastern part. The buildings burned all night and into the morning of 27 April, making it impossible to continue the offensive. There was no opportunity for bypassing the burning block, because the buildings in the neighbouring Block 153 had also been set on fire. When the fire died down, the Germans allowed the attacking subunits into the charred ruins without firing a shot, and then opened fire from *Faustpatronen*, easily destroying the burnt-out buildings and bringing down the ruins on the attackers. Losses, however, were moderate: the entire 359th Rifle Division lost on 27 April seven men killed and fifty-five wounded. Eight 'Goliaths', launched by the Germans against the burning buildings, were added to the tactic of setting fire to buildings. The area of the offensive was also intensively bombarded by *Puppchens*. On 27 April the 135th Rifle Division's losses were limited to ten killed and 67 wounded. At the same time, the employment of setting fire to buildings showed that the 'Niehoff Line', with its previously burnt and destroyed buildings, had been overcome along the western axis.

By 29 April the Soviet offensive had exhausted itself. The 6th Army's artillery had expended a significant amount of ammunition and the effectiveness of its fire had declined appreciably. The garrison had gathered its strongest units to the offensive axis by manoeuvring along internal lines. At this time the SS Besselein and Moor Regiments, which had been reinforced by individual battalions from other regiments (one battalion each from the Wehl, Sauer and Ganf Regiments, according to data from Soviet intelligence following the capitulation of Breslau, based on captured documents) were defending in the western part of Breslau, from Block 299 (adjacent to the railway lines) to the Oder.

The 6th Army went over to the defensive in the final days of April. However, this did not signify a refusal to continue the assault. Gluzdovskii ordered the relief of the 359th Rifle Division by elements of the 309th Rifle Division and the 359th Rifle Division to be pulled back into the corps reserve in the western part of Breslau. Two battalions apiece were also pulled back into the reserve of each rifle division. It was ordered to complete all the regroupings by as early as 30 April. They immediately began to reinforce the 359th Rifle Division's relieved units with troops and equipment, followed by training them and knocking them together as a unit. Ahead lay the final and decisive assault. That the idea of a new offensive had not been abandoned can be seen, for example, in an order by the 22nd Rifle Corps, in which, aside from defensive tasks, it was noted that the corps 'is accumulating forces and equipment for the decisive assault on the city of Breslau'.[77]

In order not to halt the fire effect on the Breslau garrison, the 6th Army's headquarters ordered the troops maintain a barrage from infantry weapons, heavy machine guns, 82mm mortars and 45mm guns. At the same time, the army's artillery commander was ordered to keep firing captured 75mm, 105mm and 150mm guns and individual *Katyushas* night and day, thus 'exerting a morale effect on the enemy's personnel and population'.[78] Early in the morning on 1 May the Germans withdrew from their positions facing the 74th Rifle Corps in the area of the firing range to behind the Oder to the area of the river port. As early as midday the 218th Rifle Division had occupied positions on the causeway dike along the western bank of the Oder. The division's losses during the pursuit were two men killed and thirteen wounded. The withdrawal and the occupation of defensive positions along the Oder basically put an end to the idea of rapidly breaking into the city centre. For this it would now be necessary to force the river and to assault the defences, which relied on the structures of the river port. The 218th Rifle Division's scouts could not even get into the enemy lines because of the high (4–5m) embankments of the Oder, which had been faced with stone. The plans which had been formulated earlier had estimated the opportunities for breaking into the city centre over the Oder from the west exceedingly optimistically. With the withdrawal of the defenders, the front in the city's centre grew narrower, thus easing the garrison's task.

Despite the deep penetration of the fortress's defence in the western part of the city, it's difficult to call the attackers' success in April 1945 impressive. At the same time, the army command can in no way be reproached for passivity: counting from the offensive begun on 31 March, three attempts had been made to break into the centre of Breslau in a month. The intensity of the Red Army's employment of flamethrower-incendiary weapons in Breslau in April

1945 had increased significantly compared to March. During April the 6th Army's forces had employed 2,460 bottles of KS flammable liquid and 19,533 'Molotov cocktails', that is, more than twice as many as in March. Bottle launchers, which were first employed in the March fighting, were widely used. The 46th, 47th and, until 14 April, the 37th Independent Portable Flamethrower Battalions also operated in Breslau. The 47th Independent Portable Flamethrower Battalion was attached to the 309th and 359th Rifle Divisions and the 46th Independent Portable Flamethrower Battalion to the 218th and 273rd Rifle Divisions. There are no figures for the 37th Independent Portable Flamethrower Battalion in the documents, but the 46th and 47th Independent Portable Flamethrower Battalions employed flamethrowers 144 times in April, using up 6.5 tons of fuel and losing nineteen flamethrowers. The two battalions of flamethrower troops' rank and file losses were fourteen men killed, two missing in action and fifty-eight wounded.

From 1 April through 1 May 1945 the 6th Army's losses were 3,037 men killed and 10,741 wounded, with none listed as missing in action and, taking into account those sick and non-combat losses, totalled 14,252 men.[79] Losses increased approximately 10 per cent compared to March, which testifies to the increased intensity of the fighting. The details of the losses by formation are shown in the table below.

Table 4.8: Losses of the 6th Army's Formations from 1 April through 1 May 1945.

Formation	Killed	Wounded	Total[80]
112th Rifle Div.	479	1,635	2,231
135th Rifle Div.	181	863	1,066
181st Rifle Div.	471	1,242	1,726
273rd Rifle Div.	217	985	1,238
218th Rifle Div.	396	1,743	2,197
309th Rifle Div.	294	1,491	1,872
359th Rifle Div.	645	1,848	2,499
77th Fortified Area	30	121	171

It is clear from these figures that the fresh (by the standards of 1945) 112th Rifle Division, which had been subordinated to the 6th Army at the end of March, suffered quite heavy losses. The 135th Rifle Division, which had been transferred to the 6th Army in April 1945, suffered fewer absolute losses.

Nevertheless, this loss of a thousand men is noteworthy, because the division suffered these losses in only a week of fighting.

In summing up the results for April, one should say something about the reinforcements the 6th Army received. See the table below.

Table 4.9: Reinforcements Received by the 6th Army's Units and Formations in April 1945.

Unit/Formation	From Army Resources	Replacements	Total
112th Rifle Div.	72	300	372
273rd Rifle Div.	671	132	803
218th Rifle Div.	667	600	1,267
181st Rifle Div.	346	721	1,067
359th Rifle Div.	771	1,271	2,042
294th Rifle Div.	100	–	100
309th Rifle Div.	573	270	843
Independent Disciplinary Company	109	557	666
Various Units	665	–	665
Total	3,974	3,851	7,825

The filling up of the 359th Rifle Division with reinforcements can be explained to some degree by the fact that the division was at the end of April practically only a couple of blocks from the Oder. The division was deliberately pulled back into the rear for reinforcements and training for the final attack (see above).

In spite of the reinforcements, by 1 May the 6th Army's formations were far from being in a brilliant state (see table).

Table 4.10: Strength of the 6th Army's Rifle Formations on 1 May 1945.

Formation	Personnel Strength	Rifles	Sub-machine Guns
112th Rifle Div.	3,154	1,709	917
135th Rifle Div.	3,346	2,456	1,072
181st Rifle Div.	3,288	1,590	1,135
273rd Rifle Div.	3,236	1,769	688
218th Rifle Div.	3,395	1,965	638
309th Rifle Div.	3,333	1,766	952
359th Rifle Div.	3,657	2,184	775

Formation	Light Machine Guns	Heavy Machine Guns	Anti–Aircraft Machine Guns
112th Rifle Div.	93	24	10
135th Rifle Div.	109	45	13
181st Rifle Div.	114	54	4
273rd Rifle Div.	68	32	9
218th Rifle Div.	102	34	14
309th Rifle Div.	110	36	16
359th Rifle Division	118	35	11

Given these numbers, the rifle divisions' shock capabilities had been reduced to practically zero.

During the first days of May, the 6th Army, despite the weak condition of its formations, continued to prepare for a new assault. Reinforcements were instructed according to the theme of 'A Soldier's Actions as Part of an Assault Group'. In the 359th Rifle Division and in the second-echelon regiments of the 309th and 218th Rifle Divisions they trained in the operations of assault groups in city fighting and studied *Faustpatrone* equipment. The assault on Breslau could have been repeated in the first ten days of May, although a detailed plan for a new offensive has not been located in the operational documents of the 6th Army and its subordinate corps. At that moment information about the enemy's conduct of reconnaissance in the southern part of the city and his regrouping of forces from the western part of the city to the south held Gluzdovskii's headquarters back from repeating the assault. This information forced them into the logical assumption that the city's garrison was preparing to break out to the south in order to link up with Army Group Centre's main forces, which were falling back to the west. The numerical weakness of the 22nd Rifle Corps and the extended length of its positions along the front in the southern part of Breslau, along with the simultaneous concentration of forces for an offensive in the western areas of the city, could have played into the enemy's hands. There was a precedent from the recent past of a desperate break-out attempt – that of the Buda garrison in Hungary in February 1945.

Gluzdovskii went for broke late in the evening of 3 May and demanded that the fortress commander send envoys to receive his terms for capitulation. Following this, firing was ceased for an hour before midnight. At 09.00 on 4 May, having failed to receive a reply from the commandant of Breslau to these demands, the 6th Army renewed its artillery and mortar fire against the enemy's combat formations. Simultaneously, Pe-2 bombers carried out 261 sorties. At 17.00, having ceased fire again, the commandant of Breslau was once again presented with the demand over the radio to dispatch envoys. At 18.00 on 4 May the envoys arrived and accepted the ultimatum along with the demand that representatives from the garrison staff appear to receive the terms of capitulation.

General Niehoff called the fall of Berlin on 2 May 1945 the first in the series of reasons that forced him to agree to negotiations. During his interrogation, he said the following: 'The German capital laid down its arms unexpectedly quickly, although it disposed of both forces and equipment for resistance.'[81] It's hard not to agree with Niehoff here, as Berlin fell in record time, particularly when taking into account the size of the city and the strength of its garrison.

Niehoff gave the remaining reasons as follows:

the successful advance by Soviet forces not only on the Elbe River, but also in Czechoslovakia, as well as the Prague uprising;[82]

the loss of any hope of being relieved by an attack from without, particularly in light of Schörner's[83] demonstrated incapability to put things in order, even in Czechoslovakia;

the complete lack of supply by air;

the expected concentration of Soviet forces against Breslau, because they would be freed up from around Berlin.

As F. Morzik writes, the reason for the cutting off of supply by air to Breslau was precisely the loss of territory in the Berlin area (the transport aircraft flew from Jüterbog, to the south of the German capital). It's also evident that the continuation of resistance following the fall of Berlin no longer made any sense for all the German forces remaining in isolated centres of resistance on the Eastern Front, starting from Courland[84] and ending with the troops in the delta of the Vistula River. They even lacked the theoretical opportunity of breaking out for the purpose of laying down their arms to the Western Allies.

However, the decision to capitulate gave rise to an internal conflict. Higher headquarters confirmed the order to the commandant of Breslau 'to fight to the last man and last bullet'. Among the commanders and soldiers of the Breslau garrison there were those who were preparing to fight to the end, to their deaths.

It was easiest of all to neutralize *Gauleiter* Hanke. Niehoff gave him his Fieseler Storch,[85] which enabled Hanke to abandon Breslau. To be sure, death nevertheless found him within only a few days. Nonetheless, negotiations for capitulation made do without the 'role of the party', and on 5 May a detachment of envoys, dispatched by Niehoff under the command of Captain von Buerk, crossed the front line along the *Strasse der SA*.

In light of the various readings regarding the text of the ultimatum, I will allow myself to quote it in its entirety:

To his Excellency, Infantry General Niehoff, the commandant of the fortress of the city of Breslau.

In accordance with your agreement to cease combat operations against Soviet forces, I propose the following terms for the capitulation of the encircled garrison.

1. All encircled German forces led by you are to cease combat operations beginning at 0800 on 5 May, Moscow time.
2. You are to turn over to us the entire rank and file, weapons, all combat equipment, means of transportation, and undamaged equipment.
3. We guarantee you and all of your officers and soldiers who have ceased resistance their lives, food and the retention of their personal effects and decorations, plus sidearms for the officers and a return to their homes after the war.
4. All sick and wounded will be given immediate medical assistance.

The order in which the city is to be handed over to Soviet forces, as well as the rank and file of the troops under your control, in accordance with paragraph 2 of these conditions, is attached.

The commander of the Soviet forces encircling the city of Breslau, Lieutenant General V. Gluzdovskii.

5.5.45.[86]

A definite timetable for surrendering and accepting the fortress of Breslau and its garrison was established. From the time of the cessation of combat operations, it was planned to pull back the garrison's units and subunits from the front line, where they were to lay down all their weapons and sidearms (with the exception of the officers' sidearms) and ammunition at a chosen place. Representatives of the Red Army command were to be dispatched to receive and secure the weapons. Later, the commanders of the German units and subunits of the fortress were to form up their subordinates into columns of four and lead them to three collecting areas for prisoners of war.

In all, from 6 to 11 May 1945 the 6th Army's forces captured 44,848 enemy soldiers and officers, including 6,678 men being treated in Breslau's hospitals. The equipment captured by the Red Army (according to a summary report) was: 46,608 rifles and automatic rifles, 4,864 machine guns, 559 guns, 534 mortars, 36 tanks, about 7,000 motor vehicles, 46 locomotives, and other property. The Red Army's overall losses during the assault on Breslau were 7,177 men killed and 24,427 wounded.[87]

According to an order by the Supreme Commander-in-Chief, I.V. Stalin, at 22.00 on 7 May Moscow saluted the forces 'which captured Breslau, with 20 artillery salvoes from 220 guns'.

Conclusion

At the beginning of the account of the fighting in Breslau, we referred to a passage from I.S. Konev's memoirs, where he assessed the fighting for the city quite dismissively. I will remind the reader that Ivan Stepanovich wrote that 'We had to keep the enemy in our sights and from time to time remind the Germans with ultimatums that their situation was hopeless and that there was no way out for them'. In light of the facts, it is clear that Comrade Konev is not being completely honest here. Breslau went through a number of assaults pursing the most decisive ends. Reinforcements and reserves, including tanks, self-propelled guns and heavy artillery, were transferred to the 6th Army. Gluzdovskii received fresh (by the standards of 1945) divisions several times, and the last one at the height of the fighting for Berlin. It would be more correct to say that the Red Army's chief task in Breslau was to defeat the fortress's garrison as quickly as possible and to free up men and materiel for employment along other axes. However, this did not happen until May 1945. Moreover, Gluzdovskii's army swallowed up reserves that Konev's headquarters had scraped together with considerable difficulty while facing the far more ambitious task of attacking Berlin. For example, the 135th Rifle Division would have come in very handy as the 'lid' of the Halbe 'cauldron' near Berlin.

First of all, it should be noted that insufficient forces had been gathered in Gluzdovskii's 6th Army for the rapid resolution of the task of destroying the garrison of such a major fortress. A two- to three-fold numerical superiority over the garrison could have ensured the rapid success of the assault; that is, an army numbering 100,000–130,000 men, or even two combined-arms armies. However, Konev could not allot such forces for storming Breslau and decided to resolve the task by employing the firepower of the forces assaulting the fortress. The initial failure of the assault resulted in the appearance of 'immunity' in the form of new defensive tactics in the city blocks, which made the task even more difficult in conditions of insufficient forces for the assault on Breslau. During interrogation, Niehoff took credit himself for the new tactics, but they were evidently the fruit of collective work (they had experience of blowing up abandoned buildings even before Niehoff's arrival). All of this supported the relative resilience of the garrison and even created the prerequisites for relieving it. This did not take place in light of the Soviets' March offensive in Silesia, which forced the Germans to disperse the shock group that had been gathered to break through to Breslau in order to plug gaps elsewhere.

Conclusions

I n tallying up the results of this volume, it is necessary to note the following. A city, in and of itself, can of course provide support for the defence, by forming a serious obstacle for the attacker with its buildings and factories. Even a quantitatively and qualitatively quite weak garrison may put up a serious fight on the streets against a regular army with artillery and armour.

However, in and of itself the fortress concept set out on 8 March 1944 in Directive No. 11 over Adolf Hitler's signature, proved to be quite poorly thought out. Artillery remained the god of war and the creation of large stores of artillery shells in a fortress was not possible for purely technical reasons, simply due to the absence of appropriate storage facilities in a typical city (if we exclude specialized naval bases). Armour did not actually resolve the problem, despite the effectiveness, demonstrated in practice, of it as the garrison's 'fire brigade'. The exhaustion of artillery ammunition rendered a fortress doomed in the reality of the spring of 1944. Experience also showed that fortresses in the depth of the defence have a certain chance of success. Under conditions of the overall collapse of an army group's defence, the retention of road junctions in the rear facilitated the restoration of a stable front. Besides, it's easier for fortresses in the depth to withstand the first attack by the enemy's forward detachments and by the Red Army's units separated from their rear establishments. Or, as was the case with Kovel', this worked out in special natural conditions.

It is also necessary to note some important facts. First of all, the personnel factor and the presence of a combat-capable core of the garrison, even if only of small size, played an enormous role in retaining a fortress. Without such a core of motivated officers and men intent on holding out, they were quickly abandoned or capitulated. In the case of Ternopol' and Poznań, the training units became just such a core. Secondly, the relief of the fortress was practically excluded. The relief of Kovel' was an exception that only confirmed the rule: the town was along a secondary axis and major forces, including tanks, were committed to relieving it. The absence of hope for being relieved immediately told on a garrison's state of morale.

On the whole, the fortress concept did not justify the hopes placed in it. Very often the clearly suicidal retention of a fortress was essentially sabotaged by the Wehrmacht command at various levels. For obvious reasons, the garrisons designated for defending isolated cities preferred retreat to a planned encirclement. Only in the case of the fortress of Poznań did the confluence of circumstances (the fanatical commander of the officers' school and his subordinates, a developed system of fortifications, even if old, and the length of the Soviet forces' lines of communication) had a certain influence on Soviet plans along the Berlin direction, as well as on the pace of consolidating along the Oder bridgeheads. Breslau, despite its significance as a road junction and the capital of Silesia, was on the periphery of the First Ukrainian Front.

In general, a fortress was only able to draw off part of the attacking Red Army's resources onto itself and enabled the Wehrmacht to inflict losses on the attacking formations by weakening their shock power somewhat in subsequent operations. It's possible that the rapid capitulation of Poznań and the 8th Guards Army's fewer losses in the struggle for the city might have told positively on the pace of the offensive of Chuikov's army in the Berlin operation. The capitulation of Breslau would have enabled the Soviets to free up the 6th Army for the Berlin operation and to more solidly 'seal' the encirclement of Busse's[1] Ninth Army in the woods to the south-east of Berlin and to prevent the break-out of part of the army's forces to the west.

From the technical point of view, the widespread employment of *Faustpatronen* in the Wehrmacht gave the fortress concept a 'second wind'. To a certain extent, they enabled the Germans to resolve the fortress's main problem – the impossibility of relying on artillery due to the unreliable supply of ammunition. *Faustpatronen* were a substitute for artillery and were actively employed not only against Soviet armoured vehicles, but also against infantry. It was precisely this that supported the great resilience of the 1945 fortresses and the not inconsiderable losses involved in assaulting them.

Adolf Hitler's Order on Fortresses

Führer Order No. 11 of 8.3.44

1) One must draw a distinction between 'fortresses', at the head of which stand 'fortress commanders', and 'inhabited strongpoints', with a 'military commandant' in charge.

   Fortresses must carry out the same tasks as the fortresses of old. They must prevent the enemy from seizing places of significance from the operational point of view. They must allow themselves to be surrounded and thus tie down as many enemy forces as possible. In this manner they must create the prerequisites for successful counterblow.

   'Inhabited strongpoints' are strongpoints in the depth of the defence, stubbornly defending in the event of an enemy breakthrough. When included in the defensive line, they must become its backbone, and in the event of enemy breaking through they must become the front's cornerstone and the jumping-off positions for counterblows.

2) The fortress commandant must be a soldier of firm spirit, specially selected for this position, preferably with the rank of general. The army group command will appoint him.

   The fortress commandant makes a personal pledge to the army group commander.

   The fortress commander answers with his soldier's honour for carrying out his assignment to the last man.

   Only the army group commander personally, with my permission, may release the fortress commandant from the duty of carrying out the missions entrusted to him and order the fortress to be abandoned.

   The fortress commander is subordinated to the army or army group commander, in the sector of which the fortress is located. It is forbidden to subordinate him to corps.

   Aside from the garrison, all people, both military and civilians within the fortress, regardless of their rank and position, are subordinated to the fortress commandant.

The fortress commandant is empowered by the Wehrmacht and has the disciplinary authority of a corps commander. Military-field courts should be attached to him to carry out his missions.

A staff for the fortress commandant should be created. The appointment of a chief of staff is carried out by the OKH, on the recommendation of the army group command.

3) The fortress garrison is divided into a security garrison and the full garrison.

A security garrison must be constantly located within the fortress. The commander of the army group must determine its strength. The latter depends upon the dimensions of the fortress and the missions it has been assigned (the preparation and fitting out of defensive positions, holding the fortress against surprise attacks, or local attacks by the enemy).

A full garrison must be transferred to the commandant in a timely manner in order to have time to occupy in an orderly manner defensive positions before the enemy's planned offensive and to acquaint itself with its tasks. The strength of the full garrison is determined by the army group commander, depending on the size of the fortress and the mission assigned to it (the decisive defence of the fortress).

4) The military commandant is an official person who is subordinated to the subunit leader. The latter appoints him, commands him and assigns him a mission. His rank depends upon the significance of the inhabited locale in the defensive system and the size of the garrison. This position is intended for particularly energetic officers who have proven themselves in critical moments.

5) The strength of the garrison of an inhabited strongpoint depends on the significance of the place and available forces. Its strength is determined by that unit level to which the military commandant is subordinated.

6) The missions of the fortress commandants and military commandants are in the supplement.

7) All previously issued orders concerning military commandants are rendered null and void.

Adolf Hitler[1]

Notes

Abbreviations
NARA = National Archives and Records Administration (US).
TsAMO RF = Central Archives of the Ministry of Defence of the Russian Federation.

Foreword
1. NARA, T311, R228, frame 1019.
2. NARA, T313, R70, frame 7307893.

Chapter 1: The Ternopol' Fortress: The First Attempt
1. Editor's note. This refers to the encirclement of the First Panzer Army, commanded by General Hans-Valentin Hube (1890–1944), who joined the German army in 1909 and fought in the First World War. During the Second World War Hube commanded a division, corps and army on the Eastern Front and also fought in Sicily and Italy. Hube successfully led his panzer army out of the encirclement, but died in an air crash shortly afterwards.
2. Editor's note. Ivan Danilovich Chernyakhovskii (1906–45) joined the Red Army in 1924 and served in various command capacities before the war. During the Great Patriotic War he advanced from the command of a division to that of a corps and army, and in 1944 was appointed to command the Third Belorussian Front. He was killed during the East Prussian operation in February 1945.
3. Editor's note. Vasilii Mikhailovich Badanov (1895–1971) was drafted into the Imperial Russian Army in 1915 and fought in the First World War and joined the Red Army in 1919. During the Second World War he commanded a tank brigade, tank division, tank corps and tank army until a wound sidelined him. Following the war, he commanded Soviet armoured and mechanized forces in Germany. Badanov retired in 1953.
4. Editor's note. Pavel Semyonovich Rybalko (1894–1948) joined the Imperial Russian Army in 1915 and the Red Army in 1919. During the interwar period he served mainly in the cavalry and intelligence branches. During the Great Patriotic War he served in the General Staff apparatus and the tank troops, becoming commander of the 3rd Tank Army in 1943. Following the war, Rybalko commanded the Red Army's armoured forces.
5. Editor's note. The 1st Galician Division (14th Waffen-SS Grenadier Division) was formed in 1943 primarily from volunteers of Ukrainian origin. The division was nearly destroyed in the fighting around Brody, but was later reconstituted and surrendered to US and British forces in 1945.

6. Editor's note. The T-34 was the Red Army's standard medium tank during the Great Patriotic War and afterwards. The 1941 model weighed 26.5 tonnes, carried a crew of four and was armed with a 76mm gun and two 7.62mm machine guns. A later model was fitted with an 85mm gun.
7. Editor's note. The SU-85 was a Soviet self-propelled gun which first appeared in 1943. One model weighed 29.6 tonnes and carried a crew of four. It was armed with an 85mm gun.
8. TsAMO RF, fond 3402, opis' 1, delo 82, list 21.
9. TsAMO RF, fond 1635, opis' 1, delo 129, list 127.
10. Editor's note. The U-2 (also known as the Po-2) was a general-purpose Soviet biplane that first appeared in 1929. One model had a crew of one and a maximum speed of 152km/h. It was armed with one 7.62mm machine gun and could carry six 50kg bombs.
11. TsAMO RF, 3402, opis' 1, delo 82, list 24.
12. Editor's note. '*Katyusha*' was the nickname for several kinds (BM-13, BM-8 and BM-31) multiple rocket launchers employed by the Red Army during the Great Patriotic War. These weapons first saw action in July 1941. These weapons constituted the Guards mortar units.
13. Editor's note. Erhard Rauss (1889–1956) joined the Austro-Hungarian Army in 1909 and fought in the First World War. During the Second World War he commanded panzer divisions, corps and armies, mostly on the Eastern Front.
14. NARA, T313, R388, frame 8677406.
15. Editor's note. The Panzer V ('Panther') was a German medium tank which first appeared in 1943. One model weighed 44.8 tonnes and carried a crew of five. It was armed with a 75mm gun and two 7.92mm machine guns.
16. Editor's note. The Wehrmacht encompassed the entire German armed forces.
17. NARA, T311, R228, frame 1019.
18. NARA, T313, R392, frame 8682676.
19. Editor's note. This was the German navy.
20. Editor's note. This was the German air force from 1933 to 1945.
21. Editor's note. This is probably a reference to the 1st SS Panzer Division '*Leibstandarte SS Adolf Hitler*'.
22. Editor's note. The *Sturmgeschütz* (StuG) was a tracked armoured assault gun widely employed by the German army during the Second World War. Two models were produced – the StuG III, which was mounted on a Panzer III chassis, and the StuG IV, which was mounted on a Panzer IV chassis. Both models were armed with a 75mm gun.
23. TsAMO RF, fond 323, opis' 4756, delo 31, list 21.
24. From the headquarters of the 'Galicia' Division.
25. TsAMO RF, fond 236, opis' 2673, delo 1274, list 92.
26. TsAMO RF, fond 3402, opis' 1, delo 82, list 29.

27. NARA, T313, R 388, frame 8677416.
28. TsAMO RF, fond 1635, opis' 1, delo 129, list 122.
29. TsAMO RF, fond 236, opis' 2677, delo 59, list 152.
30. NARA, T313, R392, frame 8682008.
31. Editor's note. The *Hummel* (Ger. 'Bumblebee') was a self-propelled gun employed by the German army during the latter half of the Second World War. The *Hummel* carried a crew of six and was mounted on a *Geschützwagen* III/IV chassis and was armed with a 150mm howitzer.
32. Editor's note. The StuH (*Sturmhaubitze*) was a lighter modification of the *Sturmgeschütz* self-propelled gun and was employed during the latter half of the Second World War. The StuH carried a crew of four and mounted a 105mm howitzer.
33. NARA, T313, R392, frame 8682724.
34. Editor's note. *Grille* (Ger. 'cricket') was the name given to a number of self-propelled guns employed by the German army during the latter half of the Second World War. These vehicles carried a crew of five, mounted on a captured Czechoslovak 38(t) tank chassis and were armed with a 150mm gun.
35. NARA, T313, R392, frame 8682815.
36. Editor's note. The Panzer VI ('Tiger') was a German heavy tank which first appeared in 1943. One model weighed 54 tonnes and carried a crew of five. It was armed with an 88mm gun and two 7.92 machine guns.
37. Kiselyov perished in January 1945 and made a Hero of the Soviet Union (posthumously).
38. TsAMO RF, fond 417, opis' 10570, delo 70, list 239. BT i MV 60 A.
39. NARA, T314, R1180, frame 1074.
40. TsAMO RF, fond 885, opis' 1, delo 84, list 117.
41. NARA, T313, R408, frame 8701241.
42. G. Fricke, *Fester Platz. Tarnopol, 1944* (Freiburg: Rombach Verlag KG, 1986), p. 66.
43. NARA, T314, R1180, frame 1086.
44. NARA, T314, R 1180, frame 1096.
45. Editor's note. Mikhail Yefimovich Katukov (1900–76) joined the Red Army in 1919 and fought in the Russian Civil War. During the Second World War he commanded a tank brigade, a tank corps and a tank army in several major operations. Following the war, Katukov commanded the Soviet army's mechanized forces in Germany and served in the central military apparatus.
46. NARA, T313, R392, frame 8683176.
47. NARA, T314, R1182, frame 496.
48. Editor's note. Hermann Balck (1897–1982) joined the German Army in 1913 and fought in the First World War in France, Russia, Italy and the Balkans. During the Second World War he commanded a tank regiment, division, corps, and army in the East and later commanded an army group in the West. He was convicted of war crimes, but released in 1950.

49. Fricke, *Fester Platz*, p. 74.
50. NARA, T314, R1180, frame 1120.
51. Editor's note. The ZIS-3 was a 76.2mm divisional gun produced at the Stalin Factory (Russ. *Zavod imeni Stalina*) during the Second World War.
52. Editor's note. The ZIS-2 was a 57mm gun produced at the Stalin Factory.
53. Editor's note. Lend–Lease was an American aid programme that delivered food, military equipment and raw materials to the Allies during the Second World War. In all $50.1 billion dollars of aid was delivered, including $11.3 billion to the USSR.
54. Judging from the 'Memorial' and 'The People's Feat' data bases, V.F. Rzhevskii survived the war and received the Order of Aleksandr Nevskii in 1945.
55. Editor's note. The Il-2 was a ground attack aircraft widely used by the Soviet Air Force during the Second World War. One model carried a crew of two (pilot and rear gunner) and had a maximum speed of 410km/h. It was armed with two fixed 23mm cannon, two fixed 7.62mm machine guns and one manual 12.7mm machine gun in the rear cockpit. It could carry up to six 100kg bombs, or various quantities of rockets.
56. NARA, T314, R1180, frame 1182.
57. TsAMO RF, fond. 1296, opis' 1, delo 11, list 32 (back).
58. NARA, T314, R1180, frame 1182.
59. TsAMO RF, fond 1296, opis' 1, delo 18, list 33.
60. TsAMO RF, fond 1296, opis' 1, delo 18, list 33.
61. TsAMO RF, fond 417, opis' 10564, delo 1011, list 30.
62. NARA, T314, R1180, frame 1167.
63. TsAMO RF, fond 1608, opis' 1, delo 23, list 40.
64. TsAMO RF, fond. 236, opis' 2673, delo 1274, list 35.
65. Including the 322nd Rifle Division's operationally-subordinated 1085th Rifle Regiment, or 300 active bayonets.
66. TsAMO RF, fond 417, opis' 10564, delo 1008, list 111.
67. TsAMO RF, fond 236, opis' 2673, delo 1274, list 92.
68. Editor's note. Konstantin Mikhailovich Simonov (1915–79) was a Soviet author, dramatist and poet whose works often dealt with the travails of the Eastern Front. During the Second World War he also served as a war correspondent. Following the war, Simonov became a leading figure in the Soviet literary establishment.
69. P.N. Lashchenko, *Iz Boya v Boi* (Moscow: Voennoe Izdatel'stvo, 1972), p. 262.
70. TsAMO RF, fond 236, opis' 2673, delo 1274, list 95.
71. Editor's note. The Pe-2 was a Soviet twin-engined dive bomber that saw action in the Second World War. One model carried a crew of three and had a maximum speed of 580km/h. It was armed with two fixed 7.62mm and two rearward-firing 7.62mm machine guns and could carry 1,600kg of bombs.

72. NARA, T313, R392, frame 8682008.
73. Editor's note. The StuG III was an assault gun employed by the German army during the Second World War. It employed a Panzer III chassis mounting a 75mm gun and carried a crew of four.
74. Editor's note. See Chapter 1, note 34.
75. NARA, T313, R392, frame 8682863.
76. Editor's note. The Panzer IV was a German medium tank that first appeared in 1939. One model weighed 25 tons and had a crew of five. It was armed with a 75mm gun and two 7.92 machine guns.
77. NARA, T313, R408, frame 8701243.
78. Editor's note. Otto Moritz Walter Model (1891–1945) joined the German Army in 1910 and fought in the First World War. During the Second World War he commanded a division, corps, army and army groups, mostly on the Eastern Front. Model's last command was of German forces surrounded in the Ruhr, where he committed suicide.
79. NARA, T313, R392, frame 8682010.
80. Editor's note. This refers to the SS 10th Panzer Division, which was named after the sixteenth-century military leader Georg von Frundsberg.
81. NARA, T313, R408, frame 8701250.
82. Editor's note. The *Bergepanther* (Ger. *Panzer-Bergegerat*) was a tank recovery vehicle based on the Panther tank. It carried a crew of five and was armed with two 7.92mm machine guns.
83. A conventional term that cannot be easily defined, although this most likely designated a repair facility in the army group rear.
84. NARA, T313, R314, frame 459.
85. Editor's note. The Panzer III was a German medium tank employed extensively during the first half of the Second World War. Models carried a crew of five and were armed with either a 37mm, 50mm or 75mm gun and two or three 7.92mm machine guns.
86. With the notation, 'three conditionally'.
87. NARA, T314, R1182, frame 498.
88. TsAMO RF, fond 9614, opis' 1, delo 2, list 105.
89. TsAMO RF, fond 236, opis' 2677, delo 59, list 169.
90. TsAMO RF, fond 1376, opis' 1, delo 29, list 164.
91. Editor's note. This was a Waffen-SS rank equivalent to that of a general in the German regular army.
92. TsAMO RF, fond 417, opis' 10599, delo 207, list 45.
93. TsAMO RF, fond 315, opis' 4440, delo 231, list 4.
94. TsAMO RF, fond 315, opis' 4440, delo 231, list 9.
95. Editor's note. The Ferdinand was a German heavy tank destroyer, named in honour of the designer Ferdinand Porsche, which first saw action at Kursk. The Ferdinand had a crew of six and weighed 65 tonnes. It was armed with an 88mm gun.

96. TsAMO RF, fond 987, opis' 1, delo 238, listy 25–26.

97. Fricke, *Fester Platz*, p. 120.

98. TsAMO RF, fond 9614, opis' 1, delo 2, list 113.

99. TsAMO RF, fond 9614, opis' 1, delo 2, list 113.

100. TsAMO RF, fond 9698, opis' 1, delo 28, list 19.

101. TsAMO RF, fond 9698, opis' 1, delo 28, list 20.

102. NARA, T314, R1182, frame 636.

103. Editor's note. This refers to a series of heavy tanks produced for the Red Army during the Second World War and afterwards. These included the IS-1, IS-2, IS-3, IS-4, IS-6, IS-7 and IS-10.

104. Editor's note. The IS-122 was a Soviet assault gun used in the latter half of the Second World War. It carried a crew of four or five men and was armed with a 122mm gun.

105. TsAMO RF, fond 317, opis' 4440, delo 231, list 7.

106. NARA, T313, R392, frame 8683135.

107. NARA, T314, R1182, frames 775, 788.

108. NARA, T314, R1182, frame 785.

109. NARA, T313, R408, frame 8701240.

110. NARA, T313, R408, frame 8701240.

111. TsAMO RF, fond 236, opis' 2673, delo 1274, list 57.

112. Editor's note. The SU-152 was a self-propelled gun that first appeared in 1943. Depending on the model, it carried a crew of four or five men and had a maximum weight of 45.5 tonnes. It was armed with a 152mm gun and a 12.7mm machine gun.

113. Editor's note. The SU-76 was a self-propelled gun produced in the Soviet Union during 1942–5. Using a T-70 tank chassis, it had a crew of four and was armed with a 76mm gun.

114. TsAMO RF, fond 317, opis' 4440, delo 231, list 7.

115. TsAMO RF, fond 417, opis' 10519, delo 195, list 131.

116. Editor's note. Paul Joseph Goebbels (1893–1945) joined the Nazi Party in 1924 and soon entered Hitler's inner circle. Upon the Nazi assumption of power in 1933, Hitler named Goebbels Minister of Propaganda. He kept this post throughout the war and was also in charge of the country's total mobilization drive from 1943 on. Hitler appointed Goebbels as Chancellor, but he survived Hitler by only one day. He and his wife poisoned their children and then killed themselves.

117. TsAMO RF, fond 236, opis' 2673, delo 1274, list 92.

118. TsAMO RF, fond 987, opis' 1, delo 238, list 33.

119. Editor's note. Kliment Yefremovich Voroshilov (1881–1969) joined the Bolshevik faction in 1903 and rose through the party's ranks in Ukraine. During the civil war he commanded units and also served as a political officer. An early supporter of Stalin, Voroshilov was defence commissar from 1925 to 1940. During the Second World War he held a number of command posts but gradually lost power and became a political figurehead.

120. TsAMO RF, fond 417, opis' 10564, delo 855, list 32.
121. Editor's note. The *raketenwerfer* (also known as *Puppchen*, or 'doll') was an 88mm reusable anti-tank rocket launcher used by the German army during the latter part of the Second World War.
122. TsAMO RF, fond 236, opis' 2673, delo 1321, list 8.
123. Editor's note. The *Ofenrohren* (Ger. 'stove pipe') were 88mm infantry anti-tank weapons used by the Germans during the latter part of the Second World War. It later became known as the *Panzerschreck* (Ger. 'tank bane').
124. Editor's note. The *Faustpatrone* (Ger. 'cartridge fist') was the name for a variety of infantry anti-tank weapons employed by the Germans during the latter half of the Second World War. Later models were commonly known as *Panzerfaust* (Ger. 'tank fist'), but the Soviets usually called all such weapons *Faustpatronen*.

Chapter 2: Kovel': An Exception to the Rule

1. Editor's note. The *Stavka* of the Supreme Commander-in-Chief (*Stavka Verkhovnogo Glavnokomanduyushchego*), also known as the *Stavka* of the VGK, was the Soviet Union's highest military body during the Second World War. The *Stavka* was comprised of high-ranking civilian and military personnel and functioned as Stalin's military secretariat. Stalin, as supreme commander-in-chief, was the chairman of this body and the General Staff its executive organ.
2. Editor's note. Konstantin Konstantinovich Rokossovskii (1896–1968) joined the Imperial Russian Army in 1914 and fought in the First World War. He joined the Red Army in 1918 and fought in the Russian Civil War. Rokossovskii was arrested in 1937 during Stalin's purge, but survived and was released in 1940. During the Second World War he commanded a corps, armies and *fronts*. After the war, Rokossovskii commanded Soviet forces in Poland and during 1949–56 he served as Polish minister of defence. Rokossovskii retired in 1962.
3. Editor's note. Pavel Alekseyevich Kurochkin (1900–89) joined the Red Army in 1918 and fought in the Russian Civil War. During the Second World War he commanded a number of *fronts* and armies. After the war, he commanded a military district and worked in the army's military-educational apparatus.
4. Editor's note. Fyodor Yefimovich Bokov (1903–84) joined the Red Army in 1926 and served in a variety of political posts. During the Second World War he was a member of the military council (political commissar) with various *fronts* and an army. Following the war, he continued his political work in the army and served in the military-educational apparatus.
5. Editor's note. Vladimir Yakovlevich Kolpakchi (1899–1961) joined the Red Army in 1918 and fought in the Russian Civil War. During the Second World War he served in higher staff positions and commanded a number of armies. Following the war, Kolpakchi commanded a number of military districts and served in the central military apparatus. He died in an air crash.

6. Editor's note. Pavel Alekseyevich Belov (1897–1963) joined the Imperial Russian Army in 1916 and the Red Army in 1919 and fought in the Russian Civil War. During the Second World War he commanded cavalry corps and an army. Following the war, he commanded a military district and retired in 1960.

7. Editor's note. Vitalii Sergeyevich Polenov (1901–68) joined the Red Army in 1918 and fought in the Russian Civil War. During the Second World War he commanded divisions and armies, but was later demoted to the command of a corps. He continued to command corps until his retirement in 1958.

8. Editor's note. Fyodor Petrovich Polynin (1906–81) joined the Red Army in 1928 and was later transferred to the air force, where he became a pilot and later fought in the Sino–Japanese War. During the Second World War he commanded air armies along various *fronts* and later headed the Polish air force. Following the war, he continued to command air armies and worked in the central military apparatus until his retirement in 1971.

9. *Russkii Arkhiv. Velikaya Otechestvennaya Voina. Stavka VGK: Dokumenty i Materialy, 1944–1945*, Vol. 16 (5–4). (Moscow: Terra, 1999), p. 55.

10. Editor's note. This is a large area of forest and swamp stretching from the eastern border of Poland and including southern Belarus and northern Ukraine.

11. As in the document.

12. Editor's note. Stepan Andriyonovich Bandera (1909–59) became involved in Ukrainian nationalist politics as a student. Following the invasion of the Soviet Union he was arrested by the Germans, who later freed him in the hopes of stemming the Soviet advance. Bandera later escaped to the West and was killed in Munich by a Soviet agent.

13. Editor's note. The PPSh (*pistolet-pulemet Shpagina*) was a popular sub-machine gun model in the Red Army during the Great Patriotic War. It was designed by Georgii Shpagin (1897–1952), weighed 3.63kg unloaded and had a cyclic rate of 900–1,000 7.62mm rounds per minute.

14. Editor's note. This refers to the 7.62mm light machine gun designed by Vasilii Alekseyevich Degtyaryov.

15. Editor's note. This is probably a reference to Erich Julius Eberhard von dem Bach-Zelewski (1899–1972), an SS commander in charge of fighting partisan 'bands' and others in the rear of the German army in the USSR. Von dem Bach-Zelewski was not charged with war crimes after the war, but later died in prison after being sentenced for the politically-motivated murders of opponents of Hitler's regime in the 1930s.

16. This is what the Germans called the partisan detachments. In this case, Polish formations from the Home Army also came under this definition.

17. NARA, T313, R388, frames 8677433–8677434.

18. Editor's note. That is, Hungarian troops.

19. Editor's note. The Infantry Tank Mk III Valentine was produced by Great Britain during the Second World War. One model weighed 16 tonnes and carried a crew of four. It was armed with a 40mm gun and a 7.92mm machine gun.

20. Editor's note. The M-4 Sherman was a US-made medium tank which first appeared in 1942. One model weighed 30.3 tonnes and carried a crew of five. It was armed with a 75mm gun, a 50-calibre machine gun and two 30.06 machine guns.

21. See Chapter 1, note 53.

22. Editor's note. *Gruppenführer* (Ger. 'group leader') was a paramilitary rank in the Nazi Party equivalent to the rank of lieutenant general.

23. Editor's note. The Fieseler F-156 Storch was a single-engined passenger aircraft which first appeared in 1936. During the Second World War it was used as a light passenger and reconnaissance plane.

24. Editor's note. *Hauptsturmführer* (Ger. 'head storm leader') was a paramilitary rank in the Nazi Party equivalent to that of captain.

25. Editor's note. The *Landwehr* units were staffed by men older than 35 years and younger than 45. They were generally relegated to rear-area and security duties.

26. That is, without rear units, but including headquarters elements.

27. E. Klapdor, *Viking Panzers. The German 5th SS Tank Regiment in the East in World War II* (Mechanicsburg, PA: Stackpole Books, 2011), p. 253; NARA, T354, R639, frames 23–24.

28. Editor's note. The *schutzpolizei* were the uniformed police in Nazi German responsible for keeping order in cities and large towns.

29. Klapdor, *Viking Panzers*, p. 254; NARA, T354, R639, frames 23–24.

30. NARA, T354, R639, frame 24.

31. Editor's note. Erich von Manstein (1887–1973) joined the Imperial German Army in 1906 and fought in the First World War. During the Second World War he served as chief of staff of an army group and commanded corps, an army and an army group. He was relieved by Hitler in early 1944 and never held a command afterward. Following the war, Manstein was convicted of war crimes, but served only a few years before being released.

32. Editor's note. The Yak-9 was a single-engined Soviet fighter which first appeared in 1942. One model had a crew of one, a maximum speed of 591km/h and a range of 1,360km. It was armed with one 20mm cannon and one 12.7mm machine gun.

33. Editor's note. See Chapter 1, note 10.

34. F.P. Polynin, *Boevye Marshruty* (Moscow: Voennoe Izdatel'stvo, 1972), p. 303.

35. Editor's note. This was the nickname for the Il-2 ground-attack aircraft.

36. M.Kh. Kalashnik, *Ispytanie Ognyom* (Moscow: Mysl', 1985), p. 252.

37. Editor's note. This was the numerical designation for the Sherman tank.

38. NARA, T354, R639, frame 6.
39. TsAMO RF, fond 237, opis' 2757, delo 59, list 7.
40. A village on the approaches to the city from the north.
41. NARA, T354, R639, frame 7.
42. NARA, T354, R639, frame 7.
43. Klapdor, *Viking Panzers*, p. 257.
44. Editor's note. *Standartenführer* (Ger. 'standard leader') was a Nazi Party paramilitary rank equivalent to that of colonel.
45. NARA, T354, R639, frame 2.
46. Editor's note. The *sturmgewehr* was a 7.92mm assault rifle used by the German army during the latter part of the Second World War.
47. NARA, T354, R639, frame 3.
48. NARA, T313, R388, frame 8677499.
49. NARA, T78, R719, frame 305.
50. Cited in S. Newton, *German Battle Tactics on the Russian Front, 1941–1945* (Atglen, PA: Schiffer Publishing Ltd., 1994), p. 197.
51. In his essay for the Americans, Mattenklott moved the course of events ahead by one day. The general was writing from memory and laid out the chronology of events imprecisely.
52. NARA, T313, R388, frame 8677539.
53. Editor's note. The name *jäger* (Ger., 'hunter') originally denoted light infantry, but during the Second World War came to describe various types of specialized units.
54. TsAMO RF, fond 402, opis' 9575, delo 406, list 26.
55. TsAMO RF, fond 402, opis' 9575, delo 429, list 22 (back).
56. TsAMO RF, fond 402, opis' 9611, delo 25, list 155.
57. Klapdor, *Viking Panzers*, p. 257.
58. Editor's note. The Ju-52 was a German tri-motor transport plane which first appeared in 1931. During the Second World War the plane was used to transport freight and paratroopers and was also employed as a medium bomber.
59. Editor's note. *Obersturmführer* (Ger. 'senior storm leader') was a Nazi Party paramilitary rank equivalent to a senior lieutenant.
60. Editor's note. Heinrich Luitpold Himmler (1900–45) joined the Nazi Party in 1923 and was appointed to head the paramilitary SS in 1929. As SS leader, he oversaw the Holocaust and other Nazi crimes against humanity. Himmler was captured by Allied forces at the end of the war and committed suicide.
61. NARA, T354, R639, frame 8.
62. NARA, T354, R639, frame 10.
63. TsAMO RF, fond 402, opis' 9575, delo 429, list 29.
64. NARA, T78, R719, frame 189.
65. NARA, T354, R639, frame 12.

66. Editor's note. Stuka was the common nickname of the Ju-87 dive-bomber employed by the Germans during the Second World War. One model carried a crew of two and had a maximum speed of 340km/h and a range of 595km. This model was armed with three 7.92mm machine guns and could carry 450kg of bombs.
67. Klapdor, *Viking Panzers*, p. 263.
68. TsAMO RF, fond 402, opis' 9575, delo 406, list 28.
69. J. Neuman, *Die 4 Panzer-Division 1938. Bericht und Betrachtungen zu zwei Blitzfield-zugen und zwei Jahren Krieg in Russland*. (Selbstverlag, 1985).
70. TsAMO RF, fond 1369, opis' 1, delo 43, list 107 (back).
71. NARA, T314, R1437, frame 963.
72. Editor's note. The Panzer II was a German light tank used in the early years of the Second World War, although it was superseded by heavier and better-armed models. One model had a crew of three and was armed with a 2cm gun and a 7.92mm machine gun.
73. NARA, T314, R393, frame 426.
74. NARA, T354, R639, frame 12.
75. NARA, T314, R393, frames 551, 553.
76. Strictly speaking, a battalion from the 4th Panzer Division's 35th Panzer Battalion was also removed to the west and rearmed with Panthers. It would rejoin its division in June 1944.
77. Editor's note. This was the Messerschmitt Bf 109, a single-seat German fighter that saw action throughout the Second World War. One model had a maximum speed of 520km/h and a maximum range of 1,144km. It was armed with two 13mm machine guns, three 20mm cannon and one 30mm cannon, two rockets, and could carry a bomb load of 250kg.
78. Editor's note. The Focke-Wulf Fw 190 was a single-seat fighter that gradually came to replace the Me 109 in the German air arsenal. One model had a maximum speed of 652km/h and a maximum range of 900km. It was armed with one 30mm and two 20mm cannon.
79. There are certain discrepancies regarding the number of wounded in Kovel'. On 5 April Gille radioed that there were 1,423 wounded, 243 of which were walking, while 1,179 had to be transported out.
80. NARA, T314, R1437, frame 972.
81. NARA, T312, R1304, frame 118.
82. NARA, T78, R719, frame 189.
83. K.K. Rokossovskii, *Soldatskii Dolg* (Moscow: Voennoe Izdatel'stvo, 1988), p. 248.
84. TsAMO RF, fond 402, opis' 9611, delo 25, list 252.
85. Editor's note. Ernst Bernhard Wilhelm Busch (1885–1945) joined the Imperial German Army in 1904 and fought in the First World War. During the Second World War he commanded a corps, an army and army groups. Busch was captured by the British and died in captivity.
86. TsAMO RF, fond 1369, opis' 1, delo 43, list 107 (back).

Chapter 3: Poznań: A Fortress in the Right Place

1. Editor's note. The *Volkssturm*, or people's militia, was organized in late 1944 as a last-ditch effort to stave off defeat. The *Volkssturm* was made up of males between 16 and 60 who were not already serving in the armed forces. The highest *Volkssturm* unit was the battalion. While organized by the Nazi Party, the *Volkssturm* fought under armed forces command.

2. Editor's note. *Obersturmbannführer* (Ger., 'senior assault unit leader') was a Nazi Party paramilitary rank equivalent to a lieutenant colonel.

3. Editor's note. The StuG IV was a German assault gun based on a Panzer IV chassis. It carried a crew of four and was armed with a 75mm gun and one 7.92mm machine gun.

4. Editor's note. See Chapter 1, note 45.

5. M.Ye. Katukov, *Na Ostriye Glavnogo Udara* (Moscow: Voennoe Izdatel'stvo, 1974), p. 358.

6. TsAMO RF, fond 8 gv. mk, opis' 1, delo 111, list 23.

7. Editor's note. See Chapter 2, note 5.

8. TsAMO RF, fond 233, opis' 2356, delo 547, list 6.

9. Editor's note. Vasilii Ivanovich Chuikov (1900–82) joined the Red Army in 1918 and fought in the Russian Civil War. During the interwar period he commanded an army during the 1939–40 war with Finland and was the Soviet military advisor to the Chinese Nationalist leader Chiang Kai-shek. During the Second World War Chuikov commanded an army in the defence of Stalingrad and held this post until the end of the war. Following the war, Chuikov commanded Soviet occupation troops in Germany, served as commander-in-chief of the Ground Forces, and was chief of national civil defence.

10. I.A. Tolkonyuk, *Rany Zazhivayut Medlenno. Zapiski Shtabnogo Ofitsera* (Moscow: Troitsa, 2004), p. 446.

11. Editor's note. Georgii Konstantinovich Zhukov (1896–1974) was drafted into the Imperial Russian Army in 1915 and joined the Red Army in 1918. In 1939 he defeated a major Japanese incursion in Mongolia. During the Great Patriotic War he served as chief of the General Staff and commanded several fronts. In 1942 he was appointed deputy supreme commander-in-chief, directly under Stalin. Following the war, he was relegated to several minor posts. After Stalin's death he served as Defence Minister and was a member of the Communist Party Presidium. Nikita Khrushchev removed Zhukov from all his posts in 1957 and he lived as a 'non-person' until Khrushchev's own ousting in 1964.

12. Editor's note. This refers to a series of heavy tanks produced for the Soviet army during the Second World War and afterwards. These included the IS-1, IS-2, IS-3, IS-4, IS-6, IS-7, and IS-10.

13. The ISU-152 was a Soviet self-propelled gun that saw service in the latter half of the Second World War. One model carried a crew of four or five and was armed with a 152mm gun and a 12.7mm machine gun.

14. Editor's note. The OT-34 (Russ., *ognemyotnyi tank*) was a flamethrowing version of the Soviet T-34 medium tank and was capable of projecting flame 80–120m, depending on the model.
15. TsAMO RF, fond 345, opis' 5487, delo 384, list 135.
16. TsAMO RF, fond 233, opis' 2356, delo 547, list 3.
17. U. Saft, *Krieg im Osten. Das bittere Ende jenseits der Weichsel bis Oder und Neisse* (Walsrode: Militarbuchverlag Saft, 2002), p. 151.
18. Editor's note. Posen was the German name for the city before the area was turned over to Poland following the First World War.
19. NARA, T311, R167, frames 205, 304.
20. TsAMO RF, fond 345, opis' 5487, delo 394, list 111.
21. TsAMO RF, fond 345, opis' 5487, delo 384, list 151.
22. TsAMO RF, fond 345, opis' 5487, delo 393, list 130.
23. TsAMO RF, fond 233, opis' 2356, delo 548, list 29.
24. Editor's note. The OKW (*Oberkommando der Wehrmacht*) was established in 1938 to coordinate army, navy and air force operations. As the war progressed, the OKW came increasingly to operate as Hitler's military staff in opposition to the army high command (OKH – *Oberkommando des Heeres*).
25. KTB OKW, Band 4, Zweiter Halbband, S. 1048.
26. TsAMO RF, fond 345, opis' 5487, delo 384, list 99.
27. TsAMO RF, fond 345, opis' 5487, delo 384, list 106.
28. TsAMO RF, fond 233, opis' 2356, delo 547, list 6.
29. That is, with the barrel already on the gun carriage. This was allowed when moving guns over short distances.
30. Editor's note. The FOG (*fugasnyi ognemyot*) was an ampoule-firing flamethrower.
31. Editor's note. The Heinkel He-111 was a two-engined medium bomber used by Germany throughout the Second World War. One model carried a crew of five and had a maximum speed of 440km/h and a maximum range of 2,300km. It was armed with up to seven 7.92mm machine guns, one 13mm machine gun and one 20mm cannon, and could carry up to 2,000kg of bombs in its bomb bay.
32. Editor's note. This was the Russian name for the machine gun invented by Hiram Maxim toward the end of the nineteenth century. The machine gun could fire up to 500 7.7mm rounds per minute. The Russian Army purchased a large number of these machine guns and they were widely employed during the Russo-Japanese War, the First World War, the Russian Civil War, and beyond.
33. TsAMO RF, fond 889, opis' 1, delo 96, list 184.
34. TsAMO RF, fond 91sk, opis' 1, delo 85, list 45.
35. TsAMO RF, fond 91sk, opis' 1, delo 85, list 72.
36. Editor's note. The M-31 was a heavy-calibre variant of the '*Katyusha*' rocket launcher, capable of firing 300mm rounds.

37. Editor's note. This is the German spelling for Poznań.
38. KTB OKW, Band 4, Teil 2, S. 1099.
39. TsAMO RF, fond 233, opis' 2356, delo 548, listy 136–137.
40. NARA, T311, R168, frame 243.
41. TsAMO RF, fond 889, opis' 1, delo 314, list 20.
42. TsAMO RF, fond 233, opis' 2356, delo 548, listy 167, 190.

Chapter 4: Breslau: The Reich's Last Fortress

1. Editor's note. Ivan Stepanovich Konev (1897–1973) served in the Imperial Russian Army and joined the Red Army in 1918, where he originally served as a political commissar, before switching to command responsibilities. During the Great Patriotic War he commanded an army and several *fronts*, the last being the First Ukrainian Front, from 1944. Following the war, he commanded Soviet occupation forces in Czechoslovakia and Austria and served as commander-in-chief of the Soviet Ground Forces. He later commanded the Warsaw Pact forces and the Group of Soviet Forces in Germany.
2. I.S. Konev, *Sorok Pyatyi* (Moscow: Voennoe Izdatel'stvo, 1970), p. 181.
3. Editor's note. The *gauleiter* was the Nazi Party leader of a district (Ger., *gau*), appointed directly by Hitler.
4. Editor's note. Karl August Hanke (1903–45) joined the Nazi Party in 1928 and quickly rose through its ranks. During the Second World War he was *Gauleiter* of Lower Silesia and later replaced Himmler as head of the SS at the end of the war. Hanke was killed by Czechoslovak partisans after the war.
5. Editor's note. The OKH (*Oberkommando des Heeres*) was the abbreviation for the German army high command.
6. Editor's note. Vladimir Alekseyevich Gluzdovskii (1903–67) joined the Red Army in 1919 and fought in the Russian Civil War. During the Second World War he commanded a division, was an army chief of staff and commanded armies. Following the war, Gluzdovskii served in the army's military-educational apparatus until his retirement in 1961.
7. Editor's note. The ISU-122 was a Soviet self-propelled gun employed during the latter part of the Second World War. It was mounted on an IS-122 chassis and carried a crew of four or five men, and was armed with a 122mm gun and a 12.7mm machine gun.
8. TsAMO RF, fond 236, opis' 2673, delo 2121, list 88.
9. TsAMO RF, fond 3437, opis' 1, delo 127, list 97 (back).
10. R. Hinze, *To the Bitter End. The Final Battles of Army Groups A, North Ukraine, Centre. The Eastern Front, 1944–1945* (Philadelphia, PA: Casemate Publishers, 2010), p. 110.
11. Editor's note. Aleksei Semyonovich Zhadov (before 1942, Zhidov) (1901–77) joined the Red Army in 1919 and fought in the Russian Civil War. During the Great Patriotic War he commanded an airborne and a cavalry corps,

before being appointed commander of the 66th (later 5th Guards) Army in 1943. Following the war, Zhadov served in a variety of administrative posts.

12. Editor's note. The 'Goliath' was the name given to two types of unmanned, remote-controlled vehicles designed to deliver explosives to their target. Both models were controlled by a radio operator and could carry 60kg or 100kg charges.

13. According to indirect data, there were *Panzerjäger* IV tank destroyers, with a long-barrelled 75mm gun (analogous in its ballistic qualities to the Panther's gun), in the fortress.

14. Editor's note. The '*Wespe*' (Ger., 'Wasp') was a German self-propelled gun used during the latter part of the Second World War. Mounted on a Panzer II chassis, one model carried a crew of five and was armed with a 105mm gun.

15. Cited in A. Vasil'chenko, *Poslednyaya Krepost' Reikha* (Moscow: Yauza-Press, 2009), p. 83.

16. TsAMO RF, fond 868, opis' 1, delo 47, list 79.

17. Vasil'chenko, *Poslednyaya*, p. 88.

18. Editor's note. The Hitler Youth (Ger., *Hitlerjugend*) was established in 1922 as the youth auxiliary of the Nazi Party. Once the Nazis took power in 1933, membership became virtually mandatory for German males aged 14–18. The Hitler Youth was increasingly drawn into the German war effort and the first units began taking part in combat operations in 1943.

19. TsAMO RF, fond 7322, opis' 67963, delo 18, list 17.

20. TsAMO RF, fond 236, opis' 2673, delo 2780, list 154.

21. Among the formations assaulting Breslau, only the 294th Rifle Division had the six SU-76s assigned to rifle divisions according to the new table of organization.

22. TsAMO RF, fond 236, opis' 2673, delo 2121, list 140.

23. TsAMO RF, fond 236, opis' 2673, delo 2780, list 141.

24. TsAMO RF, fond 462, opis' 5252, delo 552, list 142.

25. Editor's note. This was the Soviet name for an artillery shell, which was developed in France during the First World War, the design for which was later transferred to the Russian army, which began to produce the shells.

26. Editor's note. The Warsaw uprising was an attempt by the Polish Home Army (Pol., *Armia Krajowa*) to seize Warsaw from the Germans before the arrival of Soviet troops. The uprising began on 1 August 1944 and ended on 2 October with the surrender of the remaining Polish forces.

27. Editor's note. This refers to the airborne landing by German forces on the island of Crete, which began on 20 May 1941. Despite heavy casualties, the paratroopers were able to capture an airfield and ensure the arrival of reinforcements, which succeeded in driving the Allied forces from the island.

28. Editor's note. This refers to the Battle of Monte Cassino, which lasted from 17 January to 18 May 1944. The area was dominated by an ancient

Benedictine abbey, which was bombed and assaulted four times before the Allies finally broke through to Rome.

29. TsAMO RF, fond 868, opis' 1, delo 48, list 149.

30. TsAMO RF, fond 236, opis' 2673, delo 2780, listy 154, 162.

31. TsAMO RF, fond 236, opis' 2673, delo 2780, list 163.

32. Editor's note. Aleksandr Yevgen'evich Golovanov (1904–75) joined the Red Army in 1924. During the Second World War he commanded a bomber regiment and division and was later appointed commander of Long-Range Aviation. Following the war, Golovanov was demoted to command of an air corps and was discharged in 1953, after Stalin's death.

33. https://iremember.ru/memoirs/drugie-voyska/belik-vladimir-filippovich/

34. Editor's note. Hermann Wilhelm Göring (1893–1946) joined the Imperial German Army in 1912 and became a decorated fighter pilot during the First World War. Following the war, Göring joined the Nazi Party and became one of Hitler's trusted lieutenants and designated successor. He commanded the Luftwaffe before and after the Second World War until dismissed by Hitler in the closing days of the war. Göring was sentenced to death during the Nuremberg war crimes trials, but committed suicide before the sentence could be carried out.

35. F. Morzik, *German Air Force Airlift Operations* (New York, NY: Arno Press, 1968), p. 332.

36. TsAMO RF, fond 500, opis' 12480, delo 33, list 6.

37. TsAMO RF, fond 500, opis' 12480, delo 33, list 8.

38. TsAMO RF, fond 500, opis' 12480, delo 33, list 20.

39. Editor's note. The *Panzerjäger* IV (*Jagdpanzer* IV) was a German tank destroyer employed in the latter half of the Second World War. It carried a crew of four and was armed with a 75mm gun and a 7.92mm machine gun.

40. TsAMO RF, fond 500, opis' 12480, delo 33, list 23.

41. NARA, T78, R645, frame 523.

42. NARA, T78, R 645, frame 544.

43. Editor's note. This refers to the 20mm model 1930/1938 *Flakvierling* anti-aircraft gun used by the German army during the Second World War.

44. TsAMO RF, fond 1431, opis' 1, delo 11, list 276.

45. TsAMO RF, fond 500, opis' 12480, delo 33, list 17.

46. Vasil'chenko, *Poslednyaya*, p. 132.

47. Editor's note. '*Andryusha*' was an alternative name for the Red Army's rocket-propelled artillery known by the more popular name of '*Katyusha*'. The model referred to here was a 300mm round capable of delivering a 28.9kg warhead a distance of 2,800m.

48. TsAMO RF, fond 868, opis' 1, delo 48, list 153.

49. Editor's note. The TT was a 7.62mm pistol developed for the Red Army by Fyodor Vasil'evich Tokarev in 1930 and which was widely used during the Second World War.

50. TsAMO RF, fond 38, opis' 11360, delo 14, list 59.

51. http://iremember.ru/memoirs/drugie-voyska/belik-vladimir-filippovich/

52. Editor's note. The IS-2 (Iosif Stalin) was a Soviet heavy tank which first appeared in 1944. One model weighed 46 tons and carried a crew of four. It was armed with a 122mm gun and three 7.62mm machine guns.

53. TsAMO RF, fond 462, opis' 5252, delo 567, list 159.

54. Editor's note. Emmanuil Genrikhovich Kazakevich (1913–62) was a Soviet writer who wrote in Yiddish and Russian. Many of his works focus on Soviet heroics during the Second World War.

55. TsAMO RF, fond 236, opis' 2673, delo 2780, list 258.

56. TsAMO RF, fond 967, opis' 1, delo 70, list 1, with a clarification according to the formations' war diaries.

57. TsAMO RF, fond 236, opis' 2673, delo 2780, listy 246 (back), 1260.

58. TsAMO RF, fond 462, opis' 5252, delo 567, list 161.

59. Vasil'chenko, *Poslednyaya*, pp. 186–7.

60. TsAMO RF, fond 1679, opis' 1, delo 67, list 119.

61. TsAMO RF, fond 1679, opis' 1, delo 64, list 98.

62. TsAMO RF, fond 236, opis' 2673, delo 2780, list 250.

63. TsAMO RF, fond 236, opis' 2673, delo 2780, list 250.

64. TsAMO RF, fond. 236, opis' 2673, delo 2780, list 252.

65. Editor's note. The *Einsatzgruppen* ('task forces') were special SS death squads, which were responsible for carrying out mass murders in German-occupied territory during the Second World War.

66. TsAMO RF, fond 1309, opis' 1, delo 30, list 103.

67. See Chapter 1, note 121.

68. Vasil'chenko, *Poslednyaya*, p. 140.

69. The normal weight of a *Puppchen*, without sleds, was 105kg.

70. TsAMO RF, fond 236, opis' 2673, delo 2745, list 212.

71. TsAMO RF, fond 967, opis' 1, delo 63, list 44.

72. See Chapter 4, note 38.

73. Vasil'chenko, *Poslednyaya*, p. 195.

74. TsAMO RF, fond 967, opis' 1, delo 70, list 120.

75. According to the 218th Rifle Division's report of 18 April.

76. TsAMO RF, fond 462, opis' 5252, delo 569, list 9.

77. TsAMO RF, fond 868, opis' 1, delo 47, list 181.

78. TsAMO RF, fond 236, opis' 2673, delo 2745, list 63.

79. TsAMO RF, fond 236, opis' 2673, delo 2780, list 421 (back).

80. Counting non-combat losses and sick.

81. TsAMO RF, fond 500, opis' 12480, delo 33, list 32.

82. Editor's note. This refers to the uprising by Czechoslovak partisans and civilians against the German occupiers on 5–9 May 1945. An armistice signed on 8 May allowed the Germans to evacuate the city, although fighting continued until the next day, when the Red Army arrived.

83. Editor's note. Ferdinand Schörner (1892–1973) joined the German army during the First World War. During the Second World War he commanded a regiment, a division, a corps, and several army groups. A fanatical Nazi, Schörner was later found guilty of war crimes and was released from prison only in 1963.
84. Editor's note. This refers to the German forces holed up in the so-called Courland Pocket, in Latvia, between October 1944 and May 1945.
85. See Chapter 2, note 23.
86. TsAMO RF, fond 967, opis' 1, delo 20, list 283a.
87. TsAMO RF, fond 236, opis' 2673, delo 2745, list 67.

Conclusions

1. Editor's note. General Theodor Busse (1897–1986) joined the Imperial German Army in 1915 and fought in the First World War. During the Second World War he served as chief of staff of an army group and later commanded a division and corps. He was appointed to command the Ninth Army in January 1945. Following the war, Busse served as West Germany's director of civil defence.

Appendix: Adolf Hitler's Order on Fortresses

1. NARA, T311, R228, frames 1019–1021.

Bibliography

Babadzhan, A.Kh., *Dorogi Pobedy* (Moscow: 'Molodaya Gvardiya', 1975).
Boevye Deistviya Strelkovogo Polka. Sborniik Boevykh Primerov (Moscow: Voennoe Izdatel'stvo, 1958).
Chuikov, V.I., *Konets Tret'ego Reikha* (Moscow: Sovetskaya Rossiya, 1973).
Fricke, G., *Fester Platz' Tarnopol', 1944* (Freiburg: Rombach Verlag KG, 1986).
Fronty, Floty, Armii, Flotilii Perioda Velikoi Otechestvennoi Voiny, 1941–1945 gg. Spravochnik (Moscow: Izdatel'stvo 'Kuchkovo-Polye', 2006).
Hinze, R., *To the Bitter End. The Final Battles of Army Group A, North Ukraine and Centre. The Eastern Front, 1944–1945* (Philadelphia, PA: Casemate Publishers, 2010).
Jentz, T., *Panzertruppen. The Complete Guide to the Creation & Combat Employment of Germany's Tank Force, 1943–1945* (Atglen, PA: Schiffer Military History, 1996).
Kalashnik, M.Kh., *Ispytanie Ognyom* (Moscow: Mysl', 1985).
Katukov, M.Ye., *Na Ostriye Glavnogo Udara* (Moscow: Voennoe Izdatel'stvo, 1974).
Khaupt, V., *Srazheniya Gruppy Armii 'Tsentr'* (Moscow: Yauza–EKSMO, 2006).
Klapdor, E., *Viking Panzers. The German 5th SS Tank Regiment in the East in World War II* (Mechanicsburg, PA: Stackpole Books, 2011).
Konev, I.S., *Sorok Pyatyi* (Moscow: Voennoe Izdatel'stvo, 1970).
Kurovski, F., *Shturmovye Orudiya Vperyod! 'Shturmgeschutze: v Boyu* (Moscow: Yauza–Press, 2011).
Lashchenko, P.N., *Iz Boya v Boi* (Moscow: Voennoe Izdatel'stvo, 1972).
Morzik, F., *German Air Force Airlift Operations* (New York, NY: Arno Press, 1968).
Myuller-Gillebrand, B., *Sukhoputnaya Armiya Germanii, 1933–1945 gg* (Moscow: EKSMO-Izografus, 2002).
Nevenkin, K., *Fire Brigades. The Panzer Divisions, 1943–1945* (Winnipeg, Canada: J.J. Fedorowicz Publishing, Inc., 2008).
Newton, S., *German Battle Tactics on the Russian Front, 1943–1945* (Atglen, PA: Schiffer Publishing, Ltd., 1994).
Operatsii Sovetskikh Vooruzhennykh Sil v Velikoi Otechestvennoi Voine, 1941–1945 Tom IV (Moscow: Voennoe Izdatel'stvo, 1959).
Polynin, F.P., *Boevye Marshruty* (Moscow: Voennoe Izdatel'stvo, 1972).
Ponomarenko, R.O., *Bitva za Kovel'* (Moscow: Veche, 2014).
Rokossovskii, K.K., *Soldatskii Dolg* (Moscow: Voennoe Izdatel'stvo, 1988).
Russkii Arkhiv. Velikaya Otechestvennaya Voina. Stavka VGK: Dokumenty i Materialy, 1944–1945 Vol. 16(4–5) (Moscow: Terra, 1999).

Saft, U., *Krieg im Osten. Das bittere Ende jenseits der Weichsel bis Oder und Neisse* (Walsrode: Militarbuchverlag Saft, 2002).

Sovetskie Tankovye Voiska, 1941–1945 (Moscow: Voennoe Izdatel'stvo, 1973).

Tieke, W., *In the Firestorm of the Last Years of the War. II SS Panzerkorps with the 9th and 10th SS Divisions 'Hohenstaufen' and 'Frundsberg'* (Winnipeg, Canada: J.J. Fedorowice Publishing, Inc., 1999).

Tippel'skirkh, K., *Istoriya Vtoroi Mirovoi Voiny* (St. Petersburg: Poligon; Moscow: AST, 1999).

Tolkonyuk, I.A., *Rany Zazhivayut Medlenno. Zapiski Shtabnogo Ofitsera* (Moscow: Troitsa, 2004).

Vasil'chenko, A., *Poslednyaya Krepost' Reikha* (Moscow: Yauza-Press, 2009).

Zhukov, G.K., *Vosmpominaniya i Razmyshleniya* (two vols.), vol. 2 (Moscow: Olma-Press, 2002).